"I used to live in a one bedroom basement suite until I discovered how to buy, build and renovate homes. Now I own properties and live in a luxury renovated home and I can show you how to do it too!"

David Pocock

Disclaimer

The information contained within this book is meant to be used as a guideline only and it is the responsibility of the user to adhere to all local legislation, regulations, standards, codes and all other mandatory requirements pertaining to any and all information presented in this book.

© BuildingorRenovating.com
All rights reserved, no part of this publication can be reproduced for purposes other than personal use without the written consent of the publisher.

Acknowledgements

I would like to say thank you to the many people who helped provide professional information.

To my wife Carol Ann, for her support and perspective in many areas, especially editing and design. You are my partner in this journey that has taken us through many challenges. Without you by my side this book would never exist. Thank you!

To my son Matthew Pocock, Certified Journeyman Tilesetter and owner of October Stone and Tile (www.OctoberStoneandTile.com) for his helpful recommendations on tile-setting and to my daughter Lindsay and my son Ryan for their encouragement and support.

To Brian Tracy (www.briantracy.com) for his inspiration, wisdom and practical knowledge that I was fortunate to receive early on and continue to receive today.

To Lance Plewis from Spectrum Home Plans (www.spectrumhomeplans.com) for the house plan illustrations and the many years of supporting my clients and students with insight and value-added services in home design.

To Mike Bignell, Certified Journeyman Painter and Decorator, for his helpful recommendations on painting.

To Michael Link, roofing instructor at the (NAIT) Building Trades College, for his helpful recommendations on roofing.

To Dan Weinert, (SAIT) Carpenter and Building Trades College Instructor for his recommendations.

To Dan Swiatek, (SAIT) Carpenter and Building Trades College Instructor, for his recommendations.

To Fred Bretzke, (Sait) Instructor Pipe Trades, for his helpful recommendations on Plumbing (Visit YouTube Sait Plumbing).

To my work associates, Government Apprenticeship Trade Officers, who provided construction advice whenever I asked for it.

To my friends and business associates who have willingly answered my questions and provided me with advice, I feel a deep sense of gratitude.

To Vaughn Unick, Certified Journeyman Carpenter, for the renovating work we did together. Your knowledge and experience in all areas of renovating provided a valuable contribution.

To Dave Litwiller, Certified Journeyman Carpenter and owner of Litwiller Renovations and Custom Homes, for his practical business knowledge and experience on building and renovating.

To Joseph Cyr, Certified Journeyman Carpenter, who provided valuable additions to the framing checklists.

To the Edmonton Real Estate Board in Alberta, Canada for involving me in the industry by sponsoring my seminars for many years and providing me the opportunity to enthusiastically prepare lesson plans which led to the creation of this book.

To those real estate agents and others who attended my seminars on building or renovating who encouraged me to create more material and better lesson plans.

To Steve Wilkinson, Certified Journeyman Millwright, for his feedback and support.

To those people in the housing industry (tradespeople, suppliers and professionals) some of whom I worked with and others who have offered great advice. Thank you very much for your kind support and friendship.

© David Pocock All rights reserved. The contents or parts thereof, may not be reproduced, for any reason, without permission from the author.

Foreword

Congratulations! You are on a course for greater achievement! You have the best real estate book to accelerate your financial wealth. It is easy to follow, easy to understand and includes every significant topic dealing with four subjects which are buying, renovating, building and selling. Breaking down all the key topics into 21 single chapters helps to organize the information for quick reference of the appropriate how-to steps. Each chapter is packed with stories, information and lists to help you save time, effort and money and get you started right now and in the right direction. At the end of each chapter is an action exercise to help you set goals. You will have this excellent resource to refer to time and time again for every transaction or renovation you plan on undertaking. That's what makes this book unique. It is your action guide to help you pursue the moments that will change your life.

You will learn hundreds of ideas to save you thousands of dollars. It's not just "saving" money, the word "profit" is used often because "making" money is a key motivating factor for any transaction. I concentrated the material to specifically help you achieve profits, assuming you would never want to lose money if you were doing a deal or project for buying or improving your own residence. You will soon see I'm not being over confident in using the word profits. I'm showing you all the ideas I've used to help me save tens of thousands of dollars and they can easily save you a thousand times the cost of this book.

A self-help book, unlike most other books (novels, text books, history books, etc.) is meant to be referenced over and over again to provide constant guidance towards achieving your objectives and goals. I'm sure once you grasp the contents within these pages you will be excited with what you have and guard it as a valuable item. This is a book that you'll use often, not a dust collector on a shelf. Congratulations to you again for becoming the owner of a book that can guide you on a path of success and prosperity.

If you are serious about wanting to make and save money in residential real estate, my job is to help you get there by using this book as your "system" so you can enhance your life and reach your financial goals or your personal achievements in real estate. Consider for now that the letters of the word "system" stands for Save, Your, Self, Time, Energy and Money! The strategy is about making money as well as saving money because money saved is money earned. I'll help you achieve a financial gain by using this book as your reference to learn how to avoid potential pitfalls. This book was created and structured using real how-to information. You will learn those ideas and strategies that my wife and I and many others have used during the past thirty-seven years. If just one idea helps you make or save thousands of dollars then this book has been put to valuable use. Some of my associates have gone on to become multi-millionaires using just one or two of these ideas and I believe some who read this book will do the same and maybe that will be you.

Now you can do it like the TV personalities on Property Brothers, Love it or List It, Rehab Addict, Fixer Upper, Flip or Flop, Vintage Flip, Income Property and many other shows.

© David Pocock All rights reserved. The contents or parts thereof, may not be reproduced, for any reason, without permission from the author.

You now own the how-to book that gets you from start to finish and helps you profit in the process.

The origin of this book began with a 12-week course followed by preparation of lessons to scale down to a condensed one-day course. Consolidating information and structuring it into a simple format for teaching was one of my goals when I ran one-day seminars. I have now taken this goal one step further by focusing on the important area of money. Seminars have limitations, they require me to be there. Participants are also limited to what they can absorb and remember in a one-day seminar. A good book does not have those limitations. I wanted to give you this history because this book is much more than reading material. It is a guide with stories containing my seminar lessons with how-to checklists, steps and action activities to help you succeed now and in your future.

It's worthy to mention here that the money-making and saving ideas pertaining to building or renovating often refer to you acting as your own contractor but many others have had great success by hiring a builder, a contractor or a project manager and so can you. There are more opportunities for you to be successful. These options are clearly explained in the twenty-one chapters covering many ways to profit.

I started out in a small one-bedroom basement suite, worried that I would never own my own home. Today, I own my home and other investment property. My goal is to help you become successful owning residential real estate by sharing the conceptions which began 38 years ago when I obtained training to build my first home. During the years to follow, I was involved in almost every field related to real estate, helping thousands through courses and seminars. I worked as a bank loans officer, a government housing officer, a mortgage associate, a seminar instructor, an author, a builder, a government training consultant and a government trades officer. To create "For Profit", I've extracted knowledge taken from banking, mortgages, education, building and government administration with both housing and trades departments. I read several books and attended courses and seminars related to real estate investing, estimating and sales.

While working as a government training consultant and trades officer, I connected with thousands of people in various professional and trades industries. I also taught thousands of people on the subjects of building and renovating in seven different cities both privately and through colleges and the real estate board. I authored a book back in the 1980's called "A Complete Guide to Being Your Own Home Contractor". This book provided a foundation for seminars and the creation of additional lesson plans and training materials leading up to the writing of "For Profit".

We have used most of the strategies and ideas talked about in this book. Those not used personally were ones used by people I know very well. My wife and I general contracted our own home five times and did many renovations on other homes including fully gutting the inside of one home. We also bought homes, sold homes, rented homes and I built custom homes for others. I'll admit that we, and eventually three children, moved eighteen times which I don't wish on anyone reading this book. However, we did get to realize many rewarding times and the dream of living in homes we built as well as a fully renovated home.

Looking back we did make our share of mistakes. The offsetting benefit is the knowledge and wisdom gained giving me the incentive to help you avoid the mistakes by making better decisions. The lessons I learned and taught, the mistakes I and others made and the problems we encountered are now converted into valuable tools for your benefit.

A Glimpse at Renovating and Building

Picture yourself living in a new home in which you made all the decisions about the quality and style of cabinets, the choice of flooring, light fixtures, tile and so on. You have also made important planning decisions on energy efficiency, layout of the floor plan and lot selection. There is no doubt you will take tremendous pride in your decisions and any accomplishments using your own labor. You spend your money, you make your choices, it's your lifestyle. You get exactly what you want in your home.

Building or renovating your own home is a dream for millions of people. However, it takes a brave and somewhat ambitious person to make the decision of turning this dream into a reality. This book will outline a simple step-by-step plan for you to follow. It will give you sufficient knowledge and the confidence to do this. You can start right now and plan your renovation or new build by following the sequences outlined in the various chapters. I've included a complete renovation sequence and a new home sequence to help get you off to a quick start.

The first thing you should understand is that you don't need to know everything before you begin the planning stage to renovate or build your own home. It might be comforting knowing that before I built my first home I didn't know what soffits and fascia were. Furthermore, I had next to zero construction experience. I later realized that most trades take a three to four year apprenticeship period to gain a journeyperson certificate. With about a dozen different trades, it would take you 48 years of training to learn everything if you were doing it all yourself. That's not realistic or practical. The secret is to do only the trade work you are qualified to do and if that's none then that's okay because being a manager is also a way to gain sweat equity. What's essential is to get some key knowledge, the knowledge to take action and make the right decisions, the exact knowledge that I have put together in this book.

Technical aspects of construction such as framing, plumbing, heating and electrical are not covered in detail because there are already plenty of books on these subjects. Again, you would not be tackling these jobs unless you are working in that trade or have the training or contacts to be able to work in these trades. I have to emphasize this again, unless you have the abilities, I don't recommend doing the skilled trades work. Most imperative is how to plan, prepare and manage the construction yourself by hiring others who are qualified to do a great job. You will not require previous experience in any of the construction trades. As the owner-renovator or owner-builder you need to know how to locate, negotiate, contract and be a good manager. In this regard, I give you many construction tips, checklists and do's and don'ts on the complete art of building or renovating any home.

From a glance at the table of contents you can see that it covers a broad range of subjects. These subjects are all important and I recommend you read the whole book first and then apply the action steps from the relevant chapters referencing information specific to your goal.

Whether you are building a major addition, doing a full renovation or simply remodeling a room you will find the management tools, profit and money saving ideas offered in this book extremely valuable.

You will receive guidance on buying, selling, renovating or building. The knowledge of strategies, concepts, ideas and over 100 lists are all aimed at saving you both time and money.

The lists are valuable resource tools for anyone working in real estate. A good list will identify key points and organize them in a proper sequence. Lists can simplify a process making it easier to follow. They save time with project management and they help to ensure quality by including all important steps, reducing errors and problems. Using a good list can provide peace of mind. Think about the advantages of using a contract check list, an application checklist, a permit checklist, cost summary checklists, a tenant clean up - move out checklist. These are just a few examples of lists that can save you considerable time and save many headaches.

You now have job schedules, an estimating checklist, helpful mortgage documents, a contract reference template, sample specifications to build on and much more. Estimate accurately the cost to construct, obtain contractors discounts, apply for a mortgage, get a building permit and know what's needed to design and plan in order to save time and money. Throughout this book there are various worksheets provided for your own use. Some you can photocopy and use and some you may want to amend to suit your own needs.

The management skills required are within your capability. They become easier to understand as you gain insight from reviewing the chapters and seeing the material more than once. You will see how to maximize your savings, reduce your risks and save thousands of dollars! Remember, if you think you can, you can! With the help of this book you will succeed and profit! Whether you are buying, renovating, building or selling, you will enjoy the satisfaction of your accomplishments and take pride in doing it!

The Brian Tracy Influence

"Everyone is a Salesperson"
Brian Tracy

If you don't already know Brian Tracy, I encourage you to google him. He is a world renowned personal and business trainer. He has authored over 80 books and 300 training programs. I became a fan after attending two of his seminars, his two-day Phoenix Seminar on the Psychology of Achievement and an evening seminar on the Art of Closing Sales. The timing was perfect. The very next day after attending the Art of Closing Sales I was able to close the sale on a large custom home using three of Brian's techniques. Wow! His training was that good and I've been a fan for the past thirty years. A bit of serendipity because I'm able to now include a brief story about Brain Tracy in this book thirty years later. I have to mention this because the mindset of Brian Tracy has played a positive role in so many ways. Brian, thank you for being a great teacher and mentor. For my readers, I'll share a few tips I learned from Brian that I practiced and I know will help you with the mindset you will need to develop to be successful. In Chapter 1, I'll share another story involving selling because everyone including you is a salesperson.

To be successful in real estate, or almost anything for that matter, requires the right mindset, the right positive win/win attitude and the ability to plan and set goals. I was so lucky to have been taught by the world's best early on. I know that the key to making these money-saving ideas work for you is to become involved in personal development. I would encourage anyone reading this to subscribe to BrianTracy.com to receive information about his programs and also to receive free training segments which he often offers to his subscribers.

In Brian's training on goals, he mentions the acronym "GOSPA" which stands for Goals, Objectives, Strategies, Priorities and Activities. Using this book as a guide will assist you with choosing a strategy, setting priorities, and making a daily list of activities. It will be up to you to write down your own goals and objectives and remain focused and determined to achieve them.

Action Exercises:

Now is the time to get out there and become successful at buying, renovating, building or selling for profit. Start right now by applying the first letter in "GOSPA". Write down three goals you would like to achieve with regards to buying, selling, renovating or building a home.

1.
2.
3.

Contents

		Page
Chapter 1	Launch with a Team and Attitude for Profit	1
Chapter 2	Using Lists to Save Time, Effort and Money	8
Chapter 3	Knowing and Using Principles of Real Estate Appraisal	21
Chapter 4	Consider Economic Factors for Profit	29
Chapter 5	Negotiating for Profit	37
Chapter 6	The Right Financing for Profit	43
Chapter 7	Nothing Down Strategies for Buying a Home	51
Chapter 8	Finding Motivated Sellers and the Right Property for Profit	64
Chapter 9	Buy, Hold and Rent for Long Term Profits	73
Chapter 10	Landlord Tips for Saving Time, Reducing Stress and Making Money	80
Chapter 11	Flipping for Profit	88

© David Pocock All rights reserved. The contents or parts thereof, may not be reproduced, for any reason, without permission from the author.

Contents

		Page
Chapter 12	Renovating for Profit	95
Chapter 13	Improving Curb Appeal Profit	123
Chapter 14	Estimating for Profit	130
Chapter 15	Contracting for Profit	154
Chapter 16	Designing a New Home for Profit	175
Chapter 17	Financing the Construction of a New Home for profit	198
Chapter 18	Scheduling the Construction of a New Home for Profit	210
Chapter 19	Construction Tips and Checklists for Profit	231
Chapter 20	Selling for Profit	250
Chapter 21	Becoming a Contractor for Profit	258

© David Pocock All rights reserved. The contents or parts thereof, may not be reproduced, for any reason, without permission from the author.

Chapter 1

Launch with a Team and Attitude for Profit

*"Surround yourself with the dreamers
and the doers the believers and thinkers
but most of all surround yourself with those
who see greatness within you."*
Marji J. Sherman, writer

Starting out with No Money? This book can help you! You'll get a list of situations from which you can begin right now to look for your first home. First, obviously having money certainly makes everything easier and affords you more options presented here. Many people including myself did not start with money. I once heard a wealthy man say "it takes money to make money and if you don't have it you can't get it, and if you can't get it you will never have it so forget about it". He was joking of course because it's not true. What is true is that it takes planning and some strategy. It is a fact that you may need to make some changes, get out of your comfort zone and set some goals so you will eventually have money.

For our first home we had to sell items like a second car and some possessions that were hard to let go. Cutting back on eating out and spending lass than your means is necessary to save. We lived first in student residence, then in a very small basement suite. This was the price we paid to save our first downpayment. What price will you pay? A number of best selling books have been written on the subject of buying homes with nothing down. I'll share a few realistic strategies I've used and ones you can apply right now. Also, starting now, look at your current spending habits and payments to see where you can save money to put yourself in a position to take advantage of some of the other money making ideas which do take money to make money.

Getting Ready

Win/Win Attitude

This is all about having a positive attitude and being able to look at things as solutions not problems. Motivational speaker Zig Ziglar once said, "you can get everything out of life if you help enough other people get what they want". When dealing with others try walking a mile in their shoes and stay at all times on the positive side looking for solutions. If you have to condone an action then condone the action and not the person. Learning is lifelong so practice and develop the people skills, the communication skills, selling skills and negotiating skills that all require a win/win attitude for success.

You may already know a lot about residential real estate, buying, selling, renovating, contracting or building. If you are reading this I believe you already have the right attitude because you have the attitude of learning to find out what you don't know. I've said this hundreds of times to apprentices wanting to avoid school by challenging exams. Attend training to see what you don't know. Be open to learn the things you don't know. If it's something you already know a great deal on then maybe some of the points covered will be good reminders and help to keep you tuned up for your next project.

A colleague from the trades branch once told me that you will remember only 20% of what you read, 40% of what you read and hear, 60% of what you read, hear and see and 80% of what you read, hear, see and do. I immediately replied asking "what about the other 20%, the 80 to 100% portion?" He replied, "You never know 100%". This is a good thing to remember and the reason I'm leaving you with lists for future reference. It is also the reason you should be continuing to expand your knowledge and library with other books and courses on real estate investing. You will never learn 100% of this complex subject but you are off to a great start with many bases covered in this book.

Good Karma

What goes around comes around. There is a TV series on this with one story after another. The thing to remember is whatever you do, whatever activity you engage in, whoever you deal with, do it with good Karma. When it comes to your dealings, being creative with financing and working outside the box is only okay if everything's legal. There is a line you must draw and never cross it. Those who engage in fraudulent activities are short term thinkers who do not succeed in the long run. Some might give the appearance of success then find their health failing because their lack of integrity is causing them to be ill.

I was scammed once, it could happen to anyone. It's happened to a co-worker, a relative and even my lawyer so you have to be very careful. I know of others who had long court cases. I gained the experience and the positive side is now hopefully this will never happen to you. I'm giving you ideas and tools to save you from getting into trouble. That scammer is now in prison as bad karma has caught up to him.

Comfort Zone

It was the fall of 1979 when, as newlyweds, my wife and I moved half way across the country to secure good jobs and a greater opportunity to make a better life for ourselves. We found a little one-bedroom basement suite to rent which was close to where our jobs were. All was going well for the first month or two. Then things went downhill from there. Our landlords (who lived on the main floor) began arguing and fighting with each other both verbally and physically and more frequently. Twice EMS came to the home to take the Mrs. to the hospital. On another occasion our basement suite was broken into resulting in personal items being stolen. It was these experiences that motivated us to own our own home which seemed insanely difficult, almost impossible for us at the time.

A pivotal point came when we heard about a government-sponsored course on building your own home. That was when we decided to do whatever it took in order for us to leave our one-bedroom suite and get into our very first home. We decided to take the course and with a lot of hard work and commitment we learned what we needed to do to move forward. Since then we've never looked back and eventually I became one of the course instructors.

When we started all we had was a land line and access to a photocopier. This was in the early 1980's just before the marvel of fax machines was introduced. We had to personally visit everyone (trades, suppliers, legal, insurance, banking, designer, land developer, real estate agents, etc.) and follow up with personal communication and future visits. I can tell you that forty years later you will gain far more success from personal visits and personal contact than you will from many of the popular forms of communicating today. We had no personal computers, no internet, no Facebook or other social media, no Google, no Amazon, no e-mail, no cell phones, no text messaging, no pager, no scanners, no video games, no DVD's, no flat screen TV's. Can you guess which ones are time wasters that will keep you in a rut and which ones are tools that can help you succeed in buying, building, renovating and selling for profit?

The tools that will be useful are your personal computer with Outlook, MS Word or an Apple computer with Pages and Mail. The internet will be useful for sourcing trades and suppliers. A scanner/photocopier combination is important to have especially for estimating and contracting. A cell phone for calls, text messaging, sending photos, the camera, calendar, banking and GPS mapping are all great applications to have. The social media apps, games and others apps that are time wasters should be moved off the front page of your cell phone or deleted as they are detrimental to your time and achieving your goals and ultimately your dreams.

Your Role as a Manager

Applying good management skills is essential when contracting for renovating or building. It's a good reminder if you think in terms of the functions you will be tasked with. These include planning, organizing, hiring or contracting, directing or giving an order, controlling (meaning the financing), coordinating the activities, being innovative, motivating and acting as a representative. These are the dominant skills required for acting as your own contractor when dealing with trades and suppliers, lenders, legal, insurance and real estate professionals. Knowing the details of how to do electrical, plumbing or other trades is not necessary as you will be hiring people to do that work for you.

For all practical purposes you should act like you are starting your own small business. You will be involved in purchasing, signing contracts, scheduling and accounting with the end objective of saving or making money. Since you are performing as though you are operating a small business, you must also conduct your efforts in a professional manner as if you were a business manager. To be successful you must place yourself in a manager's frame of mind. To reduce/eliminate chaos, work with the industry professionals who can provide professional advice and assistance.

Your Role as a Salesperson

Consider for a moment that many of your activities will involve interacting with other people. This hit home for me when I was building our fourth home. It was a 1900 square foot walkout bungalow in a nice estate area. Our equity was tied up in another revenue property which meant I had very little money for construction. When I applied for the construction mortgage, a mortgage with advances, the bank declined me but offered a completion mortgage instead. The bank officer said; "we don't think you can build that home for that amount of money but we will give you the mortgage when it's built". He gave me the mortgage commitment letter and I walked out the door. I think they may not have liked the builders cost section where I included $20,000.00 for being my own home contractor.

At the time, I figured this is it and I'll never get the advances or draws required to finance the construction so I came up with an alternative approach. I asked my lawyer to draw up an "assignment of mortgage proceeds" document. It was a one page document, a commitment from myself that I would sign and give to trades and suppliers guaranteeing to pay them a portion of the proceeds from the completion mortgage. Next, I had to sell this idea to every trade and supplier.

I didn't know at the time but I was using one sales technique taught by my friend Brian Tracy. The fear of loss is greater than the fear of gain. I knew many suppliers and trades companies had lost money to builders and individuals who declared bankruptcy. They would never forget the client who didn't pay even if several years had passed. One of my associates who ran a drywall and stucco business lost over $70,000.00 to just one builder. Knowing this I went to my window supplier and asked him, "have you ever lost money to a builder or a customer?". The sales manager nodded his head and said "Yes we have". You could see the expression on his face that he was shocked with why I would ask such a question. I said, "well how would you like a guaranteed assignment of the mortgage proceeds for the house I'm building?". The answer was an overwhelming yes and every trade with the exception of the basement concrete cribber and the framer accepted the assignment of mortgage proceeds. This meant they would all (the excavator, lumber supplier, plumber, electrician, and a dozen others) have to wait until the home was built to receive payment.

It took a lot of selling but in the end I saved over $2,000.00 in interest costs. When the house was completed the bank forwarded the completion mortgage funds over to my lawyer and we sat down and I wrote out checks to all those trades and suppliers who I contracted with. All I needed to build the home was $10,000.00 for paying the two trades. It was obvious those trades who accepted a guaranteed assignment of the mortgage proceeds had to cover 100% of their labor and still make payroll.

Selling is communicating, negotiating and influencing others to work with you towards achieving your goal. You will see this more in future chapters as you read more about buying, selling, renovating, contracting and building.

Your Success Team

If you are looking to profit in real estate you want to be more analytical and less emotional. It will mean making an offer and walking away. It will mean getting three or more quotes from suppliers and trades and choosing the best one for your needs depending on a number of factors, price being just one. This is not as easy as it seems because you will have to say no to more than you are saying yes.

As you begin you will collect names and obtain references and referrals of professionals who will form your success team. This will happen naturally once you begin to search and find property so it's not critical to have a support team in place before you start. The key is to just start! You will gain good contacts in all the areas eventually requiring the services of the following professionals and trades.

Can you write a person's name beside each of the following professions?

- Real Estate Associate (Agent)
- Mortgage Broker (Associate)
- Bank Loans Officer or Manager
- Lawyer (specializing in real estate)
- Property or Home Inspector
- Insurance Agent
- Appraiser
- Contractor
- Trades and Supplier contacts (refer to Cost Summary List)
- Draftsperson (Architect)

Build Trust

Why is having good contacts with the list above important for profit? For protection, security, safety and to make money. Every money-making idea has a people element and an association with Real Estate Agents is one where it is very important to gain and obtain good relationships. Working closely with one agent and networking with many agents are explained in two of the money-making ideas. When dealing with Real Estate Agents, you want to make it easy for them to do business with you. Do what you say you will do. Don't nitpick the small things. Don't try to cut their commissions. Build trust by being consistent in your actions, keeping your promises and commitments, acting with integrity, communicating well by following up and following through and getting to know people. When problems occur you are the person who must be focused on solutions. The word problem is not in your vocabulary because a problem solver is always focused on the positive direction which is finding solutions.

The following list of benefits for ease of work and profit applies to real estate agents, mortgage associates, the home inspector, your real estate lawyer and your insurance agent.

Why use a Real Estate Associate/Agent?

- Provides access to information, listings, first to know about a listing
- Provides access to buyers and sellers, market networking
- Provides professional experience, trained in negotiating, other real estate training
- Gives professional advice
- Follows a code of ethics
- Saves time, gets quicker results
- Prequalifies buyers
- You only pay if they perform a service resulting in a successful transaction

Why use a Mortgage Broker/Associate?

- Provides the power of professional negotiating experience
- Offers one-stop convenience for access to numerous mortgage products and lenders
- Gives unbiased knowledge and advice
- Provides access to unadvertised rates
- Provides access to private lenders
- Works for you, not the lender
- They get paid a commission from the lender (in most cases)

Why Use a Home Inspector?

- Gives you an unbiased viewpoint, not emotional
- Offers another set of eyes
- Provides experience you may not have
- Checks things like insulation in attic, electrical panel, furnace, water heater
- Trained to identify a grow operation (16 things to look for)
- Inexpensive compared to the possible mistake of buying a nightmare
- Provides you a list of deficiencies you might be able to use for negotiating a discounted price
- Gives you an escape clause, buys you time to arrange financing
- Best to use your own inspector, not the sellers

Why Use a Real Estate Lawyer?

- Examines the contract and provides comments to purchaser regarding terms, conditions and other clauses
- Provides mediation on behalf of the client (purchaser or seller)
- Does a Property Title search and advises client on any easements, liens or other items on Title
- Checks to see if existing mortgages are assumable (if they are to be assumed)
- Checks to see that all utilities and property taxes are paid (orders a tax certificate)
- Prepares mortgage documents (from lender) for buyers signature(s)
- Prepares a transfer of Title
- Executes all documentation with applicants
- Forwards documentation to the Land Titles office for registration
- Reports to the lender with proof of insurance and a copy of the Real Property Report (sometimes referred to as a Survey Certificate)
- Receives deposits and mortgage advances held in a secure trust account
- Disperses funds to the lender and seller's lawyer
- Closes outstanding documentation
- Prepares a final reporting of the disbursement of all funds, tax adjustments, copies, deliveries and legal fees
- Provides buyer with a new Title after ensuring all discharges have been dealt with

Why use an Insurance Agent?

- Aware of insurance companies available in your area
- They get paid a commission from the insurance company
- You avoid dealing directly with the insurance company which may only have offices in major cities
- An agent can save you time shopping provided they deal with more than one insurance company
- Can save money by getting more than one quote
- For new construction or renovations, an agent should know which insurance companies offer construction insurance

---

Action Exercises:

Determine Your Team

1. Real Estate Associate
2. Mortgage Broker/Banker
3. Lawyer (specialist in residential real estate)
4. Property Inspector
5. Insurance Agent
6. Appraiser
7. Designer (Draftsman/Architect)
8. Contractor
9. Major Construction Material Supplier
10. Construction Trades (identify one company or person for each of the following trades)
    a) Plumbing
    b) Electrical
    c) HVAC
    d) Drywall
    e) Tilesetter
    f) Roofer
    g) Carpenters (for concrete forming, framing and finishing)
    h) Painter
    i) Siding installer
    j) Soffit, fascia and eavestrough installer
    k) Landscaper
    l) Flooring Installer

Chapter 2

Using Lists to Save Time, Effort and Money!

*"Following a written list puts activities and goals in motion,
without one is acting like a ship without a rudder."*
David E. Pocock, Author

When I ran seminars on the subjects of building and renovating, one observation was the value of having a list for each objective. A number of lists were created to make things as simple as possible and easy to follow. This idea has evolved to the extent of including lists in every chapter enabling you to take immediate steps towards achieving your goals. A list removes many unnecessary words by cutting out pages of clutter and getting right to the activities and strategies that will help you move faster in the right direction. I made using lists one of the first ideas and deserving of a full chapter to emphasize how significant this is. I believe the key to your success is knowing what to do and what to do next. Also, you save money both when you save time and avoid the hundreds of times where you might be saying, "I wish I knew that beforehand" or "I should have done that". The saying hindsight is 20/20 is true. The benefit with these lists is you get to use my hindsight.

Most of the areas involving buying, building or renovating involved working through a checklist or a to-do list. A good example is the Development and Building Permit application process. People would say that dealing with city hall and applying for permits is a lot of red tape. In other words, it's a big headache because they need to keep coming back with more information to complete the approval process. The pros get the list of documents required and treat it like a checklist of to-do items. They don't see this as a problem because they know in advance what they need to prepare and submit. They can plan, prepare and carry out this task much quicker and easier than someone without a list to follow. The same holds true for buying a home, renting homes, being your own contractor for renovating, building or hiring a builder, contractor or project manager. So whatever you do, treat it like a project to manage which involves either managing a list of activities or following a sequence. The list acts like a checklist ensuring you have completed or considered a number of items.

Building or renovating you can do yourself if you can manage a few lists. These lists include topics on house planning, financing, estimating, cost summary, contracting and scheduling. I also included a separate checklist for renovating a kitchen as well as installing a tile shower. The kitchen is referred to as the heart of the home so it's important enough to have it's own lists for design and renovating. Now if you are not comfortable acting as your own contractor, then another option is to do the up-front planning as much as possible and then hire a builder, contractor or project manager.

The first 10 chapters contain lists for buying, negotiating, selling, financing, property management and acting as a landlord. Chapters 11 to 13 have lists for flipping homes, renovating homes and curb appeal. Chapter 14 on estimating and Chapter 15 on contracting contain lists common for both renovating and building. Chapters 16 to 21 deal with building a new home, income property or retirement home. This could be any new home in any location. The lists help you with design, financing, construction and scheduling. The final two chapters contain lists that help you deal with selling a home for profit and the business of contracting.

The 21 money-making and money-saving chapters were selected because they separate all the ideas I've used or people I know have used to make tens of thousands in profit. They are all realistic and they are all practical and legal. I'll share some stories and refer you to the appropriate lists so you have some support tools for acting on these ideas. Saving money or making money is a goal for many people and I assume since you bought this book that it is your goal as well. You can achieve your goals quicker by using one or more of these lists.

Combine Lists for Maximum Profits!

As you go through the chapters and review the lists you will find that many are linked together. For example, if you are flipping a property then you will refer to the lists on appraisal, negotiating, financing, renovations, contracting and selling. On the other hand, if you are buying your first home then finding motivated sellers, negotiating for profit and buying for little or nothing down might be the most applicable areas and lists for the moment. In almost every idea discussed there is a reference to either a checklist, a document or a schedule which is for your reference to use right now or some time in the future. If your goal is to rent out properties then the list of tips on renting and property management will get you on the right path. Finally, if you want to build a new home, revenue, vacation or retirement property then the lists on designing a new home, estimating, contracting scheduling and construction tips will provide you with answers and strategies for profits, either saving or making money.

Anyone with organizational skills has a master list and underlined assorted lists. You can do nothing without a list. You will invariably forget even the most minute detail and that could make or break you! Have a Master List with you or within close proximity at any given time. Experts in their field such as professionals, instructors and certified journeyman tradespeople have either knowingly or unknowingly provided me with the ideas to create an appropriate list for the purpose indicated by the title of each chapter.

These lists have evolved over many years of personal use and improvements for seminar instructing. They are meant to be used as guides and for you to tweak so you can customize them to suit your own situation. In other words, the best list will be one you amend to meet your particular objective. Consider flexibility in their use as each person's individual goal will vary. I suggest using a pencil to check the items as you work through them. This will double as a great management tool to ensure you are moving in the right direction, the direction that will end up with you profiting financially when all is said and done.

How to Use the Lists in this Book

1. Review the entire list
2. Check items of importance and delete items not relevant
3. Determine if the list is appropriate for your goals
4. Add or amend the list to create a new list relevant to your needs and goals
5. Number or organize the items in order of priority
6. Combine lists when necessary to complete a large project
7. Add dates when the items should be started and completed
8. Review and update regularly as you complete items from your list

There are well over 100 lists to keep you on track for summarizing key points for profit. I've selected 21 of my favorite lists to explain their purpose and illustrate the value they contribute to saving you time and money by first knowing what to do and by doing these tasks in the right sequence you will get them finished quicker.

The Appraisal Considerations List

Recognizing and taking into account the principles of real estate appraisal is absolutely essential to your success. There will be several times throughout the book where Chapter 3 "Knowing and Using Principles of Real Estate Appraisal for Profit" will be referenced. An awareness of these principles provides a foundation for decision-making when buying, renovating, flipping, building and selling homes for profit. The Appraisal Considerations List in Chapter 3 is to make you aware of some of the factors that can come into play which can have a direct influence on value. For example, the proximity to the light rail train station in a city where downtown parking rates are very high. The ability to be able to walk a block and not have to drive and worry about parking can be one factor leading to an upward demand on a location. Additionally, this benefit can increase the appraisal value of properties in that area. A close review of the Appraisal Considerations List can assist you when thinking about the likelihood of a property having the potential to increase in value or not.

The Economic Factors for Profit Checklist

Is it a buyer's market or a seller's market? Whats the current trend? This information can impact what you buy, when you buy and where you buy as well as the negotiations that take place. Know what the market is doing before entering into it from either end, buying or selling. Knowing the factors that affect real estate prices therefore is a prelude to all activities. "The Economic Factors for Profit Checklist" in Chapter 4 provides a summary list to review and analyze putting you in a position of knowing the current conditions and some indication of the future trend in prices. Knowing and acting on this information is crucial for making a profit. Your real estate agent (Chapter 1, launch with a Team ...) will be able to advise you on several of the economic factors.

The Negotiating For Profit Checklist

Investors know money is made when you buy a home more than when you sell. "Buy low and sell high" is a common saying. You grow your equity whenever you can buy real estate below the market value. In Chapter 5, "Negotiating for Profit", the lists provide you with reference points to consider prior to negotiating an offer to purchase.

In the majority of cases, I would hire a professional real estate agent to handle the actual face to face negotiating. This does not mean I have no role to play. I need to work with the agent to express my needs and desired outcome. The list of ideas are therefore tips and reminders of some important elements to consider prior to buying a property. To say it's a complete list would be wrong because it cannot take into account the specific details unique to every purchase, unknown in advance and unable to be included in this book. For this reason you should ask yourself, "what is unique to this negotiation?". Add those unique points to those important for you to achieve in your negotiation and express these to your agent.

The Loan Application and Interview Checklist

Good first impressions are made when you make an appointment and you show you are prepared with the proper documentation. You only have one opportunity to make a good first impression and success is preparation meeting opportunity! Presenting the right information shows you know your stuff. You have done your homework, your due diligence. You already know you qualify, how much money you need and how you will pay it back. Chapter 6, "The Right Financing for Profit" gives you guidance to help you answer these questions and the "Loan Application and Interview Checklist" prepares you by ensuring you are ready for your meeting with the banker.

The List of Possibilities for Buying a Home with a Low Downpayment

If you are looking to purchase your first home or you are an investor, arranging the downpayment can be a barrier to achieving your goal. Have you thought of all the possibilities? The "List of Possibilities for Buying a Home with a Low Downpayment" in Chapter 7 provides you with a creative thinking cap where you can start immediately analyzing various techniques and strategies for buying a home. First time buyers often don't have the money and struggle to save the amount they need while residential real estate investors want to use as little of their own money as possible, especially when starting out.

As always, the most important step is to take action and this step does not always require using your own money. The key words are "your own money" or "money today". Nearly all real estate transactions do require some exchange of money to make the deal work. Often the difference between success and failure is just knowing one idea that would work in a particular situation. The possible alternatives for buying increase when you look at combining them. Starting with this list of ideas will help you generate even more ideas and greatly improve your opportunities for success. Take the approach that you only require one acceptable idea to be off to the races negotiating your purchase.

The Renting for Profit Checklist

The creation of the "Renting for Profit Checklist" in Chapter 10 is the result of many tenant situations and events both positive and negative. In other words, it wasn't created overnight. This particular list requires some work to complete. Words like plan, contact, explain, set up and build refer to activities required to ensure you are successful with screening the best tenants and setting up the right contract for managing your property successfully.

The Renting for Profit Checklist is to save you the costly headaches that can result if you otherwise miss these important items. Hiring a property manager may not be practical when starting out until you own larger properties or multiple units with enough income to support a management fee. Acting as your own manager can save you money, about 10% of the rental income.

The Tenant's Move-Out Checklist

When you own investment property, one of the worst things for a landlord is cleaning up after a tenant moves out. It should be the tenant that leaves you a clean property ready to re-rent. Sure you can hire cleaners and deduct the cost from the security deposit but there is also a better proactive step you can take which is to provide a Move-Out Checklist. This detailed list will bring to understanding the necessity of leaving your unit clean. It will become clear that cleaning will be a big factor in the return of the full security deposit.

I've been on both sides, one helping my son clean his suite and the other as a landlord. I can tell you this list works! The last tenant actually hired cleaners to help him and the checklist was left on the counter when they moved out. It was not tossed out, it was referenced and used.

The Flipping Formula Checklist

Are you thinking of buying a home and flipping it for profit like those experts on TV? It's very risky if you do not do the math beforehand. What numbers do you consider before you can confidently consider this money-making venture? Complete the list in "Flipping for Profit" Chapter 11.

I did say earlier that it may be necessary to combine lists to complete a large project. Flipping for profit will require you to review "The Appraisal Considerations List" and "The Economic Factors for Profit Checklist" before you buy and possibly the "Renovation Sequence List", "The Renovation Cost Summary List", "The Contracting for Profit Checklist" and the "Preparing to Sell Checklist" after you buy. You will most likely need to work through "The Renovation Cost Summary List" if there are substantial renovations to complete before you re-list the home for sale. Make sure the numbers crunch out profits before you buy, otherwise forget it. The "Flipping Formula Checklist" and "The Renovation Cost Summary List" will be valuable tools for estimating and negotiating prior to making that big buying decision. The Chapters "Curb Appeal for Profit", "Estimating for Profit" and "Contracting for Profit" have these lists that are relevant to "Flipping a Home for Profit".

The Renovation Cost Summary List

A renovation cost summary list can provide you with several uses. It can help you summarize your costs to give you a working budget. It can also be used to provide you with an awareness of the list of items for estimating or for hiring a contractor or project manager. If new financing is required, this cost summary list shows the lender where money is being spent and shows the appraiser the additional value being added to the property which can enable you to qualify for funding. Renovations typically go over budget, more so than new home construction. The reason is they are subject to a greater potential for unforeseen and unplanned items. The renovator must remove and demolish old construction before new work can begin. All kinds of things can happen such as finding mice, rotten wood and incorrect electrical installations. Also, change orders are more frequent as owners make decisions affecting product choices and installation. The renovation cost summary list will help you keep track of your costs providing you with a starting list for creating your initial budget.

The Renovation Sequence List

I was fortunate to have the opportunity to work along side a talented journeyman carpenter during a six month full renovation. Performing tasks as his apprentice kept me in good shape. It was a big job doing all the cleaning up at the end of each day. The entire inside was gutted and replaced with a new floor plan. The sequence of work was documented and formatted into an item-by-item checklist. This list, which is in Chapter 12 "Renovating for Profit", will give you a guide to keep you on track from start to finish. Edit this list and combine it with other relevant lists to make a super project management tool applicable for your renovation.

The Designing a New Kitchen for Profit Checklist

Planning a new kitchen? Where do you start? In the "Renovating for Profit" chapter, I created two valuable checklists to cover all the items critical to getting your new kitchen designed to your needs and properly installed. These detailed lists assume you are changing the entire layout therefore they are applicable if you are planning on building a new home. They reference design considerations to size, windows, flooring, electrical, plumbing, appliances, the cabinet boxes and lighting. The major undertaking of a kitchen renovation is simplified when you have a great step-by-step sequential list to follow. Whether you are making a few simple changes or installing a completely new kitchen, review this checklist and the installation checklist to make certain all the important items are covered.

I've bought many homes where you could tell the builder cut corners to save money on the kitchen. I don't want to criticize them because they also have to build a price competitive product. Those kitchens had fewer electrical outlets and lighting options, few pull-out drawers, plain doors and either no island or a small island. It's probably one reason there are so many kitchen renovations. I created these lists based on one awesome efficient kitchen we personally installed which made extreme changes and improvements to our home. I'm sure if you follow these lists you will create a kitchen masterpiece which will provide you with a great deal of pride and joy every day as well as great functionality.

Construction Checklists

Chapter 19 "Construction Tips and Checklists for Profit" covers trade checklists. This chapter was included to provide you, the manager, with awareness of the scope of work so you have reminders of items to check or discuss with trades as they work on your home. Experts in each field have provided input shown in a summery list format. The points are intended primarily as a reference but worthy of your review when the time is appropriate. If you take the time to review these lists with your tradespeople you will learn a tremendous amount about the various residential construction trades. Prior to building my first home, I didn't even know what soffits and fascia were. Today I can say I've come a long way and can perform many trade functions. Although this is covered under contracting and safety, it's important to mention that any trade work that involves safety must be completed or supervised by a qualified/certified tradesperson. This includes the mechanical trades, electrical, heating, gas, sheet metal and plumbing.

The "Painting Checklist" is one of 17 lists in Chapter 19 "Construction Tips and Checklists For Profit". I am mentioning the "Painting Checklist" because it is one task many people will tackle themselves when renovating or building. My friend Mike Bignell, a professional certified painter and painting instructor, helped me in the creation of this list which is one I reference before doing any painting work. I'm sure you will find it beneficial to ensure your work looks immaculate. These construction reference lists are all in Chapter 19 with the exception of "The Shower Construction Checklist".

The Shower Construction Checklist

Setting tiles is one thing but doing everything right to have a well built, well sealed water-tight enclosure is quite another. I learned this the hard way when I hired the wrong contractor to tile a shower enclosure which only lasted two years. My son Matthew gained his Journeyperson Certificate in the Tilesetter trade. Starting from high school he worked on everything from malls, hospitals, swimming pools and most important, high end custom homes with features like curb-less walk-in showers and drains hidden in the grout line.

It takes a professional to install one foot by two foot slabs on a ceiling, build a wave wall, complete a drain-less or curb-less shower, install schluter edging, miter the edges of tiles, install a floor heating system and perform work flawlessly to satisfy interior designers, builders and home owners. The finished look must be to perfection to obtain repeat business from those builders and designers as well as to obtain referrals from satisfied customers. By following the "Shower Construction Checklist" in Chapter 12 "Renovating for Profit", you will ensure you have taken the necessary precautions and followed the proper steps to have a shower that is properly planned and professionally installed.

The Contracting for Profit Checklist

In the Chapter 15 "Contracting for Profit", I created an all-inclusive "Contracting Summary Checklist", a list to review before signing any contracts for work. A quick run down of these items beforehand is imperative to ensure you have taken precautionary measures to protect yourself and you are moving in the right direction with a quality contract.

The "Contracting Summary Checklist" can act like a template to check against all contracts or those estimates that will be turned into contracts. Negotiate and revise any contracts that are missing vital articles prior to signing. Cover your bases, guard yourself and avoid problems by using complete contracts. This comprehensive list took into account many problems others have encountered. It's now in your toolbox to help save you time, effort and money!

The Specifications List

When hiring a contractor for a renovation, building a new home or obtaining financing, specifications provide a list of products and work to be supplied, installed and financed. Specifications often form a schedule in a contract and may be noted in your contract as "Schedule A". The list provided in Chapter 15 "Contracting for Profit" is a sample illustrating many of those items to include in your specifications. Your specifications lists will be more or less detailed depending on the scope of work. It will be a list that is applicable to you alone. To get you started, you will either revise the list provided or create a new list when you pick and choose all your products to be supplied and the work to be performed. It's not uncommon for a new custom home to have more than ten pages of specifications. It's an important list to ensure you get exactly everything you want and everything you are paying for.

The Checklist for Planning a New Home

This checklist is one of several in the "Designing a New Home for Profit" chapter. The goal is to achieve the best design for your needs and the best fit for the lot which means it satisfy's the developer's and city requirements and compliments the highest appraisal value. This list helps you to identify your needs and space requirements.

It's best to review this list and the other lists on home design covered in this book prior to spending money on working drawings. Others who had plans drawn prior to attending my seminar found out the expensive way. They needed to start over again because they made mistakes, missed items or learned better options. I've also spent money getting plans drawn up only to have them re-drawn or discarded altogether. This checklist along with advance planning can save you from making the wrong decisions and wasting money.

One of your challenges is finding a talented designer, someone who is creative, experienced in construction, layout, materials, costs and design. Check qualifications against the list provided and be prepared to pay for good drawings because they are worth it.

All the lists in Chapter 16, "Designing a New Home for Profit", have been created to take you through the process. Also reference Chapter 3, "Knowing and Using Principles of Real Estate Appraisal for Profit" and Chapter 13, "Improving Curb Appeal for Profit" to put into practice all the concepts to achieve the maximum benefits both personally and financially.

The Estimating Checklist for New Home Construction

The Estimating Checklist for New Home Construction is designed for those people who plan on acting as their own general contractor or plan to become a home builder. This checklist was created during the building of my own homes and used in my own business for estimating custom homes and later in seminars to teach others.

There was a time when the economy was in recession and margins were almost nonexistent. If I added a contingency factor to my costs, I would likely lose out to another builder. Many builders were going broke and many would leave the business. I needed to be accurate with all my costs before presenting an offer. Part of the estimating function would be to obtain estimates from all the major trades and suppliers in order to complete my estimate. It was a lot of work just to get one home to build but it had to be done because these were custom homes that were all different and each one required it's own list.

The Estimating Checklist in Chapter 14, "Estimating for Profit" is the list I used. Now you could do a Google search for example or amend this one by adding and deleting items. The one I'm giving you has all the main areas numbered and the corresponding numbers are listed in the Cost Summary and Loan Calculation List. Simply use them as they are or add them to an accounting ledger or to an Excel/Numbers spreadsheet.

The Cost Summary and Loan Calculation List

This important list summarizes the Estimating Checklist in the "Estimating for Profit" chapter and is also mentioned in the "Mortgage Application Checklist" in Chapter 17 under the heading "Costing and Mortgage Calculation". It will become one of the key mortgage documents used when applying for financing.

The design feature of this list supports you if you choose to include some dollar amount of your own appraisal of the builder's costs (sweat equity) as part of a downpayment. I've used this list to obtain financing for close to 100% of construction costs. It has the right amount of detail and is in the right format for the lender to review and approve.

The Mortgage Application Checklist for New Home Construction

When applying for a mortgage for a new construction project it's crucial to prepare and present only the required documentation and in an orderly format. Presenting a complete package tells the lender you have done your due diligence and shows confidence in you as a builder. By approving you for a new construction loan or mortgage, the lender is taking a risk by putting faith in you as a trusted builder.

The "Mortgage Application Checklist" in Chapter 17 is one I've used as an owner-builder as well as for my own mortgage clients. This list is a summary of the documents normally required to support an application when applying for new construction financing. I recommend checking your lender's requirements for new home construction and amending this list to meet the lender's request. The Mortgage Application Checklist for New Home Construction assists you with presenting your package in a neat, organized and professional manner.

The Construction Job Scheduling Checklist

Planning the construction of a new home is usually a longer process than the actual building. You go through many stages. There is the land acquisition process, the design process, the permit approval process, the procurement/estimating process, the financing process and then the scheduling process. Each process has an orderly sequence with branches like a tree from this master checklist. Chapter 18, "Scheduling the Construction of a New Home for Profit" includes both a pre-planning sequence and the actual construction sequence of a new home. The "Pre-Construction Sequence (21 steps)" precedes the "Sequence of Construction" which is an orderly list of events from excavation to move-in. This is your project management tool used to plan, co-ordinate and schedule all trade work, supplies to be ordered and delivered and inspections.

This list is meant to be amended as needed to suit your specific project. Some homes do not have basements, some have wells and septic systems, some are designed with active energy saving systems and rural and urban differences exist also. You will need to tweak these lists to suit your area, your design and any differences in construction. As a project manager, while acquiring estimates for various items, you will collect the details pertaining to the timing of each event. Add each relevant item to be scheduled to your smart phone calendar with reminders according to your discussions with those contractors and suppliers. It's now just a matter of making the calls to various trades and suppliers at the appropriate time.

This comprehensive list took many years to develop. One click today on Google can find a similar list but you will be missing some of the built-in tips that are there to save you time, effort and money. This master list I can trust to get a home built in the shortest possible time and save money by being the builder.

The Preparing To Sell Checklist

Prepare your home to sell for the highest possible dollar value by completing this list in "Selling for Profit" in Chapter 20. Check off each point as you prepare for the home inspection and while preparing to stage and list your home. This list will act as your ready made "to-do" list. By following the "Preparing to Sell Checklist" you will ensure you have done everything possible to market your home for the highest amount and obtain a quick sale. Review the sections "Prepare for the Home Inspection" and fix or repair items accordingly. Some things might not be obvious for you to see or know about. Some good advice would be to review the "Easy Do-It-Yourself Staging" with your Real Estate Agent who should give you feedback on anything unique to your own property. The list is used as discussion points to identify what can and cannot be done to support showing your property to buyers.

Toolbox of Lists

My theory in helping you achieve your goal is to not complicate things but give the information condensed, straight up and quick! The idea of having in your hands, right now, a list of activities ready to support your priorities, objectives and goals is a tremendous tool for success. I've just given you a brief description of 21 of my favorite lists. There are over 100 lists in the 21 chapters which make up your new toolbox.

Here is a snap shot of 31 lists showing how combining lists work. Consider this your new toolbox to help you establish the activities to achieve your objectives and goals.

Buying, Selling, Investing Lists

1. Seller Information Checklist
2. Financing for Profit Checklist
3. Negotiating for Profit Checklist
4. Renting for Profit Checklist
5. Rental Application Checklist
6. Selling and Staging Checklist
7. Calculating Net Operating Income (NOI) for Profit

Renovating Lists

8. Renovating Tips to Increase Value and Profit
9. Work you Might Do Yourself to Reposition a Home (sweat equity) for Profit
10. Renovation Construction Sequence
11. Renovating Cost Summary List
12. Designing a New Kitchen for Profit Checklist
13. Shower Construction Checklist
14. Renovation Cost Summary Form
15. Adding Curb Appeal to Your Design Checklist
16. The Flipping Formula Checklist

Contracting Lists

17. Contracting Summary Checklist (components of your contract)
18. Specification List

Building New

19. House and Lot Considerations
20. Checklist of Steps to Obtaining a Working Drawing for a New Home
21. Items that Affect Cost/Square Foot Checklist and Lowering Costs List
22. Financing Checklist for a Proposal
23. Mortgage Application Documentation Checklist for a New Construction Mortgage
24. Building Permit Application Checklist (example)
25. Estimating Checklist
26. Cost Summary List
27. The Construction Job Scheduling Checklist , Pre-Construction Sequence (21 steps)
28. Sequence of Construction List (Stage One, Stage Two, Stage Three, Stage Four)
29. Safety Checklist
30. Construction Tips Checklist
31. Recording and Cost Control (accounting List)

Goals List

Why work with lists? To determine activities which can be arranged into priorities to fulfill your strategy in achieving your objectives and goals. Your Goals List should be done in writing on paper with a target date for achieving that goal. This is one list that only you can create!

Date Start / Completed	Activity

Action Exercises:

1. From the 31 lists, identify the combination of lists you will use to achieve your first goal.
2. Read the entire book then review those chapters and lists that are pertinent to achieving your goal.
3. Complete a list of to-do activities on the previous page.
4. Use a pencil and the space below to record your notes.

Chapter 3

Knowing and Using Principles of Real Estate Appraisal for Profit

*"Ninety percent of all millionaires
become so through owning real estate."*
Andrew Carnegie

A little knowledge of real estate appraisal pertaining to residential real estate is paramount for making profits. To know how to increase value you need to know how properties are valued and what influences their value. This chapter gives you an overview of the basic appraisal principles you should be constantly examining with any purchase, renovation or build.

When a property is valued, appraisal principles influence the value of a property when one of three approaches are used to determine value. One of these three approaches will be considered whenever you enter into a transaction to buy, sell or build a property.

The Market Approach - used for single family homes, condo's, town-homes, vacation homes
The Income Approach - used for income producing properties, multi-family properties, commercial properties
The Cost Approach - used for new construction

An awareness of the principles of real estate appraisal will give you the mindset to keep you on the right track. Many of the profit ideas discussed in future chapters have a link to one or several of these important principles.

Location

Location, location, location! You may have heard this before and that's because "Location" is the most important value in residential real estate. A home that is appraised using the market approach will have it's valuation assessed using comparable sales and listings in the community. The range of values will therefore relate directly to the lows and highs within the vicinity of the property you are buying. Why is this important? If you buy at the top of the range there is no room to move the value upward. The saying "It's better to own a cottage among the castles than a castle among the cottages" has some truth to it. To profit when buying, stay far enough away from the top of the range of home values within an area.

When choosing a location, think of your goal. If your goal is to build wealth by accumulating real estate rental properties then the location should fit that goal. You might start with a more affordable location where there are a greater number of rental properties. On the other hand, a young family looking for a home to raise children would prefer a location with better schools, sports and shopping facilities, a lake community, a public green area or an area with less crime. To others, proximity to work, to the university, to the hospital, to a golf course or to downtown and easy access to transportation might be key factors when choosing a location.

Supply and Demand

Economics 101 teaches basic supply and demand. This applies to housing when the scarcity of a property influences it's value by creating a greater demand. There has to be demand for the price to move upward. Why is this important to know? There will always be demand for housing making it the best investment. Maslow's hierarchy chart of basic needs shows food at the top of the pyramid followed by shelter then clothing. The smart phone, nice car and TV we regard to be important but you need shelter to store them and a place to stay warm and to sleep and eat.

We bought and sold in a large community which had many three bedroom homes for sale. When we sold our four bedroom home there were only two listings in the area because the supply of four bedroom homes was few in comparison. The benefit was we could hold our price firm in a market that was declining at the time. Profit is more likely when there are fewer comparable properties listed.

Competition can be either good or bad. It's good when you are a seller and there is competition to buy your product but can be bad when you are wanting to buy and you have to compete against other buyers. Smart real estate investors use this approach to buy when everyone else is selling and sell when everyone else is buying. They use this simple theory of supply and demand to profit in real estate.

The illustration below shows the relationship between supply, demand and price when movement of supply goes up or down. When supply goes down price goes up and the opposite also occurs.

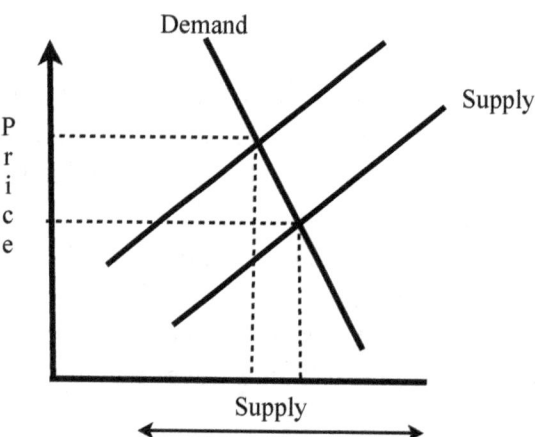

Substitution

How easily can a property be substituted for another by a potential buyer? The principle of substitution means the value of your property will be directly related to the value of similar properties that a buyer could substitute for yours. In the new home construction industry, some builders I know have used this principle to their advantage. They emphasize a feature or theme that does not exist elsewhere. Two examples of homes I know were called "The Super Kitchen" and "The Mountain Retreat". If you wanted the super kitchen design then there was only one builder offering this plan. Similarly, if you liked the mountain retreat show home you would choose that plan from that builder. Creating a demand, through the uniqueness of the floor plan, and being the only supplier, is one strategy used to raise the selling price which increases profit.

Condominiums often have more comparable listings because many units are built similar. Since property values are restricted by what can be easily substituted elsewhere, condominium values fluctuate in a more restricted range of values and are less attractive than single family homes to those people wanting to flip and renovate for profit.

Why is the principle of substitution important to know? To profit, consider how you can make your property better, different in a positive way or more attractive than the others in the vicinity. Also consider homes and renovations that will have attractive benefits not offered elsewhere. The example of having one of only two four bedroom homes for sale in the area also applies to the principle of substitution as there were far fewer comparable or alternative properties for a buyer wanting four bedrooms. Other examples where the substitution influence may come into play would be a property having a secondary/rental suite, a home having a triple or second garage, a home zoned for a business and a home on a large lot zoned for a higher use development such as a four or eight plex or a commercial building.

Highest and Best Use

The highest and best use of a property establishes the best useful benefit (the highest value) for a buyer. If a building lot is zoned for an apartment complex then that's a higher use than building a single family home. An appraisal would consider the highest and best use, the best value for the property that is to be sold. In some areas of transition, old single family homes have increased substantially in value due to zoning changes affecting the value and use of the lot. When homes are torn down and replaced with duplexes and fourplexes the land has gone through a change in highest and best use.

The popular TV show "Income Property" helps families reposition properties by adding a suite. This changes the use and has a considerable affect on valuation as the income stream makes the property more affordable and therefore more valuable.

Why is this principle important to you? To profit, consider this appraisal principle to maximize the potential value for any property you intend to build on. When building a new home, the highest and best use for the site will be the house plan that compliments the lot. Look for opportunities where you might be able to profit using this principle. A small builder or an owner/builder who is also a custom builder would have the flexibility to design the plan to compliment the features of a lot. In other words, making the best use of the lot which increases it's future value.

A friend of mine (Jim) used this principle when he designed his home to take maximum advantage of a lot having a front view of the mountains. Jim had the only home with a view from the kitchen, dining and main living area. The other homes along the street were built by builders who used their show homes and other existing plans having the kitchen, dining and main living areas located in the back of the home. Those homes, on these front view lots, had all the main rooms viewing the back lane and a row of houses behind. Step out on to the back deck and wave to all your neighbors! Those builders, because they were not custom builders, paid no attention to the uniqueness and the highest and best use of the lots on that particular street.

Principle of Anticipation

The Principle of Anticipation is that the value of a property today depends on the income or increase in value or other benefits that will accrue to the property owner in the future. In short, it is the present value of the sum of anticipated future benefits. According to this principle the value of the property depends on the anticipated utility.

Considering buying or building an income property? The anticipated rental income would be capitalized to determine the value of the property. Why is this important for profit with single family homes? Adding a rental suite or buying a home with a rental suite may allow you to use the anticipated appraised amount (check lender's requirements) of rental income in the financial calculations that determine the maximum mortgage qualifying amount. In addition, when you add rental income you correspondingly raise the property value.

Another interpretation of this principle considers that property values will rise or fall in anticipation of some future occurrence. For example; the migration of baby boomers retiring in the area, the creation of jobs with a major announcement creating an influx of workers, the anticipation of development following winning the bid for the Olympics or a new rail transportation line to the community. Why are these examples important? To profit through anticipation or speculation, you would recognize and consider future benefits, trends or other factors which increase demand and price.

Principle of Balance

The principle of balance states that value is created and maintained when the factors of labor, capital, land and the amount and location of essential types of real estate are in a state of equilibrium. The principle refers to the relationship between cost, added cost and the value it returns. Why is this important for profit? For each dollar you invest, the value should increase by more than one dollar.

The most sought after communities have schools, bus routes, shopping, parks, transportation, a good location and a well planned mix of housing. These communities maintain their high value and continually increase in value through inflation. Alternatively, a decrease in value may result if a neighborhood is not in good balance. When buying for profit, drive around the neighborhood, check out all the services, learn the history and find out about any planned future developments.

Principle of Conformity

The home you buy, renovate or build needs to conform to the design and quality of other homes to maintain maximum value. In new neighborhoods the land developer will mandate architectural controls just to maintain conformity. You can tell by driving through communities if they were built with architectural controls or not. The developer will ensure homes are built in the same style as the other properties in that same area, because the values will go up.

In smaller cities and towns, land is often developed by the municipality. Individual lots are sold off by the town with no architectural controls and design approvals. This leads to a mixed bag of old and modern designs where nothing seems to conform to one style. You might buy or build a nice looking home and save a lot of money because you learned how through this book only to find out later that your neighbor is building a weird or ugly looking house next to yours.

Why is this important for profit? When buying, ask yourself if the home conforms to the others on the street? Will this purchase be beneficial for future profits? When renovating, maintaining conformity is also of great importance for profit especially when making changes to the front elevation because visibility (curb appeal) from the street is very important.

Principle of Contribution

Like the law of cause and affect, Principle of Contribution means what you put in you get out. Your goal is to get out more than what you put in. If you spend $50,000.00 on a renovation then the property should go up accordingly and preferably much more than the $50,000.00. I once spent an extra $3,000.00 on windows for a home I built. When I sold the home I asked the agent what the buyer thought about the windows. The agent said, "Windows!, he bought the home for the steel beam in the garage so he could hoist motors out of his cars". That was $3,000.00 I could have saved. All home builders are very careful to spend only what will contribute to value. When multiplied by hundreds or thousands of homes, spending a little extra here and there would cost millions. Builders know what to put in and what not to put in to obtain the maximum value for a home in an area and for contribution to their profit.

Market Value

Market value takes into consideration location and comparable sales along with a host of other factors giving pluses or minuses to those comparable homes recently sold. Market price is what the property actually sells for, which ideally should be the same as market value. The expression "the buyer paid more than the market value of the property" refers to when a home sells higher than the market value.

It can be an advantage or disadvantage if there are no homes recently sold. The advantage is if comparable homes sold for much higher. The disadvantage is the opposite, if homes sold for less than you expected. When there are no comparable sales then other approaches to value such as the cost approach are often considered in addition to the most relevant market sales.

Principle of Progression

Some neighborhoods go through rapid change when the area becomes trendy causing an increase in appeal and demand. Old homes are sold for land value, demolished and replaced with far more expensive homes or multi-family properties. New shops and stores are built and land values start to rise upward. This movement is progression.

If you are selling an old home in an area where many homes have been replaced or renovated, the price of your property will also be pulled upward because of the state of progression the neighborhood is going through. Why is this important? When you hold property that is in a state of progression, you profit over time from values trending upward.

Principle of Regression

When a property is negatively affected through comparison of lower valued properties, the neighborhood is in a state of decline or will likely be very slow to change. Why is this important to know? You should be mindful of the principle of progression and regression and make the necessary adjustments by considering selling in an area of regression and targeting your resources into an area of progression.

Investments in renovations generally will produce a lesser return in an area that is regressing. This should impact what amount you spend and what you spend it on. For example, instead of spending a large sum of money building a new home in an area that is not progressing, you might be better to do some minor renovations to increase value or add a suite to increase income. This is exactly what we did when we came to realize that the prevailing winds, which drifted over the sewage ponds delivering a pungent smell to the immediate area, would discourage any nice new developments that would appreciate the value of our two properties. We minimized our investment in the renovation, sold the homes and left that area.

As you can see by now, many of the principles of real estate are linked together. It is also easy to see why many real estate people say "location, location, location" because all the principles have a direct link to location. Location within the city or location outside a city, location by neighborhood, location by street and location on the street are all analyzed into a property's valuation for appraisal purposes.

When buying, renovating or planning to build for profit, spend a considerable effort researching various locations. You might be the one saying "I'm glad I bought in this area when I did" which is better than saying "I wish I had bought over there". Knowing all the principles of real estate appraisal will be very valuable for making those big decisions. Several of these principles will be referenced in future chapters. You will be reminded of the forces and influences enabling you to increase your property value and profit through knowing and using principles of real estate appraisal.

Put the principles of appraisal into action. Consider all the factors in the following list that affect the value of a particular property you are interested in. Next, consider all those things you can change that will contribute to value more than the cost to change.

Appraisal Considerations List

Location
Value of neighborhood, progressing or regressing
Proximity to downtown, a major center, employment location
Proximity to services, schools, shopping, transportation, recreation, parks
View, exposure
Street particulars, busy, quiet, available parking
Lot location, corner, end of street, lane access to back yard
Sun, trees, slope
Zoning

Home
Curb appeal
Size of home, # of bedrooms, is size a factor to consider?
Style of home
Kitchen (size, design suitability, condition, age)
Extras and features
Quality of construction (heating, roof, windows, plumbing)
Income potential if renting is possible (depends on zoning and city/town by-laws)
Comparable homes sold, size, value per sq. ft. and other features
Adjacent homes conform to the street and area?

Interior Floor Plan
Suitable to add suite for rental considerations
Quality and potential for improvements
Things you can touch and see are important
Open concept, neutral colors
Wow factor ?
Quality and attractive tile and hardwood, stainless steel appliances, granite counter tops
Fixtures, plumbing, lighting
Ceiling height on all levels
Railings, headroom on stairs
Storage space
Hallways, too much wasted space or can make changes?
Renovation considerations, kitchen, baths, bedrooms
Potential to re-design floor plan

For Building a New Home
Lowest cost per square foot, size, style, shape, specifications
What is in demand today?
Consider principles of appraisal in location, lot features and house design
Style considerations for a rental property
Refer to the Chapter 16 "Designing a New Home for Profit"

Action Exercises:

Perform your own appraisal test by asking these questions before you buy, build or renovate for profit.

1. Is the *location* attractive? Close proximity to important facilities/amenities?
2. What is the current *supply and demand* of similar homes?
3. Are there many similar listings that can be easily *substituted* for mine when I sell?
4. What is the *highest and best use* for this property?
5. Are property values *anticipated* to rise or fall?
6. Is the area in *balance*? Are values being maintained and moving steadily upward?
7. Does the property *conform* to others in the vicinity? Are there other non-conforming properties close by that may affect the sale of this property?
8. Will my renovation *contribute* to added value and future profit?
9. What is the *market value* of other homes recently sold?
10. Is the neighborhood going through a state of *progression or regression*?

...

Chapter 4

Consider Economic Factors for Profit

*"In the real estate business, you
learn more about community issues,
you learn more about life,
you learn more about the impact of government
probably than any other profession that I know of."*
Johnny Isakson

By now you might be anxious to get to one of the chapters on flipping for profit, renovating for profit or building for profit. Do not skip this chapter because it relates to all of the chapters to follow. You will see that it's of great importance for profit to get in the game when the game is good to get into. It's much easier paddling a canoe downstream than it is against the current. For just a minute, compare purchasing a home as an investment with investing in stocks. Those who trade in the stock market know about trends and follow indicators to determine when to buy and when to sell. Does this same strategy work for buying real estate for profit? Absolutely! There are indicators that show which direction real estate prices are heading and it's vital for profit that you take these into account.

Many people have made fortunes buying low and selling high. In comparison, many people have lost money because they sold or bought at the wrong time. I've experienced hard times and good times and now I know there are times to buy and times to either wait or calculate in a risk factor. The economic indicators in this chapter will help you formulate the right buying and selling decisions, otherwise you can lose money very quickly. Hopefully, sharing some experiences and instilling some awareness of observing what the outlook is for the local, regional (State or Province) and National economy will give you tools to help you approach your buying decisions with the right confidence and knowledge needed to profit.

Marshall Field said, "Buying real estate is not only the best way, the quickest way, the safest way, but the only way to become wealthy". Under the right conditions this is true. But what about those people who bought before the 2008 crash? I'm sure some would disagree. Blanket statements don't take into account the "what if's" that could happen. Economic factors like inflation and interest rates can be major trend changers. Major announcements can have a dramatic influence on the movement of residential real estate prices. Local supply, demand and price indicators should never be ignored if you want to profit. Once you know all the factors influencing real estate prices, you should know where to buy, when to buy and what to buy.

Let's start with the local supply, demand and price indicators. Ask yourself what is happening in the market right now? Is it an emerging real estate market? Are real estate prices holding their value or are they declining? Some of the indicators you may know off hand or have a gut feeling because you live and work in the area, read the newspaper, listen to the radio and talk to co-workers and friends with similar interests. For other indicators you may need to ask an industry expert, your agent or associate, the local real estate association or seek out the facts from the city or municipality.

Number of Listings

Number of Listings going down indicates a reduction and eventually a lack of supply. This was covered in the previous chapter as a "Principle of Real Estate Appraisal". Your agent can advise you on the number of properties listed and what is considered a balanced number, a shortage or a surplus. A swing in home prices can occur either way when the numbers reach either a critical high or a critical low. Generally, it's a "buyer's market" when there is a surplus of listings and a "seller's market" when there are fewer listings. You should know what market you are buying in.

Movement in Purchase Prices

When there is a lot of interest in buying (demand), prices trend upward. You can check the statistics on the average and median price of homes recently sold. Ask your real estate agent, the real estate association or read the real estate association news bulletins to get the information which will tell you how prices are trending at the moment.

I remember listing one home and within hours there was a rush of vehicles driving by, followed by several bookings for viewing. I knew something was up but I didn't know all the economic factors that were playing out. A strange thing happened after we listed the home. There was a political decision which scared away buyers causing an immediate turn in the market. Demand fell and so did prices.

Volume of Sales, Momentum is Increasing

When a train starts slow and gains speed it gains momentum. In real estate, momentum is indicated by the speed at which homes are selling. In other words, the number of days on the market. When homes sell in fewer and fewer days on the market, it's an indication of rising demand. Similarly, when the number of sales increases that's also an indication of momentum, greater demand and likely rising prices to follow. Check with your agent on the average number of days that homes sold were listed on the market. Check how many homes sold last month in comparison to previous months and last month compared to the same month last year and the year before. These statistics are common ones that real estate associations track to keep their members informed so they are better equipped to advise their client which is you.

Rental Rates

Are rents increasing, decreasing or remaining steady? As a landlord I know that when there are an increasing number of properties for rent it's bad news. You have to be more competitive with your price and with what you offer. You may have to lower rents to attract and keep tenants. Opposite to this is a dwindling supply of rental units which is an indication of rental increases and rising home prices. Knowing the rental rates is very important if you are planning on becoming a landlord.

Vacancy Rates

The easing of vacancy rates is a factor which contributes to the stability in the housing market. The local real estate association would be the best source for current statistics and forecast information. A decreasing vacancy rate indicates migration to the area, a reduction in the supply of properties for rent, a stabilization and upward direction of prices. On the opposite side, a vacancy rate trending higher can lead to a reduction of rents, weaker home sales and softening prices. Knowing the vacancy rate is important for competing in the business of renting properties where the goal is to have your properties rented at all times.

Costs More to Rent than to Buy

Another supply/demand indicator is when the cost of renting is above the cost of building new rental units. This indicates an opportunity for construction of new rental units. It also means rents are also stable and on the rise due to a shortage of available homes. Higher rents allow for higher financing. A lower supply of both rental units and homes to purchase translates to higher property values.

Housing Starts

Housing starts, building permits and housing completions can indicate increases in demand for newly constructed homes which indicates increased prosperity and the possibility for a tightening supply of existing homes for sale. This indicator can also be a sign of job growth in the construction industry, including companies that act as suppliers to home builders. Although it focuses on one area of the economy, there is the ripple effect as new homes require appliances, furniture, and consumption of other items leading to economic growth.

An increase in housing starts is a good indication of the population expanding in a region. You would assume that demand is on the rise when housing starts are increasing. Builders need buyers and it would be foolish to build new properties if there were no buyers willing to pay the full price of a new property.

Housing starts may have seasonal highs and lows so comparing yearly numbers is often needed to determine a trend.

Costs more to Buy a New Home

Replacement costs have an influence on the existing market price. When you can buy comparable existing homes for less than the cost to build a new one, building new is not a good option. This is when new home builders reign in their production because demand is low and carrying inventory is just too costly. If it's your own home that might make a difference but I doubt you would want to go through all that work unless you were gaining some equity. You would certainly have the advantage to save money if you were acting as your own builder, doing all the pre-planning, performing all the project management activities and also rolling up your sleeves and getting into your old jeans to put in a little sweat equity. The chapter "Building a New Home for Profit" will give you what you need to be on top of this game.

National Influences

Interest Rates

I remember my parents having a 6% fixed mortgage rate, a rate that was given to war veterans. When we entered the housing market we could only dream of having a rate as low as 6%. How times have changed! A 6% rate today would bankrupt many people. In the early 80's we witnessed interest rates reach highs of over 21%. I was fortunate when my lending officer backdated my application so I could get a better rate of 15.75%. This is unthinkable in today's terms where rates are in the 2.5% to 5% range. Rate changes will directly impact values which are a direct link to your monthly mortgage payments and affordability. The record low rates we are enjoying today represent tremendous opportunities for buying a home or investing in homes.

Mortgage rates can vary daily as a result of economic events, political activity, news and reports, or things like Fed meetings. The mortgage rate for which you qualify may vary from the national average based on your personal financial situation. Your credit rating, beacon score, job security and other factors will also have some influence on the best rate you can qualify for. Keep a close eye on the movement of the five year closed mortgage rate and what the Fed's announce when setting their prime rate for indications in the movement of interest rates in the fixed term and variable rate mortgages. Check the "Bankrate daily" website for current rates.

Inflation Factor

Landlords love inflation because they know that leverage and inflation combined leads to profits. If you have a few revenue properties, a modest amount of inflation and time can make the shift towards having a comfortable retirement. Building wealth through accumulation of revenue properties is a well known practice. Investment groups where you can meet other investors and share ideas is one good way to get involved. I've dedicated two chapters "Buy, Hold and Rent for Long Term Profit" and "Land-lording Tips for Saving Time, Reducing Stress and Making Money" to get you started right away with lists to guide you in the right direction.

How would your investment portfolio grow if you were to purchase one home every year for seven years? The example below assumes a 2% inflation rate and a purchase amount of $300,000 to illustrate growth in equity. You can easily see that owning real estate can make you rich very quick when there is some amount of inflation. The example does not take into consideration the mortgages being paid down, monthly rental income, taxes, maintenance, vacancies or other factors.

After first year $300,000 x 1.02 = $306,000

After second year $306,000 x 1.02 = $312,120 plus $306,000 = $618, 120

After third year $618,120 x 1.02 = $630,482.40 plus $306,000 = $936,482.40

After fourth year $936,482.40 x 1.02 = $955,212.05 plus $306,000 = $1,286,436.29

After fifth year $1,261,212.05 x 1.02 = $1,286,436.29 plus $306,000 = $1,592,436.29

After sixth year $1,592,436.29 x 1.02 = $1,624, 285.02 plus $306,000 = $1,930,285.02

After seventh year $1,930,285.02 x 1.02 = $1,968,890.72 plus $306,000 = $2,274,890..72

After buying seven properties at $300,000 each for $2,100,000 the total gain from a 2% inflation is $174,890. This only illustrates what happens when you accumulate properties. In reality, you may go through several years with no inflation then be hit with a major jump. This will happen when those economic indicators all point upward. History has shown times when increases were much higher than 10%. In some instances higher than 100%! Barbara Corcoran (Shark Tank) said, "*A funny thing happens in real estate. When it comes back, it comes back up like gangbusters*".

Theodore Roosevelt said, "*Every person who invests in well-selected real estate in a growing section of a prosperous community adopts the surest and safest method of becoming independent, for real estate is the basis of wealth*". It's important to note Mr. Roosevelt put a caveat on this when he included the words well-selected, growing and prosperous. This relates to that key word "location" again. Obviously, if you buy swamp land or a piece of the open prairie somewhere you won't see returns in the short term. If you don't analyze all the factors that influence value beforehand, you could be making a very bad investment. On the other hand, if you are cognizant of major changes, interest rates, world and business events, political announcements, appraisal principles, real estate trends and other factors, you could be making a profitable investment decision.

Inflation and Return on Investment

One of the goals of people who invest in homes is to use as little money of their own to obtain the property. Chapter 7 "Nothing Down Strategies for Buying a Home" deals with this subject. For now, how does a return on investment change when there is inflation? The example below considers only inflation and shows a $400,000 home adding $8,000 after one year with 2% inflation. The rate of return based on a 20%, 10%, 5%, and 2.5% downpayment varies from a 10% return to an 80% return on money invested. The power of leverage and inflation is what landlords and investors bank on to get a higher return on their investment.

$400,000.00 home @ 2% inflation after one year = an $8,000 increase or profit

- purchasing with a 20% downpayment of $80,000 = 10% return after one year

- purchasing with a 10% downpayment of $40,000 = 20% return after one year

- purchasing with a 5% downpayment of $20,000 = 40% return after one year

- purchasing with a 2.5% downpayment of $10,000 = 80% return after one year

Presidential Elections

It's often been said that an election year is a good time for renewing a mortgage as rates generally do not go up during the election year and there could be uncertainty after the election. Chances are no matter who wins the next federal election, the governing party will be interested in keeping interest rates low, because that is what will appease voters. Circumstances that require raising rates do not depend on who wins the election but on the policies the president and congress pursue following the election. How the next president will impact the U.S. Federal Reserve's (the Fed) monetary policy may have some influence on interest rates and mortgage rates. The posing question is, will there be a status quo on many policies or can we expect the Fed's to raise rates?

Political Announcements

A political announcement can have an immediate impact of the housing market by bolstering sales or stagnating them. A political decision to add tariffs on products either bought or sold in the community can impact jobs and influence home prices. A political announcement of a large financial investment in infrastructure or any major Government undertaking can impact the local area altering real estate values.

I can remember one political event that was like flipping a light switch off on home sales. It was very dramatic and quick as home buyers became nervous of something negative that was going to happen in the economy. This was called "The Meech Lake Accord" and it was in Canada. This National interest event came to a climax involving the potential separation of the Quebec province.

Oil Prices

The price of any commodity can be a factor affecting real estate prices in a region. The price of lumber in a region supported by lumber mills, the price of wheat, corn or pork bellies in farm regions and the price of steel in those steel manufacturing regions. If you live in a region which depends on oil production where revenue and jobs are affected by oil prices then you live in an area where home prices may be impacted either up or down by the price of oil. One thing about the price of oil is that many items in home construction rely on oil in the manufacturing process plus every product requires transportation. When the price of oil goes up so does gasoline and everything else causing some inflation which we know will raise home prices.

Local Indicators

Employment and Migration

Ask yourself, "what is happening to the population?". Are there any new major projects in the works in the areas of Government or Industry? Examples are a new hospital, university expansion, Amazon depot, oil refinery, home office relocation, a new manufacturing facility, Olympic or other sport projects, tourism or expansion due to people relocating to retire in the area.

When a city or town attracts a major new development, employment opportunities rise and there is migration of people to fill those jobs. Accordingly, everyone needs a place to hang their hat which makes for a strong real estate market. A hot market is a good one to invest in. A boom in a major city will have spillover to surrounding towns where land and housing is more affordable making these small towns attractive places to invest in housing. The opposite scenario where people are vacating the region represents a land mine you want to avoid.

Here's an example of how new home prices can take an overnight jump. The city council is considering adding a tax to developers of new subdivisions to pay for the cost of new services such as fire halls and police stations. This will add an extra 10 to 20 thousand to the cost of a building lot. Land developers and builders will pass this cost along to new home buyers with a resulting ripple effect on resale home values.

Know what's happening today in your city or town. Are the demographics changing? Aging baby boomers retiring in record numbers means more seniors and demand for wheelchair access homes. Bungalow style homes will be more attractive to seniors than the common two story. Some people will downsize while others renovate and some will just do nothing. Young families moving in is a good sign of a growing population and an attractive community.

When many of the indicators show a downward trend it will mean either the timing is bad for buying or you must take extra precautions by factoring in the added risks. This means negotiating a better deal with consideration for the current economic climate. Chapter 5 "Negotiating for Profit" explores some ideas and tips on the art of negotiating.

When many indicators are pointing up you want to be buying for profit. If all are pointing up it's a hot market and you definitely should not be selling any properties. I've seen this more than once where prices jump $100,000.00 in one year on single family homes in the $300,000.00 and up price range. This is a time when you are using leverage and you are really gaining so hang on during upswings whenever possible. When the indicators turn, you can sell and take profits.

Economic Factors for Profit Checklist

List of Supply, Demand and Price Indicators

1. Number of listings, are they going up, or going down indicating less supply?
2. Movement in purchase prices?
3. Volume of sales, momentum is increasing indicating more demand?
4. Rental rates (rents) are increasing?
5. Vacancy rates declining indicating more demand?
6. Costs to rent are more than the costs to own?
7. Housing starts are increasing indicating demand is on the rise?
8. Costs more to buy new, replacement costs have an influence on the existing market price. Are replacement costs moving higher or lower?

National

9. Interest rates, moving upward is an indicator of rising mortgage costs?
10. Inflation rate, higher inflation means higher leverage by owning real estate?
11. Political announcements? Are there any that will affect real estate in the area?

Regional (State or Province)

12. Boom in a major city, spillover to towns?
13. Migration to area?
14. Employment opportunities, professional, technical, trades, services, other?
15. Major construction projects?
16. Changing demographics, trends indicating opportunities?

Action Exercises:

Identify the indicators that are affecting real estate prices right now in your community. Use the above list as a guide and mark each one with an arrow either up (positive moving upward) or down (indicating a negative downward trend).

Chapter 5

Negotiating for Profit

*"Price is what you pay.
Value is what you get"*
Warren Buffett

Many books have been written and courses taught on the subject of negotiating. Let's just target some key ideas for buying one property for profit. Profits can get lost quickly when you become emotionally attached to a property. When you buy revenue property you are at a slight advantage because it's strictly for investment. When looking for a home to live in, emotion sets in which can put you at a disadvantage when negotiating. Make sure to apply all the factors talked about previously to get the right sense or feel for the property and awareness of the market conditions.

Setting the Asking Price

Investors know that you make money when you buy the right property therefore getting a good deal is where it's at. This does not always mean a discount as there are some profit ideas discussed where that is not the case. It means you need to know if it's a good deal or not so you have to do your homework before you make the offer. Negotiations work well when you are working towards a win/win situation.

Real Estate professionals know how to massage deals so both sides are happy. Acting for you as a facilitator they predetermine and consult with the buyer what would be a good offer knowing in advance that it will either be accepted, countered or declined by the seller. You set the stage like goal posts on a football field with buyer and seller at opposite ends. The plan is that you will eventually end up at the fifty yard line with an accepted offer. This is one strategy to keep in mind but certainly it's not the only one because if there is the expectation of multiple offers then this is likely not going to work in your favor.

Negotiating is like playing chess. You anticipate the other players next move and you move according to your prediction. Under most circumstances, noting that there are exceptions, you **will not** go with your best offer right up front. If you state this is your final offer you have no room to negotiate.

Terms

Sometimes the seller is only concerned with getting their asking price. If it's a FSBO property (for sale by owner) you might have a seller who is focused just on price and getting it sold. Like this for sale by owner example, a husband may say, "Honey, you just watch, we can sell this ourselves and save the commission". What the seller may not realize is that terms can be structured to be more significant than price. An example might be a longer possession time, the addition of a carry back mortgage for a portion of the price offered or other favorable financial terms for the buyer. If you disagree that terms are more important than price then here's my offer to you. I will buy your home for your full asking price, the terms are you carry the financing at zero percent and I'll pay you $100.00 per month until it's fully paid.
You see, terms can be more important than price.

One strategy for buying is to add in some items you are willing to remove. This gives the seller the feeling of winning with the negotiation.

Here are some examples of terms that might be negotiated to benefit a buy/sale agreement.

Terms for Negotiating a Purchase

- The initial down payment
- Financing to be arranged by the seller (provided the mortgage can be assumed)
- Closing costs paid by the seller
- A carry-back mortgage (Vendor take back) for a portion of the purchase price
- Possession date
- Improvements to be made prior to possession (i.e. new furnace or hot water tank)
- Conditional sale (i.e. conditional on sale of another property, conditional on financing, conditional on home inspection)
- Trading an item like a motor home, vehicle, time share or a service for work

Renovations/Repairs

When a home is in need of repairs or renovations, the costs of these renovations should be reflected in the lower asking price or they need to be included in your offer or a combination of both. Having good knowledge of construction costs, I often shake my head when I see properties listed where they require repairs and the asking price is too high. I think it's because the owners are emotional about their property having lived there for a long time. It could also be that they are unaware of the repairs or renovations I foresee as being needed and what they would cost. In any case, your offer, if presented properly, may make them change their mind regarding their asking price. This may not happen immediately but through the negotiation process, time and circumstances can sway the seller to accept a lower offer. Your real estate agent might need to work harder to complete the negotiations. Furthermore, this means you need a good agent who is up to the task of presenting a low offer and pleading your case to the other players, the sellers agent and the seller.

A home inspection can help in this case and the offer should be made subject to a home inspection. We offered 25% less on one home because it needed a full renovation. We did come up on price but saved $35,000.00 off the asking price. This was one purchase where the seller was not aware of the extent of work needed to be done to bring the home up to what I would consider the current market standards of acceptability. If you are looking at a home needing renovations and you are considering flipping it for profit it's really important to know what needs to be done and what the costs are going to be to complete these repairs. Before you make the offer have a meeting with your real estate agent so he or she is fully informed on what deficiencies exist and has some idea on the associated costs which he or she can use when explaining the offer to the seller's agent.

Negotiating Land or a Building Lot

There is more than just the price to negotiate but if you can't agree on price, forget it! There is no point in discussing any of the terms or conditions of the agreement until after "price' is settled or within an acceptable range. If the price doesn't work out the way you expected then at least you haven't engaged the services of a lawyer and incurred legal fees.

When comparing building lots there many factors to consider and the chapter on designing a new home for profit covers a long list. Prices can vary according to desirability reasons such as a view lot, parking access, location on the street, physical attributes such as the slope of the property allowing a walk-out basement, proximity to a park or playground, amenities and the size of the lot. You can divide the cost by the number of square feet to determine a cost per square foot figure. This can be one measurement useful for making comparisons.

The Land Agreement

When you have found a building lot that meets all your requirements, take time to consider the agreement before signing. Don't sign any document unless you have given it at least 48 hours consideration. Read your land agreement carefully then bring the agreement to your lawyer before you sign. Discuss any articles or concerns with your lawyer. Once you sign it is a binding contract and you have to live with the terms regardless of how harsh they are. This is an important transaction and the cost of having a real estate lawyer review and advise you on the contract beforehand is well worth it. The lawyer will provide insight into what's in the agreement and also what's missing from it. It's the "what's missing" part that you might not have considered and a second set of eyes by an experienced real estate lawyer can identify and inform you on these matters if they exist.

Here's some points to consider followed by a good checklist to review before you buy a building lot.

Points to Consider when Buying a Building Lot

- Remember those that hold the land also hold all the cards. Many land developers won't even talk to you unless you are a builder putting up a show home and prepared to build on twenty or more lots. You may need to find the right developer who is willing to sell, the right lot to purchase and the right timing of your offer. Look for a lot requiring a custom builder.
- Infill properties for demolition and new construction allow you to avoid dealing with land developers and can offer opportunities to build for profit in established communities.
- Avoid package deals. You want just the lot, not a package scheme where the land owner is also the builder. I'm assuming you are going to do the planning and select your builder or be the builder.
- Reduce any risk of the other party not following through on verbal promises. Ask which article in the agreement covers that particular promise.
- Place a time limit on your offer. Deals can be lost if the other party has too much time to think it over.
- Prepare how you intend to ask for something. The proper choice of words can make a difference in how it will be viewed by the other party.
- Sometimes it pays to be a tough negotiator provided you know when to quit. Be prepared to make some concessions. You may underestimate what the other party wants.
- Have provisions to legally cancel the agreement if things go wrong before the closing date. Be sure any deposits are refundable if this happens.
- Have your lawyer draw up a purchase agreement if the developer's standard agreement is unfavorable to you. Your lawyer should have copies of agreements on file to work from.
- After an agreement is reached place documents in a safe place for future reference.
- Think about all financing points, the amount of downpayment, the security deposit, the payment timing for the balance of the purchase price and the interest rate on any balance being carried by the developer.
- Consider an option to purchase agreement initially to allow time to start the planning process, determine a suitable floor plan and complete a rough estimate on the cost of construction to establish feasibility of building. Simply, an "option to purchase" helps you buy some much needed time before you make this important commitment.
- Consider a conditional offer to purchase if you need to verify or check something critical such as arranging financing, getting permits, checking acceptability of a plan or anything else deemed necessary to complete the purchase.
- Recap important points by reviewing the Checklist for Buying a Building Lot.

Buying a Building Lot Checklist

Read the land agreement and note the following items:
- deposit required and payment terms
- building commitments
- architectural controls
- setbacks (front and back) and side yard measurements
- required location of garage
- information on grades and location of all utilities
- building restrictions

Why consider an option to purchase?
- lower interest carrying charges
- time to get a suitable set of building plans
- time to get estimates and pre-plan construction
- if time of year is not good for building (a delay will benefit you)

Deposit, initial downpayment, security deposit and full payment
- from line of credit, 2nd mortgage, other source
- consider interest free time (if possible to negotiate)
- payout from other source of credit or 1st mortgage advance or private lender

Contacting Developers, what to look for?
- disadvantaged lots where a custom plan is required, not in the interest of other builders.
- subdivision near completion, now willing to sell some lots to private builders
- selling to a small builder (that's you) not an individual
- lot sales to builders is slow and the developer would like to see more homes being built

City, Town or Township
- city/town developed lots
- tax sale

Infills and Acreage Lots
- examine the cost of a development permit, new services, utilities and demolition costs
- review subdivision or neighborhood restrictions, zoning and bi-laws
- know the costs and other particulars (rules, environmental regulations, by-laws, facts) of installing a water well and septic system if one is required

Negotiating for Profit - Checklist

- Hire a good Real Estate Agent who is licensed, has references and was referred.
- Be prepared to negotiate everything and anything!
- Set a goal or target price and establish a ballpark like you are on each end of a football field and you will move towards the center.
- Set your initial distance from the target price (like the 50 yard line on a football field).
- Allow plenty of room to move as you don't know the seller's motivation
- In theory, each party starts at one end and moves to the middle. This will depend on the seller's motivation and other factors.
- Identify all the negatives and be careful not to discuss positive features with the seller.
- If possible, try to find the other party's needs and/or hot button (e.g. quick sale and possession date). Knowing their motivation for selling could help you close faster with a win/win scenario.
- Your mindset should be to know that the sales process can take up to 6 times. It would be rare to close after the first offer.
- Add in a statement (if not in the sales contract) that the seller provides a current satisfactory "Real Property Report".
- Adding in an escape clause such as "subject to home inspection" and/or "subject to financing" are common. "Subject to viewing by a partner" is another example.
- Add in things of little value to you that you can give up or change later in the negotiation. Some examples are; all appliances, longer possession, small deposit, removal of something unwanted in the yard or house, a repair item, and the escape clauses above. Stay calm, flexible and listen. Silence is golden.
- ASK - What's the lowest price and best terms you would accept for a quick sale?

Action Exercises:

1. Determine the best negotiating strategy for a property you are considering to purchase.
2. Review the Negotiating for Profit Checklist.
3. If possible, ask questions to identify what the important "Hot Buttons" are for the seller.
4. Review "Gold Mines versus Land Mines" in Chapter 8.

Chapter 6

The Right Financing for Profit

*"It is not necessary to do extraordinary things
to get extraordinary results."*
Warren Buffet

My first job after graduating with a degree in commerce was a bank loans officer. I'll never forget the day a client walked in for a $7,000.00 car loan. The manager who was training me told me that his personal accounts were at our branch and his business accounts at another with the same bank, about a mile down the street. He was working as a contract engineer. Interest rates were high and the economy in the early 80's was weak. His loan request was just declined at the other branch. He came into our branch and within ten minutes he was approved by my manager. The manager came to me later and explained that he takes the attitude of looking for ways to approve loan requests whereas the other manager was looking for reasons not to approve him. One manager looked at the glass as half full and the other as half empty. I realized at that time it's important to be dealing with the right person when applying for any type of financing. It's often the person and not the bank that turns you down. Sometimes it's best not to deal directly with the bank and to go through a broker for reasons previously covered.

A year later, I starting with the Co-op Housing branch as a Housing Officer. My boss took me out to the college and introduced me to a class of 20 families who were attending evening classes to learn how to be their own home contractor. It was my first day on the job and I was ready to learn too. He introduced me to the class and said, "Dave worked for the bank and just completed his own home. He is going to talk to you about interim financing". Then he patted me on the back and walked out the door. It was a case of OMG, what now? I struggled through it and afterwards began to prepare all my lessons. My excitement grew when a year later I taught a three-hour class on interim financing and the class gave me a standing ovation. That was very motivational and it eventually led to my first book "A Complete Guide to Being Your Own Home Contractor". As a result of this experience, I'm motivated to help you with the nuts and bolts on financing for profit. My goal is to pass along many points to you to enable you to become successful as financing will be one of the most important keys to your success.

Determine Resources

How do you begin to implement an idea? Start by appraising present and potential opportunities, resources, strengths and weaknesses. Second, carefully consider the alternatives, the advantages and disadvantages and potential costs of each. Third, decide which alternative is best to achieve your end objective. Finally, begin to carry out your plans.

I can remember planning for the construction of our third home. We had no money to buy the building lot and pay for blueprints. How did we do it? Well, we took out a $15,000.00 second mortgage on our existing property to cover the deposit on a lot, the drafting of house plans and the cost of a building permit. The terms of the land agreement allowed us one year to pay the balance and the plan was to pay it out with the new construction mortgage. We obtained all the estimates from suppliers and trades and prepared the cost summary and other documents for the construction (draw) mortgage. The mortgage was approved conditional upon the sale of our home. The building permit was approved and we were ready to start construction the day our existing house sold. Our home was listed and sold with a ninety day possession which is what we requested. To facilitate the sale of our existing home we carried a private second mortgage of $20,000.00 which helped the buyer to qualify. We later sold the second mortgage to a finance company at a small discount which gave the finance company a good rate of return. We started construction immediately and completed one week before the end of the ninety days. Pre-planning really paid off, we were able to move once and construction went smoothly.

Planning is an exceedingly practical job. Be realistic; objective honesty is essential. Guard against allowing your plans to wonder off into dream world.

Write down the answers to the following questions.

- How much money do I currently have for a downpayment or to invest?
- Do I have funds for closing costs, legal, property tax adjustment, insurance, moving?
- How much can I borrow or refinance to invest?
- How much mortgage do I or we qualify for? What will the new payments be?
- How much money do I need to turn the property into a rental or to add a secondary suite including carrying costs, renovations and advertising costs?
- How do I fund these improvements and carrying costs?
- What strategy would I follow for building a new home? (see Chapter 16 and 17)
- What deposits have I already paid? How much money can I save prior to construction? What work can I do myself? Who can assist me with financing or with work?
- How long will it take to renovate or build?
- What will the house cost?
- What will it be worth?

Know Your Maximum Qualifying Mortgage Amount

In order to qualify for a mortgage, you may have to reduce your consumer debt payments from their current level to an amount allowable by the mortgage lender. Often payments that are more than 10% of your gross monthly income will reduce your maximum qualifying amount. You maximum qualifying amount will be determined by the combined applicant and co-applicant's total income. It will change depending on the amortization and rates for the various terms offered. A typical allowable amount for mortgage payments is 30 to 32% of the applicant's gross monthly income with 40% being the total amount allowed for all payments associated with loans including credit cards, student loans and car loans. You can use a payment table to work out the various mortgage options but an easier approach is using the bank websites that do all the calculations for you. Alternatively, you can get the assistance you need from a mortgage broker.

Getting Approved

You need a good solid plan when approaching a bank. When I worked with the bank, the criteria for approval was Ability, Stability, Security, Age and Health. Later, when I worked as a mortgage associate, it was known as the five C's of credit. These are Credit, Capacity, Collateral, Character and Capital. Age and Health were no longer applicable, at least on the surface. Here's what the five C's represent, the way I see them.

Credit — Your credit score according to the credit bureau
Capacity — Your ability to make payments (your maximum qualifying mortgage amount)
Collateral — What are you putting in? The home is collateral or security for the mortgage
Character — Your job/employment history and personality traits
Capital — The principal amount you require to finance compared to your net worth

The Loan Application and Interview Checklist

- Always make an appointment first.
- Introduce yourself to the lending officer.
- If married, both should attend.
- Leave children with a sitter to give all your attention to the lender.
- Know you already qualify for the amount you are applying for.
- Dress accordingly, first impressions are important. Approach the lender as though you are a business manager.
- Be prepared with the required documentation and identification.
- Only provide the information that is asked for. Do not give extra irrelevant information.
- Be positive and optimistic at all times.
- If this is your first home and you have little experience, don't remind your lender of this when you are trying to gain his or her confidence.
- Negotiate the best rate.

Creative Financing

How do you define creative? I would say it's an uncommon way to finance a property and does not involve the normal 25 year amortization with the required down payment. It might equate to a "low" or "no" down payment or any financing option that is not standard but is legal. This could involve a line of credit, a family loan, a co-signer, an investor or partner, sweat equity, a lease-to-own, a vendor take-back (seller holding part of the financing), an assumable mortgage, a bank or government program or a creative offer such as delaying payments, possession dates or other terms. Incidentally, I've used them all! The profit ideas to follow will expand on some of these creative financing possibilities.

The rules change frequently. There are different rules for rentals, self-employed persons, new immigrants and for people with poor credit scores. Find out what types of mortgages are available, who has the best rates, the options that meet your needs and what prepayment privileges are available at what cost to you. Be fully aware of the rules that apply to your application and situation.

It might be a possibility to finance the purchase price plus improvements. Here's an example, but check with your lender, as this is only one lenders' rules. Purchase price is $400,000, improvements $40,000, lender will finance 95% of improvements or $38,000 plus 95% of mortgage or $380,000 for a total loan of $418,000.00. In this example, improvements are added to the purchase price. In certain situations and with the right lender, it's possible to finance up to an additional 20%.

Self Employed Applicants

If you are self employed, you will most likely need to have your last year taxes done to show proof of income. Some lenders relax the rules knowing self-employed small business owners have more write-off's and strive to lower their income to save on taxes. In the lending industry, there are lenders known to mortgage brokers as A lenders, some as B lenders and some as C lenders. The B and C lenders are Trust companies, Credit Unions and other Finance companies who are less strict with their lending rules than the A lenders which are the banks. Your mortgage broker should know these lenders and know if one is willing to accept "Stated Income" in their application. This is simply the applicant stating their income. Self employed individuals like consultants, contractors and trades have irregular incomes so stating income on a yearly basis makes sense. Accepting stated income provides the advantage for a B or C lender to gain a client. If the deal can't fit with an A lender, the mortgage broker would know to present it to a B lender as an option for approval.

Rental Properties

Mortgage rules differ between owner-occupied properties and property for investment. Check what amount lenders will finance as far as loan to value ratio and their requirements for various property sizes and types. The rules change with each lender so the only rule is to verify what each lender is offering so you can then choose the best lender with the best terms for your application. The income generated by a single rental home or duplex home in some cases could be added to your personal job income for the purpose of qualifying for the mortgage. The rental income could one of the qualifying factors. Adding a suite adds income (Capacity) which can also help you qualify for a larger mortgage. This approach has been demonstrated many times on the TV show "Income Property". Check with your bank and a mortgage broker because rules vary, not all lenders accept rental income for a property that is not currently rented.

Some commercial real estate investors have said it's easier to finance a four-plex or a larger multi-family building than it is a single family home. The reason given is that your income could either be of little or no significance on a larger property which is appraised based on the income approach to value. Larger properties generate more income and qualifying is based on a business plan versus your personal income. The land and building cost is easier to cover as they have many tenants paying rent, therefore more revenue covering total costs. Calculating the Net Operating Income (NOI) would be one part of your analysis and becomes a document to form part of a proposal for funding. See Chapter 9 "Buy, Hold and Rent for Long Term Profits" and the "Calculating Net Operating Income Worksheet".

For Sale By Owner (FSBO) Financing

The FSBO properties are what many investors target because the benefit can be a nothing down deal. To achieve nothing down it usually means the buyer would assume the seller's existing mortgage. There is also no real estate agent involved and therefore no commission to be paid. What remains is the difference between the existing mortgage and what the seller is asking. Carefully negotiating some creative financing for this difference is one method many investors have used to purchase multiple properties. The most common strategy is for the seller to carry a second mortgage for a portion or all of the remaining amount. When calling on a FSBO property, you should create a seller information sheet to record the answers to your questions. Sample questions are provided in Chapter 8.

Assumable Mortgages

You will notice that I have been using a lot of words like often, usually, could either be, likely, and check with your lender or broker. Ever since the economic crash in 2008, lenders have been tightening their rules and closing loopholes in order not to get caught with either over-funded properties or with under-qualified owners. Lending rules change frequently. Mortgages that were assumable in the past may require the buyer to qualify today. When buying a property you can inquire if there is existing financing on it, how much and if it's assumable. When an investor can obtain a revenue generating property without qualifying, the investor has gained an asset and his future qualifying ability increases.

Finding the Downpayment

Lenders today are careful to scrutinize the source of downpayment by requiring a paper trail to show where the source of funds came from. Some options may exist for you to help with obtaining the required downpayment. Here are some ideas to consider:

- An applicant with strong income and good net worth can borrow funds from a line of credit, a credit card or a second mortgage.
- A lender may accept a gifted downpayment which might only be acceptable to help a family member.
- The bank may have a program for first time buyers allowing financing up to 100% of the value. The downpayment is paid with a 5% cash back added to the mortgage over a term such as five years. The interest rate would be slightly higher.
- Money taken from a retirement savings plan.
- Sell some items to raise the downpayment.
- Find an investor as a partner.
- Seller assists with financing by carrying back a second mortgage to help facilitate the sale.

See "Chapter 7" for additional ways to finance your purchase and fund the downpayment.

Closing Costs

In addition to the downpayment, some lenders may want to confirm that you have extra funds on hand for the closing costs. The amount they look for could be 1% or 1.5% and it's to cover your costs for legal fees, any tax adjustments, costs for an appraisal or home inspection, moving costs and other expenses such as insurance and setting up accounts with the utilities. Make sure you have funds set aside where you can show the lender you can cover these additional expenses.

The Right Product

The financing must suit your goals. If your goal is to flip the property in a month or within a year then going with a five year closed mortgage wouldn't be a good plan because an early payout would come with a penalty. On the other hand, a five year fixed closed mortgage would suit a property purchased for a rental that you intend to keep for long term.

For a property you are renovating to sell or live in, an interest only line of credit may work best to lower payments while under construction. The loan amount would be determined at the end of the renovation.

For any property you are looking at flipping, you would want to first use your own cash, use lines of credit with suppliers, use open financing in the form of a line of credit based on existing equity or use an open mortgage and a shorter term. This way you avoid getting locked into a contract with payout penalties. Shop around for the best rates and the best financing product or combination of products (mortgages, loans, lines of credit, etc.) for your needs.

New Construction Financing

The ideal method to finance a new home is with your own cash or line of credit. But often the project requires some amount of mortgage financing. The most common approach to financing an owner-built home is with a construction or draw mortgage. This process ensures the security of the lender by not advancing funds until work has already been completed. Guidelines, qualifications and documentation required may vary depending on the lender's policies. The basic procedure on a draw mortgage is as follows:

- You own the building lot and have some equity which contributes to the downpayment.
- You get approval prior to starting construction.
- Begin construction using your own money or an interim financing loan from the bank.
- Once you reach a certain stage (foundation and subfloor complete) which is determined by the bank, call the lending officer for an inspection.
- The inspection identifies the appraised percentage completed and the first advance (example 16%) is advanced.
- Lawyer (acting for the lender) receives the first advance from the lender and any land advance at this time.
- Lawyer searches title for any liens, pays out the balance owing on the land, registers title securing lender's interest, processes mortgage documents with owner-builder, and advances the first advance to the builder or his bank.
- At this stage the builder brings to the lawyer the survey certificate and proof of the required fire insurance specified by the lender.
- The mortgage advance pays down the revolving interim financing loan which helped finance the first stage.
- Steps are repeated at different stages of construction until completion.

When to Apply for a New Construction Mortgage

Imagine for a minute someone walking into a bank, talking with the manager and saying, "I'd like to build my own home. Do you think I can get a mortgage to do it?". What's the manager thinking? He/she is thinking this person hasn't got a clue and obviously he is not a builder because he has no application or documentation. The manager is likely also thinking, "I'm not going to babysit this person for the next year and worry that I might end up with a half-built home", remembering other horror stories of people who didn't know what they were doing. The expected response will be one of trying end the conversation and quickly get the customer out the door. Don't be a "walking generality" when dealing with the bank for any loan. Be specific, know you qualify, and be prepared! Be ready to talk dollars!

Before you even make the appointment have a complete package ready which gives the lender confidence in you as a builder who understands what he is doing. After all, there is a lot to know about building a home and the lender doesn't know the answers to it all so you need to show that you are competent and capable. To assist you with this type of request, refer to Chapter 17 for the documentation checklist for a new construction mortgage.

Do your Due Diligence; Physical, Financial and Legal

Prepare a budget and do some financial homework before applying for financing. Prepare for the loan application by creating in advance a personal statement with personal, job, and income information and a financial statement listing assets and liabilities. Know the amount you qualify for and be specific on what you are asking for and how you intend to pay it back.

The property inspection will determine if the home was a previous illegal grow-op, has mold, termites or other issues as well as needed repairs. This important inspection is best if it's completed by an independent expert who is trained in this field. Even though I have gained a lot of experience building homes, I still hire a home inspector for an independent unbiased view and second pair of eyes to provide a valuable opinion. The findings in an inspection report have saved me thousands of dollars when used to negotiate a discount with the seller for covering the costs of the needed repairs. More than often it pays for the cost of the inspection. The inspector will check the roof, the attic, the electrical panel, every switch and plug. Everything that's possible to check they check and this can take several hours to complete.

Obtain all the information on the property. For a condominium you would obtain the financial report from the management firm or the board to determine if the property has any special assessments on it. Also review the reserve fund to check if it's reasonable for the age of the property and in line with the engineer's recommendations for the size of the fund.

When buying a home to renovate or add a suite you would check the zoning, permits required and what work would be needed to add a legal suite.

For building a new home you would check the building lot for easements and utilities. In a planned subdivision you would need to know the architectural controls for building a home. These would include things such as size requirements, style, garage location, exterior finish, roof finish, grades and other items identified by the land developer's architectural coordinator. You would need to know if there is a security deposit required prior to construction for potential damage to sidewalks or services due to your construction as well as all the building permit requirements, inspections and safety rules. The lists under construction in Chapter 17 and 18 are guides to assist you when planning, financing and building a new home.

Always seek out expert advice in everything you do as this is how you gain expertise and minimize problems. Focus on those management functions including financing and only plan to do the physical work you are qualified to do.

Action Exercises:
1. Work out your qualifying mortgage amount by visiting a bank website or by contacting a Mortgage Broker (Associate).
2. Prepare a Personal Statement and a Financial Statement.
3. Source out different lenders and their various lending products and features or locate a Mortgage Broker (Associate) who can act as your representative.
4. Get pre-approved before purchasing a property.

Chapter 7

Nothing Down Strategies for Buying a Home

*"Life is about accepting the challenges along the way,
choosing to keep moving forward, and savoring the journey."*
Roy T. Bennett , Author

What is meant by the phrase "Nothing Down"? Real Estate Associates will laugh at these words saying "there is no such thing as nothing down". In nearly all contracts they are correct because "nothing down deals" really just mean none of your own money, but money from somewhere else. Even if you can structure a nothing down purchase you still have some associated closing costs to deal with. You would have to be very crafty to end up with a true nothing down purchase. To be realistic, let's discuss nothing down as nothing out of your own pocket. The different approaches identified in this chapter will be the tools you can add to your toolbox for use whenever the opportunity is presented to you.

The nothing down phenomena began in the 1980's with Robert Allan's book "Nothing Down". There were many entrepreneurs to follow offering seminars and books and still today real estate seminars continue to run on this subject. A true nothing down deal means the buyer has nothing to lose by walking away from a property. It puts the lender at risk because the buyer has no vested interest in the property. Over the years, lenders and mortgage insurers changed their guidelines to reduce both risk and also reduce the number of fraudulent mortgage deals. This happened following the 2007-2008 world economic crash led by subprime lending.

In the United States, subprime loans are usually classified as those where the borrower has a credit score (Fico Score) below 640. The term "subprime loans" was popularized by the media during the subprime mortgage crisis or "credit crunch" of 2007. Those loans which do not meet government sponsored enterprises like Fannie Mae or Freddie Mac underwriting guidelines for prime mortgages are called "non-conforming" loans. Many of these mortgages were packaged into asset-backed securities that corporate investors could buy. The end result was far too many properties funded too high by many people with little to no equity in the property where they could easily walk away if values were to fall or from loss of income.

Following the 2008 housing crash was a time where investors could scoop up great deals on vacant foreclosed properties. The idea of using little to none of your own money is still an investor strategy used today to afford to purchase more properties. Lending guidelines change and investors change their financing strategies to accommodate the new rules. There are still legitimate ways to buy property using little to none of your own money for the downpayment.

The methods I've used and ones our children have used to purchase a home with little to no downpayment would fall under the following headings:

1. Bank program
2. Gifted Downpayment
3. Lease to own
4. Motivated and Flexible Seller
5. Investor (family member) financed
6. Sweat Equity for new construction

Bank Program

Bank promotions come and go like a sale; however, far less frequent than your local clothing store. When they are offered they can be considered. One example used by a family member to buy his first home involved the bank allowing financing up to 100% which provided certain qualifying criteria to be met. The bank rate of interest for the first five years was slightly higher so the accumulated difference in monthly payments would add up to the downpayment required to meet the high ratio insurance guidelines. This program was created as an incentive for first time home buyers. The point to be made here is to check with your bank to see if any programs exist to help you obtain your first home.

Gifted Downpayment

This was another option to assist a family member with a first home purchase. The bank required a gift letter stating it was a gift and the money did not have to be paid back. In other words, it's a pure gift not a loan. One family member paid the gifted downpayment and the other family member became the owner using none of their own money.

Lease to Own

A "Lease to Own Contract" would need to be reviewed by your lawyer who would amend the terms of the lease and detail the amount of rent which could be applied towards the future downpayment and purchase price. I used a lease to purchase contract for a twelve month period. The length of time would depend on factors such as what is the seller willing to allow, how much is being applied towards the downpayment and the time required to accumulate an amount which will allow you to finance and purchase the property. If prices are going up it's definitely to the buyers advantage to complete the contract by buying the property. If prices decrease, the contract would not be fulfilled and the portion of rents to be applied towards the purchase would either be kept by the home owner or refunded depending on the terms of the contract.

The amount which can apply towards the downpayment must meet lender and insurance guidelines and there would be limits on the acceptable amounts. A copy of the contract I used is included here for you as a working document should this opportunity present itself. This is the actual agreement we used to secure a home and purchase it a year later with no downpayment other than legal costs.

Lease to Own Agreement
(Agreement of Purchase & Sale and Interim Lease Agreement)

THIS AGREEMENT made, as of the date of acceptance hereof by the owner, between:

_____

_____
City, Province
and

_____

_____

_____

WHEREAS the Owner is the owner of Certain Lands described legally as:
PLAN _____
BLOCK _____
LOT _____

EXCEPTING THEREOUT ALL MINES AND MINERALS

which lands, together with the buildings, improvements and appurtenances thereon and thereto are hereinafter called the "Property";

NOW THEREFORE:

1. Subject to the provisions hereof and the conditions contained herein, The Purchaser offers to purchase, and the Owner by acceptance hereof agrees to sell to the Purchaser, the Property as of the Date of Closing (as that term is hereinafter defined).

2. The price to be paid by the Purchaser to the Owner for the Property shall be _____ Dollars ($), subject to adjustments as hereinafter provided, to be paid in the following manner:

    $_____ As initial deposit by Certified Cheque non-refundable payable _____

    $_____ to be in the form of ____ post-dated cheques dated the first day of each month commencing _____ and running through to _____, each such cheque to be in the amount of $_____ and to be payable to the Owner (or as the Owner shall designate), (the aggregate amount of which shall have been cashed from time to time are hereinafter called the "Deposits") and

$_____   subject to adjustments as hereinafter provided, in cash, bank draft, or solicitor's trust cheque, such funds to be paid to the Owner's solicitor, on trust conditions satisfactory to the solicitors for the Owner and the Purchaser acting reasonably, on or before the Date of Closing. Owner acknowledges that all or part of the purchase price may be raised by way of a mortgage or mortgages of the Property which shall be arranged by and at the expense of the Purchaser, on terms satisfactory to it. The obligation to complete the purchase is subject to the purchaser arranging satisfactory financing on or before _____.

$_____   TOTAL

3.   (a)   All taxes, rents, security deposits, insurance, local improvement levies, and all other items normally adjusted in transactions similar to that contemplated hereby (with the exception of utilities which shall be adjusted as of the Lease Commencement date hereinafter set out), shall be adjusted as at the Date of Closing, (with the Date of Closing to be for the account of the Purchaser) subject to the terms hereof being complies with the parties hereto.

      (b)   Any money not paid when due hereunder shall bear interest at the prime rate charged by the (<u>name of bank</u>) from time to time plus __% per annum, from the date the same is due and payable, to and including the date the same is paid in full.

4.   Owner covenants and agrees that following acceptance hereof and during the duration of this agreement, the owner shall not solicit or accept any offers to purchase the Property, nor sell, lease, mortgage, encumber, to otherwise alienate its interest in the property or any part thereof.

5.   The Owner agrees to provide to the Purchaser, within five days of the execution of the Agreement, copies of all leases, easements, agreements, contracts, drawings, plans, surveys, specifications, and other documents in its possession (or available to it) related to the Property.

6.   The Date of Closing shall be _____. Provided the Purchaser has fulfilled the obligations under this agreement, vacant possession of the Property shall be given to the Purchaser as 12:00 o'clock noon on the Date of Closing, subject to the Purchaser's right of possession granted hereinafter, the rights of any tenants under leases, or licenses of which the Purchaser shall have been made aware of prior to the condition Date and Subject to the Purchaser's being in earlier possession in accordance with paragraph 8 hereof.

7.   The purchase price shall include all buildings, equipment, fixtures and chattels on or utilized in the Property including, without limiting the generality of the foregoing. All non property items shall be at the Purchaser's risk and the Property shall be and remain at the risk of the owner until the Date of Closing, and all insurance policies and any proceeds thereof shall be held in trust for the parties as their interests may appear.

8.   The Owner shall at 12:00 noon on the _____ day of _____ 20,_____ (hereinafter referred to as the "Lease Commencement Date") provide to the Purchaser

vacant possession of the property. The Owner hereby grants to the purchaser, as of the Lease Commencement date, a Lease (the "Lease") of the Property for the term and on the conditions set out in Paragraph 8.

(a) The term of the Lease (the "Term") shall be a period of _____ months, commencing at 12:00 o'clock noon on the Lease Commencement Date, and fully to be ended and completed at 12:00 o'clock noon on the Date of Closing.

(b) The Purchaser shall pay to the Owner, a monthly rent of $_____ each such payment of rent to be due and payable on the first day of each and every calendar month throughout the Term. The post-dated cheques paid by the Purchaser to the Owner as Deposits under the provisions of Paragraph 2, 8 (b) hereof shall, when honored by the Purchaser's bank, constitute satisfaction of the Purchaser's obligations to pay rent under the provisions of the sub-paragraph 2, 8 (b).

(c) Throughout the Term, the Purchaser shall be responsible for the payment of the costs of all utilities and municipal services consumed on the Property, directly to the provider of such utilities or services. To the extent that any such payments are not made when due, the Owner may (but shall not be under an obligation to) make such payments on behalf of the Purchaser, and the amount of any such payments shall be immediately due and payable from the Purchaser as rent under the Lease.

(d) Throughout the Term the Owner shall be responsible for all taxes, rates and assessments due or payable with respect to the Property.

(e) Throughout the Term, the Purchaser shall peacefully posses the Property for its own use, under the provisions of the Residential Tenancies Act of the Province of _____, and shall be entitled to sue the Property for any legal purpose.

9. The transfer of land shall be prepared at the expense of the Owner and shall be forwarded to the Solicitor for the Purchaser on or before the date of closing. Any mortgage or other instrument required by the Purchaser to secure its financing (other than such instruments as may be required to give effect to the intent of the following paragraph 10) shall be prepared at the expense of the Purchaser.

10. The cost of discharging any encumbrance which the Purchaser has not agreed to assume shall be borne by the Owner. The Owner shall have a reasonable time following the Date of Closing to discharge any encumbrance which is not a permitted encumbrance and to provide the Purchaser with a Certified Copy of Title evidencing such discharge.

11. The Owner represents and warrants that:
(a) It is not now (nor will it be within 60 days of the Date of Closing), a non resident of Canada within the meaning of the Income Tax Act of Canada;

(b) It is not the agent or trustee for anyone with an interest in the property who is (or will be within 60 days of the date of Closing) such a non-resident; and

12. The purchaser agrees to purchase the Property as it stands, and there are no representations, warranties, or conditions made by or on behalf of the Owner or its officers, directors, employees or agents, other than those expressed in this agreement.

13. If the Purchaser fails to comply with the terms hereof, then the Deposits referred to in the Paragraph 2,8. (b) hereof and all interest earned thereon shall be absolutely forfeited to the Owner as liquidated damages and not as a penalty. The parties acknowledge and agree that the damages payable to the owner in the event of such failure shall be limited to the total amount of such Deposits together with the interest earned thereon.

14. The Owner shall be responsible for the payment of all Real Estate commissions or fees payable with respect to the purchase and sale of the Property, and is unaware of any person who is entitled to any such commissions or fees.

15. The Owner agrees that the Purchaser may not assign it's interest in this agreement to any person, corporation, partnership or other entity, or may not designate any entity to take title to the property on closing.

16. Any notice or correspondence between the parties contemplated by this agreement shall be in writing, and shall be deemed to have been received by the addressee when delivered to an officer or employee of the addressee, at the address of such party first set out herein, or at such other address of which the addressee may have advised the sending party by notice in accordance herewith.

Until any such notice of change shall be delivered, the address of each party for the purposes of this Agreement shall be the address of each first set out hereinbefore.

17. This Agreement shall be interpreted in accordance with the laws of the Province of _____. All references to time are to Mountain Standard, or Mountain Daylight Savings Time in effect on the date in question. This Agreement shall be binding upon the parties hereto, their executors, administrators, legal representatives, successors and assigns. Time shall in every respect be of the essence hereof.

18. Price to include all appliances, _____

19. This Agreement shall be open for acceptance by the Owner until _____ p.m. on the _____ day of _____, 20____. If the Owner and the Purchaser have not each been provided with a fully executed copy of this agreement by that time, any Deposits shall be returned to the Purchaser, this agreement shall be at an end, and neither party shall have any further obligation to the other with respect hereto.

IN WITNESS WHEREOF the purchaser has caused this Agreement to be executed as of the _____ day of _____, 20_____.

_____   _____
Witness   Purchaser

_____   _____
Witness   Purchaser

We, _____ and _____, the Owner herein, hereby accept the within offer to Purchase together with all terms and conditions herein contained, Dated this _____ day of_____ 20_____.

_____   _____
Witness   Owner

_____   _____
Witness   Owner

Option to Purchase

When buying a building lot it's best to ask for an option to purchase for a month or longer in order to allow time to research the lot, get an acceptable plan (main floor drawing and sketch of front view) and arrange financing. The more time you have the greater the opportunity to opt out if things don't work according to your plan.

A good example would be if you were looking at buying a property with a characteristic that you need to examine such as an easement, a utility right of way, zoning, or architectural controls to see if your design will fit and suit the property.

On one occasion the land developer just put our name on the lot giving us a thirty day window to check out floor plans and work out financing details. This required no formal agreement. The deal was that if another builder wanted to buy the lot, I would have the first option to buy and be required to bring in the downpayment of 15% of the lot value and sign for the purchase. Within less than a month we were able to close the purchase. An option can allow you to tie up a property without using any money and with no risk. If you are building homes to sell then holding options on building lots is very valuable. You have inventory you can use to market to the public.

Another trick with options has been used by some skilled real estate individuals/investors as a means of obtaining the right to buy a property for a predetermined price allowing the investor to show and sell the property to another party at a higher price. Assume you have negotiated an option to buy a home for a good discount. You find another buyer, at a higher price or one close to the original asking price, before the option runs out. Basically, you use none of your own money and on closing (double closing) the lawyer essentially hands you a check for the difference. You have no closing costs, no financing to arrange and no risk. This is one amazing strategy if you have the excellent selling skills needed to deal with both sellers and buyers.

A simple "option to Purchase Agreement" is illustrated as an sample to work from should you be in a position of this particular need and negotiation. As you can see it is much shorter than a real estate purchase contract which would have many articles dealing with the closing and possession. This agreement is only showing an option where the seller is agreeing to sell you the property at the agreed upon price. This form is not approved by a real estate association. It is intended for an interim agreement until the option is exercised. When this occurs, an official real estate purchase contract should be completed.

This agreement as with the others in this book are for illustration purposes to help explain strategies for buying a home. It is recommended you review any agreement with a lawyer who can advise you on all legal matters and provide the best documentation for your purpose. When you are dealing in real estate you should always check if a real estate license is required for whatever you are doing.

Option to Purchase Agreement

THIS AGREEMENT made this _____ day of _____ 20_____

BETWEEN

_____

                                                            Hereinafter called "the Vendor" of the First Part.

_____

                                                            and

_____

                                                            Hereinafter called 'the Purchaser" of the Second Part.

_____

Witnessed that in consideration of the sum of _____Dollars now paid by the Purchaser to the Vendor (the receipt whereof is hereby acknowledged), and the Vendor hereby gives to the Purchaser an option, irrevocable within the time of acceptance herein limited, to purchase, free from encumbrances and encroachments, the land described as follows:

The purchase price of the said lands shall be the sum of _____Dollars, which upon acceptance of this Option, shall be paid as follows:

The said sum of _____Dollars, now paid to the vendor as consideration for the within Option shall be applied on the purchase price and the balance in the sum of _____Dollars shall be paid as follows:

_____

_____

_____

The within Option to Purchase shall be open for acceptance up to twelve (12:00) o'clock Noon on the _____ day of _____ 20_____, but not after, and may be accepted by written Notice to that effect delivered to the Vendor or his solicitors, and upon acceptance thereof, the same shall constitute a binding agreement of purchase and sale.

Provided that if the Purchaser fails to accept the within Option within the time and the manner provided herein, the Purchaser shall forfeit to the Vendor the said sum paid by way of consideration for the within Option and the option shall be determined at an end.

All adjustments of taxes, insurance premium, rentals and all other adjustments shall be made as of _____, 20_____. Vacant possession of said land shall be given to the Purchaser on _____ 20_____.

Time shall be of the essence of this Agreement.

The within Agreement shall ensure to the benefit of and be binding upon the Vendor and the Purchaser, their respective heirs, executors, administrators, successors and assigns.

In Witness Whereof the parties have hereunto respectively set their hands and seals on the day and year first above written.

SIGNED, SEALED AND DELIVERED
      in the presence of

_____
      Witness

_____   _____
      Vendor   Purchaser

To purchase a home using little or none of your own money requires one or a combination of a number of possibilities. Find one that will work for your situation or find a property where one will work. Here is a list of possibilities for you to examine regarding your personal financial situation as well as the property and seller's motivations.

List of Possibilities for Buying a Home with a Low Downpayment

- Access to a personal line of credit or HELOC (Home Equity Line of Credit).
- Equity in another property which you can access.
- Credit from a loan or credit cards that won't affect qualifying.
- A gifted downpayment from an immediate family member. The letter must state that the money is a gift, not a loan.
- A parent who can co-sign to help qualifying (increase "capacity" for making payments).
- An investor or partner who is part owner. The investor provides personal financing for the downpayment and closing costs, co-signs the mortgage and is on title for 50%. The investor benefits from leverage and also has the other invested party living there, paying the bills and maintaining the property. For the investor this is better than a rental tenant. The buyer now owns 50% and benefits from inflation. The buyer can sell at a later date when there is equity in the property. It's a win/win for both parties.
- An investor who finances the entire property where there is no downpayment. The investor has access through personal or business accounts and can structure a cash purchase.
- A motivated seller who is willing to allow you to assume the existing mortgage where there is little to no equity for the seller.
- A motivated seller willing to participate by carrying paper, a vendor take-back or second mortgage. The seller is flexible in some way on the difference between the mortgage and the negotiated purchase price.
- A motivated seller willing to trade something for the equity.
- A repair allowance where the purchase is structured to give the buyer cash back on closing for needed repairs. The amount must be reasonable to a lender, keep it under 3% of the purchase price.
- The buyer sells some items to come up with the downpayment.
- The buyer can access money from a registered retirement savings plan or other retirement investments.
- Money is borrowed from or secured by an existing whole life insurance policy.
- A "rent to own" also known as a "lease purchase" where the terms of the lease show that a portion of rents, for a pre-determined period of time, are applied towards the purchase price. The deposit is shown on paper as paid at a future date from the total portion of the accumulated rent payments paid by the tenant. Lenders have restrictions regarding what they will accept. They like to see the paper or money trail. It's important and necessary for you, as the tenant, to sign a formal contract. The property may appreciate and without a contract the offer will be retracted. After a period of time, if and when the property appreciates, you will want to pursue purchasing the home to take advantage of the equity you would gain from the increase in property value.

- A Government or bank program allowing a zero down option to help first time home owners. The downpayment was provided by the lender and repaid during the first five year term by applying a slightly higher interest rate. Buyer must have good credit and be able to qualify at the higher rate. Check availability of government programs nationally and also in your region.
- An income property where the closing date is after the first of the month (example 3rd of the month) allowing the buyer to collect the rents (28 days or rents prorated by lawyer) prior to making the first of the month mortgage payment. These rents could also help with repaying the downpayment and funding closing costs.
- An income property where the combination of financing covers 100% of the purchase price.
- A pre-foreclosed property where the lender allows you to assume the mortgage and there is no equity for the seller and no downpayment.
- A real estate agent participating in a deal where no commission is paid by the buyer.
- You assume the existing financing equal to the purchase price. There is no commission or the commission might be paid by the seller or the lender if the property is listed.
- A property that is inherited. Title is simply transferred into your name and the legal fees are paid by the estate.
- A new owner-built home where the owner uses sweat equity as the downpayment. To achieve this, the owner-builder would need to understand appraisal and costs per square foot, build the right property, know how to prepare and present the application including how to complete the "Cost Summary Form", act as the builder and perform some minor trade work/sweat equity during construction.
- Private financing during construction with bank financing at the end. The advantage is the new completion mortgage financing is based on the appraised market value not your construction costs (cost approach) which may be significantly lower. The downpayment shows as the difference which makes up the 20% or more for the downpayment.
- An option to purchase for negotiating a short-term hold on a property or a building lot. The option is a signed agreement specifying a time period or a condition such as the buyer having the first option to buy if another party is interested in buying.

As you can see there are many ways you can cover the downpayment and associated closing costs without using cash from your personal account. All you need is the right one to work for your purchase. Use this list to creatively select one of the possible options. It may require you to practice your selling skills. It sure did when I built a home using an assignment of mortgage proceeds to sell to all the trades and suppliers. That took a lot of selling. It's very important to note that not all of these options may exist with your lender, with the insurance provider and with the seller therefore inquiries need to be made. Also, as discussed in Chapter 1, this is the time when you have to use your selling skills to negotiate the deal.

If you are prepared to roll up your sleeves and get out there, view properties, talk to real estate agents, sellers and lenders, you will find the solution you need to buy your own home starting now. Don't wait until you have saved a downpayment. If you are month to month with paychecks it will take too long or it may never happen. You need to take action right now.

Action Exercises:
1. Check current rules with your mortgage broker examining the possibilities listed above.
2. Review the qualifying criteria pertaining to financing a property in Chapter 6.
3. Talk to an investment planner to see how you can save the downpayment faster. Don't buy more than you can afford.
4. Study the Cost Summary form for a Mortgage Application in Chapter 17. This document is used when applying for financing for an owner-built home. Where is the "Builder's Cost" listed?
5. Select one or more ways from the list of possibilities provided that you could act on for your first or next home purchase. You can combine ideas to structure your financing.

Chapter 8

Finding Motivated Sellers and the Right Product for Profit !

*"People work for money but go the extra mile
for recognition, praise and rewards!"*
Dale Carnige

Finding a good property to invest in often means being in the right place at the right time and talking to the right person. It means finding motivated sellers as long as the motivation is not to get rid of what we can consider a land mine. It also means when a good deal comes along it's often the "first with the most" who ends up being the buyer.

Get on the Agents Hot List

When you know how much financing you qualify for you are ready to invest and positioned to make an offer. You are the person a real estate agent wants to call first when a hot new listing comes into the office and is presented to all the agents. I went one step further by contacting several agents in different offices. I informed them on who I was and what kind of property I was looking for and the important fact that I could buy on short notice with no financing condition. This put us on their hot list. I wanted to be on the top of that list so I advised them I could take immediate action if the right property came up for sale.

The plan worked well! I got a call within a week to view a duplex (two properties with a common wall). The owner had already moved two thousand miles to Toronto and he just wanted to get rid of the property. He was a motivated seller because he had already moved. The asking price reflected that motivation. It was going to be a quick sale, likely the same day, to the first person who could make a reasonable offer. The asking price was just $89,000.00 for both sides which were already rented. I knew immediately this was a great deal because we had bought other half duplexes for $60,000.00. I know what you are thinking, you can't even buy a garage for that amount today! Remember, it's not the amount that matters, it's the strategy of networking with Real Estate Agents.

My plan was working because I was on the top of the agents hot list and I got the call first. I must have done a good job selling myself to the Agent. Now we needed to drop everything and view the property immediately to be the first one with an offer before it sold. The listing was time sensitive. It was imperative for us to take immediate action and for the Agent to be the first to present an offer to the seller's Agent and the seller. As it turned out we were able to view one side and make the offer immediately for the full asking price with no conditions. There was no reason for the seller not to accept the offer and there were no other offers being presented at the moment.

The listing was so new it wasn't even marketed to the public on the multiple listing service (MLS). It was a situation where it was a win for everyone. The full price offer was so our Agent could capture the sale immediately rather than allow time for back and forth negotiations and the possibility for other offers to be presented on the same day. Sometimes you just have to be "the first with the most" and this was one of those times. It's not every day you can make a $30,000.00 profit buying one property by *being ready, being fast and being first*!

Playing The Numbers Game

We bought two rental properties from an investor who was relocating 250 miles away to another city. These purchases required some negotiating and sales skills because it was a for sale by owner (FSBO) situation. I learned that selling, or the sales process, means you need to ask as many as six times, ask in a different way and ask at a different time. It means listening to the seller and paying attention to their needs and any hot buttons. A hot button is something important they need to gain from the transaction. It paid off, we negotiated back and forth a few times and finally completed both transactions. There were no Agents involved in these purchases and I was able to complete both with a very low downpayment.

Over the coming weeks I learned the investor's strategy for picking up properties in the new city which was Edmonton, Alberta Canada. He was relocating there because prices were favorable and the economic signs showed things were just starting to pick up for the city. He met with his Agent in the office and identified many properties in several locations that fit his criteria. On the most wanted list was a single family home with three bedrooms, a basement suite and a garage. His objective was to rent all three separately to have three rents coming in. This is a great plan because it provides the benefit of positive cash flow. Having three tenants lowers his risk of having negative cash flow. With three rents, should one of the three areas become vacant for a month or two, he still collects two rents. He prefers to rent the garage separately for the same reason. There would be some headaches with tenants and I did experience some hiccups with the two properties I bought. I was prepared to deal with the issues because I was ready and up for the game.

To find motivated sellers in the new location, the investor and his agent did one thing unusual. I don't think all Agents would endorse this plan but like I said earlier some selling skills are needed to be successful when dealing in these matters. The investor had his Agent send out conditional offers on many properties for 20% less than the list price. This was done prior to viewing with the condition "subject to viewing" added to every offer. This was the starting place knowing that a motivated seller would either accept the offer or counter the offer with a discount from the listing price. In short time the investor had regained a full portfolio of rental properties. He also knew that equity or profits are gained when you buy a property, especially when you find a motivated seller and negotiate a discount off the list price.

Work with Your Agent

To your Agent, you are the client and repeat business is what every agent loves to have. Bill (not his real name) was a flooring supplier I knew quite well. He supplied floor covering for many of the homes I built and others we bought. Having good trade and supplier contacts is very beneficial when you are buying properties. Bill, who was in his seventies and financially very well off, told me what he was doing that was making him a pile of money. A million dollars in two years flipping homes. I was all ears to hear his plan. He was working with one Agent in a different city three hours away where the market met the right conditions. These economic conditions are discussed in Chapter 4 and they cover supply, demand, the market condition and trends which can really determine opportunities that exist for flipping homes.

Bill set the parameters to buying single family three bedroom (bread and butter) homes in the $300,000 to $400,000.00 price range. This was determined to be the sweet spot where the highest number of sales took place. The higher demand was due to the ease of more buyers qualifying for financing under $400,000.00. Bill knew he could buy and sell staying within this price range and profit from a quick sale. He picked established communities, closer to amenities, schools, shopping, the university and transportation to the downtown core. These areas would have few homes for substitution and allow better opportunities to negotiate a discount considering most required some cleaning up and updating. The newer subdivisions would not be the market for his profit strategy.

Having the funds to finance 100% through lines of credit gave Bill the advantage to buy over the phone based on the word of his Agent who described the properties and facilitated the negotiations for all purchases and subsequent listings and sales. He would buy and sell with the same Agent who would become a close business associate.

Bill's strategy was to immediately remove the old flooring, apply a clean coat of neutral paint to all the walls, install new modern broadloom if required and update the tiling and fixtures in the kitchen and/or bathrooms. Note: paint before the new flooring arrives, otherwise the painters have double the amount of work. From start to completion this work took less than two weeks. Bill re-listed the property with enough room to cover real estate fees, legal fees, renovations and generate a profit between $10,000.00 and $50,000.00 per home. Not too bad and when you can afford to buy one or two homes every week you can see how fast you can make a million dollars.

We covered three examples, my plan for buying a property, the investor's plan relocating to a new city and Bill's plan for buying and selling homes. In each case, the Real estate Agent played a key role for success. Developing a good relationship with one or more professional licensed Real Estate Agents positions you in the market as a ready buyer and a future potential seller.

Homes For Sale By Owner

For sale by owner properties can offer some unique opportunities but requires you to be extra careful to ensure you are dealing with actual owners. If you do any deal and you are not using a licensed real estate agent you absolutely must ensure you handle all your affairs through a real estate lawyer. For sale by owner (FSBO) properties are the target of investors looking to negotiate a low downpayment deal because there are no commissions to be paid and there might be an opportunity for creative financing. One aspect is asking the seller to carry financing (seller provides a second or carry-back mortgage) on the equity part of the purchase. Creative financing can also mean working outside the box by structuring a contract that's not the standard one requiring the buyer to put up the required deposit and qualify for financing. It's not a free fall today like it was before the economic crash. Today the rules for assuming mortgages are not as loose, lenders may require you to qualify. This is a question you will need to investigate when you evaluate a purchase. I will also be sharing a long list of potential situations to get you thinking about creative solutions for buying.

Newspaper classified ads used to be the medium for sellers. Today, websites that allow you to list for free have almost entirely taken over as the go to place for advertising. I can list my house in a matter of minutes on the same website I use to sell a piece of furniture. As a buyer, this is where you should look. Check the photos on line, check out the street view on Google maps and reply directly to the seller with the goal of setting up a phone conversation allowing you to ask some of the other prequalifying questions. If you don't know the best websites for your area just ask around and you will find them. Kijiji is popular where I live but it's area related. There are many others such as homesbyowner.com and Comfree.

The beauty of websites is you can view the photos on line, check out the street view on google and reply directly to the seller to set up a viewing. I suggest you carefully check out the property, get the address, do a drive by to view the outside and confirm it's the property for sale. Also, it's a good idea to pull title (do a title search) before any offer is made so you know you are dealing with the registered owners. All the steps of using a lawyer to hold deposits in trust and checking picture ID need to be taken. Trust me on this one. I met up with a team of scammers who were acting like real estate agents however they were unlicensed. They used websites to sell properties they didn't own. Their goal was to take possession of your 20% deposit. They set up a very complex system involving buyers, sellers, land titles, fake mortgage documents, invalid contracts and a commissioner of oaths working with them to make it all look real. This group of low life's would work both sides (sellers and buyers) offering fantastic deals to lure people in then transfer title using fake mortgage documents. Once the buyer (who is an unknowing participant in their scam) is on title, the fraudsters could sell their fake mortgage, which was never funded but is now registered on title, at a discount to an investor. Police had a real hard time figuring things out and it took years before they could lay charges.

When I tried to explain their scheme to a lawyer he told me it would take him a whole day to figure it all out. His fee was $450.00 an hour so that would sure cost a bundle. It would cost far more if you got involved with this group and ended up in court. Two of these crooks ended up doing some jail time but not before taking more than a dozen families for hundreds of thousands in deposits. I'm telling you all this because the critical objective here is you *must* do your due diligence whenever you are dealing with a property not listed with a licensed real estate agent.

For sale by owner properties are certainly the target for investors because of the opportunity they might have to negotiate a low down deal directly with the seller. As the buyer, you would start a friendly conversation asking them about their property followed by an open question regarding the existing financing. You want to let the seller know who you are and that you are looking to buy a home in the area for either yourself or as an investment. Telling them a little bit about yourself helps to build a rapport which opens the conversation up for future questions. It also helps to open up the conversation if you can complement them on something about their home. Basically, you want to save time when qualifying sellers and viewing properties. You want to know if the financing is assumable and if the seller needs all their equity out of the property. Finding out their motivation for selling can help when you structure an offer. A seller who doesn't require money right away could be one who agrees to carry back a mortgage (carry back paper) for the difference between the existing amount owing and the final price you agree on. The bank certainly doesn't want to own the property and may allow you to assume the existing mortgage with or without qualifying, depending on the circumstances and their rules.

Practice making those phone calls because this will save you time, effort and eventually money. Tell yourself "I can make these phone calls, I can do it! The phone does not weigh 50 pounds". Just go to a quiet place and do it. If you think you can, you can!

Questions to Ask the Seller
- Can I ask you a few questions about your home?
- How much are the taxes?
- What's the property like?
- How many bedrooms?
- How many bathrooms?
- Is there a garage or street parking?
- Is there a suite?

- Sounds like a nice property. Can you tell me why you are selling?
- Do you know if there are other homes rented or for rent in the area?
- Do you know what rents go for in the area?
- Is there existing financing which can be assumed?
- How much are the mortgage payments?

As I just mentioned, websites have almost completely taken over since they can offer much more information including photos of the property. And again, remember to carefully check out any property advertised on a website by getting the address, completing a drive by to confirm it's the property being advertised for sale and checking the title.

If you make a purchase, all the steps of using a lawyer to hold the deposits (if any) in a trust account and checking the seller's ID need to be taken. Your lawyer will disperse funds at the appropriate time when all documentation and the title transfer is complete. If anyone says to you, we don't need a lawyer, we can save the legal fees, that's a red flag telling you to run. Your goal is to make profits, not allow others to steal from you!

To find motivated sellers let's look at reasons why people would be motivated to sell. The answers help identify the source of these potential leads. Think of this as coming to their rescue because they win when you buy. I don't think either of us would feel good with a win/lose contract especially when the motivation is for an undesirable personal reason. Here's another phone tip, your tone of voice and mannerism is important when dealing with a stressful state of affairs, i.e. sellers who may be emotionally sensitive.

The following list identifies some of the sensitive reasons for a seller to be motivated.

Reasons Homeowners Might be Motivated to Sell
- A personal or business bankruptcy (forced to sell to pay creditors)
- Need money now for another purpose (investment, pay taxes, law suit etc.)
- Retirement (need to lower cost of living)
- Health reasons needing a change to a condo or a bungalow with less stairs
- Death, estate sale
- A transfer, or job loss
- A divorce
- A worn out landlord who wants to sell his properties
- A motivated home builder holding too much costly inventory
- A builder starting a new construction project or a new area offering incentives
- Property is vacant and costing money every month to keep

To be aggressive in your search you would do more than one thing to find that home. You could do several things;

Taking Action to Finding a Property
- Network with real estate professionals you know as well as others you have yet to meet
- Check out FSBO websites, do internet searches
- Network with everyone you know, tell them what you are looking for
- Drive around looking for signs of vacant homes in the areas of interest
- Advertise using flyers, posters, news ads and the internet for sale by owner websites
- Join an investment club
- Visit the courthouse to look up foreclosures
- Talk to bankers and mortgage brokers

Joe Girard, who is listed in the "Guinness Book of Records" for being the worlds greatest salesperson and Author of "How to Sell Anything to Anybody" said, "The elevator to success is out of order. You'll have to use the stairs... one step at a time". He also said, "Start doing what's necessary; then do what's possible; and suddenly you are doing the impossible". These words really do apply to becoming a real estate investor. Starting out, you have to be determined to look, ask, investigate and make offers. Sometimes many offers just to get one property. It may take you out of your comfort zone and it may be difficult delaying gratification by re-investing current equities but the payoff in the long term means living financially free.

Condominiums

I do not consider all condos to be a bad investment. I own one that looks like a single family home but has an attached home on one side. It's been a great investment. I attended my first annual general meeting (AGM) and was nominated to become a board member. The following year I was nominated board president. I have my preferences on property types and you will have yours. One that is not my preference is a multi-unit wood frame building. I'm thinking of those four story wood frame condo buildings and remembering those 65 families who narrowly escaped the four alarm fire. Owners have no control over others negligence. They are vulnerable to someone leaving a barbecue on, a stove on or not properly discarding a cigarette. They have less effective sound barriers between units. Who wants to listen to their neighbors or not be able to play your own music. On the other hand, a steel and concrete building has a much higher fire safety rating and better sound control. I own one in a thirteen story concrete building. The condo fees are higher but they also include the heat and insurance. Right now there is a $9,000.00 special assessment for elevator maintenance. The total cost of over a million dollars is not covered by the reserve fund and must be paid proportionately by the owners. Be aware of these possible expenditures when you purchase a condominium.

Here are a few things I learned that you should research prior to buying a condominium.

Condominium Checklist

- Read the minutes of the previous meeting for the past year to get a feel for the state of repairs and Board activities.
- Obtain a copy of the latest reserve fund study and request the status of the reserve fund.
- Inquire with the management company about current or pending special assessments.
- Read the by-laws to understand the rules pertaining to pets, repairs, maintenance, tenants and other rules and regulations.
- Find out what the condominium fees are and what they include (insurance, maintenance etc.) Review the last AGM so you are aware of any planned increases/changes in fees.
- Condo Boards rely on owners to volunteer time as a Board member. Be prepared to do your time on the Board.
- Make sure that your own insurance (i.e. not the insurance covered by the condominium board) covers the deductible amount in the event there is a claim and/or an unforeseen special assessment. You could be required to pay a substantial sum as these deductible amounts can range from $5,000.00 up to $50,000.00.

Buying Gold Mines NOT Land Mines

Your first task is to determine if the home fits your criteria for investment. Is there potential for a future higher price if you make improvements? Can the property value increase based on other properties in the vicinity? Considering the principles of real estate appraisal, does the property fit your profile? Most importantly, do the numbers crunch?

The second thing to do to stay clear of land mines is to obtain a home inspection from a qualified home inspector. Ask him what the indicators are for determining if the home was used as a previous marijuana grow-operation. My home inspector is very thorough. He takes 3 to 4 hours to complete an inspection on an average home under 2,000 square feet. He is aware of 16 indicators for determining if a home was a previous grow operation, a land mine you want to avoid unless you have remediation skills and financing to support the purchase, renovations and and other carrying costs. A good home inspector should know this and have some trade background or has attended training courses dealing with inspections. I also look for a home inspector with some knowledge of the electrical building code. A certified electrician would be best because it's rare an inspector would hold that trade certificate. Being able to identify electrical problems is one of the critical items of a home inspection.

My preference for an investment property is a single family three bedroom home preferably with a suite or potential for a legal suite. Having a separate garage which can also be rented is a bonus.

Here is a list of some areas for consideration which is not to be taken as cast in concrete or to make or break a deal. These items are to get you thinking and provide a starting point for evaluating a property for profit.

Buying Gold Mines or Land Mines

Gold Mines	Land Mines
Newly renovated	Previous grow-operation
Needs lipstick - flooring and paint	Structural problems
Suited and has a garage	Poor grade / not easy to improve landscaping
Reno potentials, has a problem that can be fixed resulting in greater value being added	Rental home with only one tenant possible
Great location / lot / exposure / view	Bad location, backing on to traffic, overhead power and phone lines
Good windows, furnace, floor system	No potential to improve curb appeal
Can easily add a legal suite	Water problems, low area
Zoning / Bylaws allow for a suite	No potential to add a secondary suite
Several units and already rented	Electrical, plumbing and heating concerns
Trees on property	Bad basement development, low ceiling
Potential to enhance curb appeal	Requires work in many areas, evidence of rotten wood, asbestos, termites, mice
Close to everything - schools, work, transportation, amenities (i.e. retail, restaurants, etc.)	Over-priced and/or outdated, too much work required for the asking price (needs a complete renovation or should be demolished)
Motivated seller, great price and terms	No garage or parking area

Action Exercises:
1. Determine the ideal property and your strategy for locating it.
2. Contact a Real Estate Agent and present your criteria for a property you would like to purchase for your home or investment.
3. Search the internet multiple listing service and other homes for sale websites in your area to look at listings.
4. Collect business cards from real estate agents when you view properties. Write down any information on the back of their card for future reference.

Chapter 9

Buy, Hold and Rent for Long Term Profits

*"Real estate cannot be lost or stolen, nor can it be carried away.
Purchased with common sense, paid for in full,
and managed with reasonable care...
it is about the safest investment in the world."*
Franklin D. Roosevelt

My opinion is that holding property is the best plan for financial gain if you are young enough to hang on for several years. Long term could mean 25 or more years if you are under 40 years of age or it could mean 5 years if you are 60 years old. Remember the latin phrase "Tempus Fugit" (Time Flies). My father-in-law used to say this all the time "Tempus Fugit - Memento Mori" time flies, remember death. I think it was his way of saying get on with it, have your family when you are young because time goes by fast. You will have to determine what is long term for you and when, if at all, you should sell. Hanging on and never selling is definitely an option for property you want to keep in the family and pass along to the next generation.

Holding property for a long term can create a guaranteed retirement income. Most pension plans today (with the exception of Government plans) are defined contribution. This means you need to manage your own investments and plan for a future retirement income. Having one or more income producing properties in your portfolio is a proven secure way to ensure that an income will be there for you sometime in the future. Along the road to achieving residual income you are potentially applying seven ways to make profits. These seven way are difficult to achieve through stock investments, registered retirement savings plans, GIC's or any other investment. They are only achieved through owning real estate. These seven ways make investing in real estate, under normal economic conditions, a secure and safe place to put your money.

Seven Ways You Profit with a Revenue Property

1. Leverage   (Bank financing 80% of purchase price)
2. Appreciation   (Equity through inflation when the property goes up in value)
3. Monthly Income   (Residual rental income when property has positive cash flow)
4. Pay Down Mortgage (Portion of mortgage payments applied to the principal amount)
5. Sweat Equity   (Acting as a property manager and improving the property)
6. Taxes   (Certain tax benefits such as depreciation and improvements)
7. Equity Position   (Beneficial for future personal or business loans)

To be successful holding property you must be determined to hang on, think long term and set long term goals, maintain the property in a good state of repair and deal with all the issues of being a landlord. A big motivating factor to keep your property is the thought of paying commissions, legal fees and taxes when you sell. A second factor is knowing you can refinance and pull out equity funds tax free at a later date.

Holding property long term allows you to profit from upswings in real estate. In some markets property values may seem like they are going nowhere then all of a sudden they begin to shoot up due to a number of those economic factors discussed in Chapter 4. For example, what is happening when the number of listings is considered low, the cost to build new is higher than existing homes, land values have risen due to a shortage of available serviced building lots, the job market is positive and families are moving to the area creating a demand for housing? If you guessed prices of home are rising you are correct. Now add another factor, interest rates are declining making home ownership more affordable. You now have a scenario where demand is high and supply is low. This is the recipe for soaring real estate values.

Here's an example of two homes that we purchased and held for five years under these conditions.

	Home 1	Home 2
Purchase price	$165,000	$132,000
Improvements	20,000	2,000
Rents covered 100%		
Sell after holding for five years	$440,000	$300,000
Profit before taxes and fees	$255,000	$166,000

It really makes "dollars and sense" to buy a home for profit. In the example above, home number two underwent minor improvements to make it ready for new tenants. This home was not a good home for major renovations due to it's small size, age and overall condition. The resulting equity gain was primarily due to appreciation in land values. Home number one underwent interior renovations as well as a new roof and substantial improvements to the exterior to improve curb appeal. These renovations combined with the rise in land values provided a great return on investment.

The next example illustrates a potential rate of return for a 20% or $100,000.00 investment in a home which also has a secondary suite and a separate garage providing three rent incomes. This example shows how leverage can greatly increase your rate of return. However, before you buy a home with a suite or add a suite to a home there are important things to research to ensure you are following all the rules, city by-laws and safety codes.

Secondary Suites

Failure to follow the rules can result in injury or death of a tenant. In consideration of this, the courts have been known to order substantial fines for violations in safety codes. It's important to do your due diligence and know the rules before you begin renting out secondary suites. The following list touches on some of the things that you may need to consider when becoming an investor/landlord of a property with a secondary suite.

Secondary Suite Checklist

- Does the zoning allow for a secondary suite
- Does the suite need to be registered with the city and inspected
- Is a development permit and/or a building permit required to make an application to install a secondary suite
- Are secondary suites allowed in the land use bylaws for my property
- What are the city/town fire codes and other codes for a secondary suite
- Does the suite have the required bedroom window size in the event of emergency, check local codes (example 3.75 square foot window and the required portion above grade for a basement suite)
- Are there electrical, plumbing, heating and air conditioning codes that need to be met and/or inspected (does the suite require a separate heating source)
- Does the existing suite have proper smoke and carbon monoxide alarms installed
- Does the existing suite have a separate direct entrance (is one required for a legal suite)
- Does the suite have a proper fire barrier or fire resistance rating (FRR) and sound transmission barrier (STC) separating floors, adjacent suites, garage, furnace/utility room and the living areas (what are the local code requirements i.e. fire rated drywall etc.)
- Is there available parking and will the suite meet the rules for parking spaces
- Is there a maximum size restriction the suite needs to be to conform to city bylaws
- Are backyard suites (detached from the home) allowed in the community and what are the rules

As you can see from the above list, whether you are repositioning an existing suite or renovating to add a suite, it's very important to check out all the regulations and do it properly. You do not want tenants to be living in an unsafe unit. Also, it's to your advantage to be able to advertise your suite as a legal and if possible, a registered legal suite. Chapter 1 provided you with a list "Why Use a Home Inspector". This is one of those areas where a professional home inspector can advise you on the particulars of a suite prior to purchasing a property. Get it inspected to ensure it meets all the requirements of a legal suite and know what the costs are to make it a legal suite before buying.

A legal suite can help you obtain positive cash flow, give you peace of mind knowing your tenants are safe and increase the appraisal value of your property which is what you want when planning to invest in a suited rental property for profit.

Example of Investing in a Home with a Secondary Suite

Example - Investment $100,000.00

Purchase Price 475,000 + Improvements 25,000 = $500,000

Mortgage amount (80%) $400,000   Rate 3.25%

Frequency (monthly), Payment $1,944.66

Assume the property appreciates 2% per year with no allowance made for vacancies. Improvements are made to increase rentability of the property.

Monthly Rents		
	Upstairs	$1,300.00
	Suite	900.00
	Garage	300.00
	Total	$2,500.00

Monthly Mortgage Payments	$1,944.66
Monthly Taxes	250.00
Monthly Insurance	100.00
Monthly Maintenance / Repair Allowance	100.00
Total Monthly Expenses	$2,394.66

Net Monthly Operating Income	$105.34
Amount paid to principal starting on the first month	$868.59
Monthly appreciation at 2% per year x 500,000 = $10,000.00 ÷ 12 =	$833.33
Total Monthly Investment Return	**$1,807.26**

The yearly rate of return as a percentage of original investment of $100,000 would be the total return for twelve months divided by the investment.

Potential Return on Investment in this example is: 1,807.26 x 12 = 21,687 ÷ 100,000 = **21.69%**

When evaluating a property to hold and rent you would do the math calculations to determine the rents less all the expenses. The result is the Net Operating Income or NOI. The purpose of this calculation is to determine if the property has positive cash flow, otherwise, it could be one you would need to supplement through other income.

A property you supplement might still be an okay investment because the mortgage is being paid down. This calculation is left out of the NOI because it's an assessment of the risks of having positive versus negative cash flow which answers the question "can the property I'm considering buying cover itself when rented for the going rents?". If not, the question is do I have the monthly cash flow to support the property? Supporting a property can act like a forced savings which will provide a future benefit. While you are delaying gratification today by reducing your monthly disposable income, you are gaining equity through inflation while paying down a mortgage at the same time.

If you own a business which has a shop or store you would want to look at the long term benefits of owning versus renting. I know many entrepreneurs who have bought their own buildings. They range from trades people owning a cabinet shop to one owning an auto repair shop to professionals operating financial and legal businesses. Owning their own building is their future exit strategy. Without this asset there would be no future income stream to afford retirement. On the other hand, those who rent their space do not gain equity and never have the control to eliminate this substantial overhead expense. I know of businesses that have gone bankrupt due to running out of money. If those same businesses had built up equity owning their property they may have been able to refinance to survive the down times. The ones who buy real estate have a greater chance to enjoy the benefits of cash flow later in life and have the means to travel and have more fun completing their bucket list. It's your time to get started by buying a property for profit. Assuming even a small amount of inflation, the sooner you buy, the better. The real estate tycoon Robert Allen said, *"Don't wait to buy real estate. Buy real estate and wait."*.

In summary, owning some real estate is a good investment philosophy because it's generally regarded as low risk and a safe place to invest for the long term. A cash-flowing property is not subject to the daily ups and downs of the markets. Houses are generally the first type of property you would buy.

Calculating the Net Operating Income (NOI)

The following example provides a list of the common expenses associated with owning a small rental property. Use this page to determine if the property you are considering will have positive or negative cash flow. Remember to factor in the amount if you will be making monthly payments on borrowed funds used for the downpayment. The best plan for profit is to have positive cash flow to cover maintenance, repairs and to build up funds for another property to invest in. Look for properties where you have more than one suite paying rent to maintain some cash flow during a vacancy. We covered one good example which is a home with a legal rental suite and a garage that can be rented separately.

Buying for Rental - Calculating the Net Operating Income (NOI) for Profit

Total Rents

    Monthly rent _____ x 12 = _____

    Monthly rent _____ x 12 = _____

    Monthly rent _____ x 12 = _____

    Monthly rent _____ x 12 = _____

TOTAL YEARLY RENTS _____

Expenses

    Principal and Interest x 12 _____

    Monthly Taxes x 12 _____

    Insurance x 12 _____

    Utilities not paid by Tenants x 12 _____

    Allowance for maintenance x 12 _____

    Allowance for vacancy x 12 _____

    Management Fees x 12 _____

    Other fees (Condo Assoc.) x 12 _____

TOTAL YEARLY EXPENSES _____

NET OPERATING INCOME (rents - expenses) _____

Rental Property Expenses

As a landlord you can claim eligible property expenses. You need to determine if the expense is a current expense or a capital expense. Expenses with lasting benefits such as a new roof, new windows, new siding, adding a garage and a renovation that improves the property would be considered capital expenses. These expenses should be capitalized over a longer period of time. Generally these expenses are of considerable value in relation to the property and they improve the property over its original condition. If in doubt, check with an accountant or a tax professional.

Expenses that are current are ones that simply repair or maintain your property like painting, new carpeting, appliances or any repair that replaces something in your rental property. Maintenance like repairing the driveway, replacing rotting deck steps and landscaping are short term repairs and are generally considered current expenses. Current expenses reduce your net income in the current year providing a tax advantage for you as a property owner.

Stick to Your Plan

Owning your own home can be an important part of one of the four cornerstones to a financial plan (short-term reserve fund, income and asset protection, intermediate-term goals, long-term goals). A second property can improve your lifestyle by providing a long-term goal for additional financial security upon retirement. A vast number of people have become millionaires and multi-millionaires simply by owning a million dollars or more in property. It's important to know what properties to keep and how to manage them so you can easily keep them for the long term. Stay the course and don't sell. If you become frustrated, you may end up selling which could hamper your strategy for long term success. There are two directions landlords often go, one is the rich landlord and the other is the burnt out landlord. In the next chapter you will learn many property management tips enabling you to easily become a landlord. Armed with this information you will save time, have far less stress and make more money!

Real estate always goes up and down but in the final analysis you make money when you hang on for the long term because they are not building more land.

Action Exercises:

1. Explore neighborhoods in the area that are good for a rental investment property.
2. Test the market to determine if there are tenants looking to rent in the area.
3. Investigate current rental rates.
4. Ask a mortgage professional what lenders are requiring for a downpayment on a rental house and other small investment properties.
5. Check the zoning to determine if a suite is allowed in the area.

Chapter 10

Landlord Tips for Saving Time, Reducing Stress and Making Profits

*"The two things in life
you are in total control over
are your attitude and your effort."*
Billy Cox
Motivational Speaker

Every landlord has stories of bad tenants. I have a few myself. I'll spare you the details seeing as I've also had many great tenants and I'd rather focus on the positive side here. I will give you many tips that will save you plenty of headaches and allow you to profit by being your own property manager. You can never be 100% sure you will get the ideal tenant. Review what I do and then you choose how you will manage your rental property to your satisfaction.

As an investor, you should build a contingency fund of at least $5,000.00 to allow for times when tenants don't pay and as an emergency fund for any repair you need to make or appliance you need to purchase. This contingency fund will certainly reduce any financial stress. I would ask my students the question "who has a big problem if the tenant does not pay the rent?". It should be the tenant and not you. With a fund there is less stress because you have the money set aside for this purpose. It is part of your plan. You knew in advance it could happen at some point in time, it was expected and therefore it is no surprise. If rent is not paid, it is your tenant that has a big problem. The tenant is faced with a late fee and possible eviction notice if the rent is not paid before a specified time which is very often before the middle of the month.

I have given 14-day eviction notices in the second week of the month and have had new tenants by the end of the same month. I like to make the eviction notice look as official as possible quoting the applicable legislation whether that be the Landlord and Tenant Act or the Residential Tenancies Act or under some other name depending on your State or Provincial laws. It's advisable to obtain a copy of the legislation and know what can and cannot be done as a landlord. For example, you might be required to deliver a formal eviction notice providing a minimum 14 days' notice. It is very important to know the rules.

Many tenants are misled by landlords advertising first and last month's rent up front. The intent is that the last month's rent is to be used as a security deposit. Tenants often believe that the last month's rent has been paid and when they give notice to vacate they do not wish to pay the last month's rent. A better practice is to refer to the security deposit as "the security deposit" and explain to the tenant that it is to be returned to them following the termination of their lease contract, after they have completely moved out and the property has been inspected. Any damages, not including normal wear, that were not on the original occupancy inspection list will be noted during the time of the inspection and may result in a decrease in the amount of security deposit being returned.

Tenants who meet all my criteria may also be picky with where they live. It's a two-sided street here which means the tenant will be evaluating whether or not the property is clean, has no foul odors, is in a good state of repair and has all the things they are looking for. It goes to say then that if you want to gain a high quality tenant then you need a high quality property to rent. I always look at the unit and ask, "Would I rent here?". If the answer is no then it needs to be cleaned up and potentially newly renovated. Primarily, this means new paint, flooring and new appliances but sometimes also plumbing or other small renovations.

My ideal tenant would be willing to sign a lease that will go from year to year beginning the first of the month starting either May 1, June 1, July 1 or August 1. These months are higher move in and move out months so it's easier to find a new tenant after the existing tenant terminates their lease. The worst time for a tenant to leave is December or January, especially if you live in a cold climate. Fewer people are looking to rent so it's not a good time to have a vacancy. This strategy supports one of the objectives of having the property always rented so you avoid making a mortgage payment. More people plan their move in late spring or early summer to get settled before summer holidays and before school starts in September. If you buy the property in November or December, make the first lease for six or seven months ending May 31 or June 30th then start again with year long leases so the lease ends at the same time the following year. What would you look for in an ideal tenant?

Characteristics of an Ideal Tenant

- Tenant provides an e-mail to landlord so tenant can e-transfer rent on the first of each month. Cash and Post-dated checks are not preferred methods of payment.
- There is a higher probability that the tenant who is neat in appearance and keeps a clean vehicle will also maintain the property and keep it neat and clean. It can be helpful to sneak a peek inside their vehicle before you agree on a lease. To do this, meet with the prospective tenant(s) outside at their car before viewing the rental unit.
- Tenant has no pets, no large dogs and no cats.
- Tenant is employed and has a stable income. Tenant is able to pay the first month's rent on time and the full security deposit up front when the lease is initially signed.
- Tenant is willing to provide ID and references.
- Tenant is quiet and does not smoke
- Both parties complete the application form in full followed by a lease agreement. See the sample application in this chapter (contact the government rental advisory authority).
- Tenant has no issue with your explanation of the security deposit and when and how it will be paid back.
- Tenant has a good attitude and is able to communicate well with the Landlord.
- Tenant thoroughly cleans and removes garbage when vacating the property.

Rental Application Form

Full Legal Name(s) of Applicant(s): _____

_____

Address: _____

_____

Phone Res: _____ **Bus:** _____

Cell: _____ **Other:** _____

Number of people to occupy premises: Adults _____ Children _____

Ages of Children _____

Employment Information, occupation, name, address, phone #, how long there, supervisor's name, monthly income

Name, address, phone # of present landlord (and previous landlord if less than two years)

References: name, address, occupation and phone numbers

Rental Application Form pg. 2

Person(s) who can be contacted in case of emergency.

Names, address and phone #

Describe any pets you may have: _____

Do you have contents insurance for fire, theft?   Name of Insurance Company

_____   _____

This application pertains to a fixed term contract rental agreement to be signed upon acceptance. A security deposit equal to the first month rental is required when the contract is signed along with post dated checks for the contract term.

I/we acknowledge that the security deposit is for any rent owed and/or property damages caused by the tenant and will be returned (less any rent owed and/or property damages) after inspection following vacancy. The security deposit is under no circumstances to be considered as the payment for last month's rent.

I/we will request and submit an online credit report or provide my written permission for a credit check.

_____   _____
         print name   signature

_____   _____
         print name   signature

Please attach a photocopy of two pieces of ID (Government issued ID and other) to this application. All information provided will be kept confidential.

Sample Eviction Notice

LANDLORD'S NOTICE TO TENANT

(EVICTION NOTICE)

TO: _____
   Names of Tenant(s)

_____
   (Address)   (Postal Code)

In Accordance with the Landlord and Tenant Act I hereby give you a 14-day eviction notice between me as landlord and you as tenant for the following reasons:

(examples)
- Non payment of rent
- Continuous late payments of rent
- Insufficient security deposit
- Noise disruption to other tenants
- Allowing other occupants not approved in lease agreement

Vacant possession must be provided by 12:00 noon on ___ day of _____, 20 ____.

The past due rent and utility owing is: $ _____

The late charges amount owing is: $ _____

The total amount owing is: $ _____

* Note: As you have broken the terms of your lease, a re-rental is required to minimize damages. Additional charges will be applicable (subject to outgoing inspection, advertising and re-rental).

_____
Landlord's name and phone number

The application form sets the stage by getting all the pertinent information on paper before choosing the tenant and meeting to sign a lease. The following checklist will help you with selecting and setting up the right tenant.

Renting for Profit Checklist

Ask Questions

- Reason for leaving previous home?
- Who will be living here and renting?
- Any pets?
- Work information?
- Tenant's lifestyle (noise, any musical instruments, smoking, clean, go look inside their car!).
- Can they sign a one year lease? How long are they looking to rent?

Application and New Tenant Set Up List

- Personal data (get all information on an application first).
- ID (copy ID for identity confirmation and possible Credit Check).
- References (two or more), previous landlord or whatever else you can get.
- Statement pertaining to payments with post-dated checks.
- Statement pertaining to security deposit, not used for last month's rent.
- Contact "State/Provincial Consumer and Corporate Affairs" to obtain a copy of the Landlord and Tenant Act.
- Contact "State/Provincial Residential Rental Association" to obtain a forms package which includes Residential Tenancy Agreements and a number of other useable forms.
- Contact the city or township for "Land Use Bylaws and Zoning" rules pertaining to secondary suites.
- Choose "Fixed Term" or Month-to-Month depending on your intentions for the property. If holding the property for a long term choose a fixed term.
- Plan for rental periods to start between May and August and to extend for 12 months. Try to keep rental contracts closed from September to May. Go for a long lease, one year preferred!
- Diligently explain late fees, and NSF fees when signing the rental Agreement.
- Set up electronic e-mail transfer for rent payments and ease of making deposits.
- Remember, good contracts make good tenants.
- Build a contingency fund for incidentals and possible non-payment from a tenant. Get rid of non-payers, late payers and any criminal element. Their problems should not become yours!

In addition to an a move-out inspection form, a move-out checklist such as the one on the following page clearly targets the issue of making sure the property is left clean. E-mail a copy of this page to your tenant a week before they move-out so they clearly understand their responsibilities and the amount of work required to leave the property in a re-rental state.

Tenant's Move-Out Checklist

Please ensure the property is left in the condition that was provided upon move-in ensuring the same condition for the next tenant. Otherwise, costs for cleaning and expenses for the repair of damages may be deducted from your security deposit. Normal wear and tear is acceptable.

Personal Possessions, Garbage and Mail List

- Remove ALL personal possessions from property, garage, storage areas, yard
- Remove all garbage from property
- Set up automatic mail forwarding with the post office
- Provide all keys and forwarding address during final walk through

Clean-up List

- Vacuum all floors, remove carpet stains using only carpet cleaning chemicals or have professionally steam cleaned if needed. Includes cleaning under stove and behind fridge
- Damp mop/wipe hardwood and tile floors
- Dust, vacuum and/or wipe clean all baseboards, door and window trims, sills, light fixtures, closet shelving, counters
- Clean kitchen sink and taps
- Clean inside stove including oven racks, use stove cleaner or self-clean option. Clean top and elements.
- Thoroughly wash clean all shelves and storage areas inside the fridge
- Clean inside the microwave oven
- Clean outside of appliances using stainless steel appliance cleaner or other non scratch cleaners
- Thoroughly clean toilet, bathtub/shower stall and sink
- Wipe out the inside of all kitchen and bathroom cabinets
- Check washer and dryer are empty and clean
- Return outside yard to move-in condition (grass, flowerbeds, snow removal, etc.)

Repairs Required

Please list any repairs that should be attended to by landlord (toilets, taps, stove, windows, furnace, hot water, floors, lights, etc.)

_____

_____

_____

Upon completion of move-out and cleaning, contact the landlord to set up a final inspection and to <u>return all keys.</u>

As the owner and property manager you want to focus on these three key responsibilities:

Key Responsibilities for Making A Profit

1. Collect all the rents on time when they are due.
2. Keep the property occupied.
3. Maintain the property in good repair.

It's important to take a pro-active approach to managing these key responsibilities. Be respectful to tenants, listen to them and follow up with repair requests. You are best to keep a business relationship with all tenants as you never know if or when you might have to evict them or not renew their lease.

Action Exercises:

1. Contact the Legislative Authority governing Landlord and Tenant Laws to obtain information including the government approved lease forms (if provided).
2. Create a legal file for forms such as Lease Agreements, Application Forms, Property Inspection Forms, Tenant's Move-Out Checklists and other notice letters, examples include; notice to enter premisses, tenants mandatory notice to vacate, notice to terminate lease, pet agreement and notice of rental increase.
3. Investigate rental rates in the area you are looking at investing in.
4. Investigate the zoning and track down the local rules for secondary suites in the community.

Chapter 11

Flipping for Profit

"The person who is ready, is fast and is first,
is often the person who makes the profit."
David Pocock

The television shows on flipping homes make it look easy. It seems like anyone can do this and profit. That's show business and although those shows are fun to watch, doing is a whole different ball game that requires a great deal of analyzing, planning and performing.

Can you always make money flipping or is it sometimes you win by making money and sometimes you lose if you make the wrong decisions. I wish I could say all you need to do is refer to the flipping formula and crunch the numbers; however, life is not that simple as there are other factors you need to consider when looking at a property to buy and flip for profit.

Run through this list of considerations and questions when evaluating a property to flip for profit.

Evaluating the Flip Property

- Consider real estate principles of appraisal in Chapter 3. Can this property be purchased and renovated and still remain within the range of property values for the location or community?
- Consider the economic factors that influence real estate prices in Chapter 4. Are the conditions favorable (supply, demand, price) for making this investment or is the risk too high at this point in time for the area?
- Rate the curb appeal as acceptable, potential to improve appearance or unacceptable for purchase.
- Ask the question, can the property be purchased at a reasonable price? Is the seller motivated?
- Do the math following the example below to determine Risk and Profit potential. Plug in all the numbers in the flipping formula. Allow a contingency factor for renovations and for carrying the property until it sells. Don't get emotional! Get mathematical!
- Determine structural integrity, is the foundation in good condition? Is there evidence of rotting wood? Does the property have good bones (i.e. good foundation and structure)?
- Determine items which could result in unknown costs such as mold remediation, asbestos, the presence of rodents, termites, radon gas or other volatile organic or fungal components.

The following examples are hypothetical to illustrate the calculations one should make when evaluating flipping a home for profit. Some of the calculations will require your estimate based on listings and sales data to determine how long you might end up carrying the property.

As a flip investor you will need some construction estimating experience to determine the estimate for renovations and holding costs. Real estate commissions can be based on a flat percentage, a split percentage or a flat fee. All costs must be calculated and estimated when doing a flip for profit. The purchase and selling costs are fixed costs which can be determined ahead of the purchase. You or your real estate agent must have a good market awareness and know what impact these improvements will have on the future resale value. Study the following three examples and the flipping formula showing all the associated costs.

Evaluating the Buy and Flip - Example 1 (minor renovation)

ARV (After Renovation Value)   **$500,000.00**
- Desired profit $30,000.00
- Renovations $30,000.00
- Purchase Costs
  - (inspection, legal, appraisal, tax adjustment) $3,000.00
- Holding Costs
  - (financing costs, utilities, property taxes, insurance) $6,000.00
- Selling Costs
  - (legal, staging, Real Estate Commissions) $21,000.00
- Contingency factor $10,000.00

= MPP (Maximum Purchase Price)   **$400,000.00**

Evaluating the Buy and Flip - Example 2 (major renovation)

ARV (After Renovation Value)   **$680,000.00**
- Desired profit $100,000.00
- Renovations $130,000.00
- Purchase Costs
  - (inspection, legal, appraisal, tax adjustment) $3,000.00
- Holding Costs
  - (financing costs, utilities, property taxes, insurance) $8,000.00
- Selling Costs
  - (legal, staging, Real Estate Commissions) $29,000.00
- Contingency factor $10,000.00

= MPP (Maximum Purchase Price)   **$400,000.00**

After reviewing these examples it's easy to see where the money can disappear. Flipping homes requires some deep pockets because you have to not only finance the purchase but also the renovations and all the other costs noted in the examples above and you still need to sell the property within the parameters of the home prices within the community.

For someone starting out, the key is to have an investor or investor partner, a good contractor or carpenter who is experienced in all aspects of renovations as well as availability to other trades and suppliers and a good Real Estate Associate. These three team players make the perfect fit for flipping homes. One puts up the money, one provides the labour and one helps find and sell the property. I followed a similar team of home flippers for three of their projects. They profited on the first two homes and lost a little on the third due to changing economic conditions covered in Chapter 4. Remember, if you don't respect the principles of appraisal in Chapter 3 and the influencing factors in Chapter 4 you are taking a gamble, not a calculated planned approach.

Here is a look at the numbers in John's quick flip strategy. John financed the purchase and renovations therefore the holding costs were only taxes, utilities and insurance for a couple of months. John did not request an inspection report other than what his Agent was able to advise him on. No lender financing meant no appraisal was needed. John's Agent was his partner and they negotiated a flat fee for service on commissions. The homes were not staged. The renovations were all based on contribution to value. These included all new flooring using carpet $4,000.00, some minor tiling $2,000.00 and $4,000.00 for painting.

Evaluating the Buy and Flip - Example 3 (quick flip)

ARV - After Renovation Value $362,500.00

- Desired profit $20,000.00
- Renovations $10,000.00
    - (flooring, painting, tiling and minor repairs)
- Purchase Costs
    - (inspection, legal, appraisal, tax adjustment) $1,500.00
- Holding Costs
    - (financing costs, utilities, property taxes, insurance) $1,000.00
- Selling Costs
    - (legal, staging, Real Estate Commissions) $10,000.00

- Contingency factor   0

= MPP - Maximum Purchase Price $320,000.00

The Flip Formula

ARV - After Renovation Value $_____

Subtract

- Desired profit $_____

- Renovations $_____

- Purchase Costs

    - (inspection, legal, appraisal, tax adjustment) $_____

- Holding Costs

    - (financing costs, interest estimate) $_____

    - (utilities, property taxes, insurance) $_____

- Selling Costs

    - (legal, staging, real estate commissions) $_____

- Contingency factor $_____

= MPP - Maximum Purchase Price $_____

The idea of flipping homes is simply the same as buying low and selling high. The "low" is obtained by negotiating a good deal from a motivated and flexible seller. The "high" is the sale price after the improvements are made to maximize the appraised value. Improvements could be anything from minor renovations (referred to as lipstick) to major renovations to the interior, the exterior or both.

What work you do and to what extent will be influenced by many factors which should relate back to the appraisal principle of "contribution to value". Improvements that you choose to do, such as changes to curb appeal, renovations to the kitchen, bathrooms, flooring, paint, roof and other areas are typically evaluated according to contribution to value because the intent is to flip the home for profit. Here's a summary list of some tips for profit!

The Flipping Formula Checklist

- You are searching for motivated sellers. You need to make offers to find them. It's not about taking advantage of a seller, it's about helping a motivated seller with a win/win contract.
- Ask your Real Estate Agent for "value-added deals". Properties with a problem that you can fix and realize a sizable appreciation in value.
- A majority or vast amount of the profit is achieved by negotiating a low price.
- You will probably make several offers to buy one property 10% or more below market value.
- Consider contribution to value with all improvements.
- Consider the range of property values within the location.
- Add some sweat equity if you are capable and have the time to do some work yourself.
- Key areas are curb appeal, flooring, paint, kitchen and bathrooms.
- Fix the problems that may exist such as leaky faucets, rotten deck, weeds in lawn, ugly paint color, damaged walls, old appliances, old light fixtures, old roof, outdated kitchen, old tiles, old bathroom fixtures and cabinets.
- Do your calculating before making an offer using the flipping formula and take into account some room for negotiations and a healthy contingency factor.
- Seek open financing that will compliment your goal to flip the property.
- When starting out, take care of existing cash needs first.
- When the market is strong and momentum is upward, look at holding on to the property and consider the renting for profit ideas discussed previously.

- Be considerate to your support team, real estate associate, contractor or experienced carpenter, trades and suppliers, lender, investor, lawyer and your insurance representative.
- When you make the offer to buy put in "and/or assigns" after your name. This allows you to assign the contract to a third party before closing and to receive money right away when the third party completes the purchase.
- Put the property up for sale as soon as you have closed the purchase contract. You don't have to wait for possession. You may end up with a buyer and do a double closing.
- As the "prime contractor" for renovations you have an obligation and responsibility for safety and liability of those working on the job site. Ensure you have liability insurance and all workers are covered for worker's compensation and also have liability insurance.

To be confident flipping homes for profit, you should become a student of this book and reference the information over and over until you have the insight and the feeling that you can make the right decisions. People working in the real estate and construction industries have some advantages with exposure to properties and experience in construction renovations. Look at any gaps that might exist in what you know and what sweat or elbow grease you can contribute. Contract work to others who have the expertise or get sufficient training to fill in the gaps.

Motivational speaker and trainer Tony Robbins would advise you to find out details of what experts in this field know and train yourself to duplicate them. A good place to start is to review the qualifications of a real estate flipper.

Qualifications of a Real Estate Flip Investor

- An access to a source of funding
- A vision to see the before and after picture
- A support network of key people
- A willingness to work hard and get involved in the process
- An understanding of construction renovation costs
- Knowledge of local real estate property values
- Knowledge of real estate principles of appraisal and factors affecting values
- A good negotiator and a good communicator
- An ability to calculate and analyze the flipping formula
- An access to trades and suppliers
- An understanding of trade contracts
- Awareness of applicable zoning and building codes
- Knowledge/awareness of environmental issues such as lead paint and asbestos removal
- Ability to obtain fire and liability insurance before every project
- Practices safety on the job site

Action Exercises:

1. Review the list, qualifications of a flip expert, evaluate your present skills and determine any gaps in training or experience.
2. Study the Flip Formula and perform dry runs on paper (similar to an investor who would paper trade stocks or commodities) before making your first flip for profit. Note the difference between the Maximum purchase Price (MPP) and the After Renovation Value (ARV) in the examples given.
3. Keep reading as future chapters will provide helpful tips on renovations, estimating, contracting and selling for profit.
4. Ask a real estate agent what commission rate would be charged for an arrangement to buy and sell? Would it be a flat fee, a percentage of the sale price or a split percentage?
5. Review the "Tips for Profit" list before making a purchase.

Chapter 12

Renovating for Profit

*"In every area of life there is a cheaper alternative
but don't forget the bitterness of poor workmanship
stays long after the sweetness of low price is forgotten"*
Benjamin Franklin

In this chapter we take a closer look at analyzing the actual renovation including the strategy, the work, the sequence and the costs. Let's assume your objective is to increase the difference between the appraised or future resale value and your construction costs. In other words, you want to gain far more than what you spend.

When I drive around some areas I can tell a renovation that was planned and expertly done from one that looks like something was scabbed onto the front of a house without any thought to design and curb appeal. These are homeowners who just don't know about appraisal and how to go about making the right changes. The experts know because they plan and design the changes with a lot of thought put into the products and color choices as well as the design itself.

I remember seeing one house and not liking it. My wife, who completed an interior design program, could visualize the home differently. Everything in this 1980's home was pink. The carpets were dusty rose, the blinds were dusty rose, all the walls were painted dusty rose, the countertops were pink. There was pink in the bathroom sinks, the front floor tiles and the kitchen linoleum floor even had some pink flowers. I called it the pink flamingo house. Others called it a life size barbie's playhouse. Our mission was to change everything that was pink. Fortunately, we were able to "see beyond the cosmetics".

When we sold the home several years later there was nothing pink. We changed the tiles in the front entrance, added hardwood in the main area, installed new neutral broadloom up the stairs, hallways and in the bedrooms, changed the light fixtures, changed the counter tops to granite, made some minor additions to the kitchen cabinets and changed the kitchen flooring to tile. In one four-day weekend, I painted the entire inside with a modern neutral color.

Using some carpentry skills and tools, I added a porch on the front which complimented the design by visually shortening the front walk along the garage. I remember building the porch myself but I contracted a stair company to build the front steps in order to ensure a professional job with the exact rise and run specified. I specified the steps to be built with double 2 x 6 treated wood treads and a longer than normal run. It's important to know your strengths and weaknesses and only do what you can do well, with the tools you own and within reasonable time.

On another home we did a complete gut of the inside and changed the entire main floor layout. We redesigned and renovated all three bathrooms, redesigned and expanded the kitchen, eliminated one bedroom and opened up the hallways. This was a major renovation. The demolition and construction sequence of undertaking a complete renovation is included in this chapter as well as a cost summary page. In addition, you can follow the sequence for a complete new kitchen design and a new tile shower installation. You can create your own sequence and cost summary using these examples.

If your objective is increasing the appraised value then you need to identify what the value-added features for profit are. Review the following list of renovation tips to expand your ideas and establish a plan.

Renovating Tips to Increase Value and Profit

- Consider the principle of contribution and doing value-added renovations.
- What improvements can be made to the curb appeal?
- Painting is the least expensive way to make a substantial visual change.
- Today's market prefers tile, hardwood flooring and granite counter tops.
- Older plans have more hallways and wasted space. Consider removing walls to open up the floor plan. Before you remove any walls, determine what walls are bearing walls and can't be removed without adding support. Also be careful with walls where plumbing and duct work are present as this can be costly to re-locate.
- Large kitchens with storage space are attractive, so consider alterations that will improve the kitchen. Entertainment today is often centered around cooking and eating and large islands are in style. If the kitchen is small, check to see if it can be extended and if an interior wall can be removed.
- A large full ensuite is preferable to a half bath if you are doing a major renovation.
- Storage space is important to consider as buyers look at where they can store items.
- A separate suite could be an asset depending on the location.
- Have a plan (on paper) of what you want done.
- Note the bearing points and avoid changes with load bearing walls or add plans for any structural changes that might be necessary.
- Have a plan for interior design (flooring, paint, cabinets, railings).
- Get organized and prepare a list of trades (plumbing, electrical, heating, paint, etc.).
- Determine specifications, style, model and brand names.
- Do your shopping for appliances before cabinets, including hardware and countertops, plumbing fixtures (list only because Plumber will supply), flooring (hardwood, tile, slate, carpet), light fixtures, paint, any windows to be replaced, interior finishing (doors, casings, baseboards, hardware), bathroom tile and kitchen backsplash tile.
- Look for trades in new areas under construction. Obtain referrals from other trades and suppliers and see projects in progress or completed.
- Get several quotes to compare prices.
- Walk through home with the Electrician, Plumber and HVAC Contractor (recommended).
- Check dimensions and clearance for appliances and fixtures.
- Place your orders (items requiring manufacturing like cabinets and items requiring delivery like appliances, flooring and the finishing materials package).
- Check lead times for scheduling and set some deadlines.
- Determine sweat equity (any work you will do yourself).
- Hire a good contractor for gutting, framing, finishing (provide a plan and specifications).

- Outline in detail what's included and what work meets the minimum building code (i.e. height of handrails and railings, distance between spindles, minimum percentage for glass/windows, electrical codes, etc.)
- Gut areas that will be changed and remove garbage from home to bin or truck.
- Remove all old drywall during the gutting stage (trying to match old drywall with new is often harder than replacing it, blending old drywall may require several coats of paint).
- Determine if you should remove drywall from ceilings or scrape ceilings, apply primer sealer and add new knock-down ceiling texture. Painted ceilings require drywall to be finished to the same finish quality as the walls.
- Remove ceiling drywall if you are adding lots of pot lights. Hire a professional to ensure everything is done to code (must be in boxes with zero clearance for insulation).
- Remove old wallpaper or cover with new drywall (3/8 inch) if the wallpaper is difficult to remove.
- Save by shopping for and supplying your own hardwood flooring (i.e. spend $5.00 per sq. ft.) or spend $10.00 per sq. ft. for comparable material supplied by a contractor. When buying flooring always check the quality (i.e. mill runs, fit, widths, domestic vs import, and buy an extra 10% to compensate for waste) See Flooring Checklist in Chapter 19.
- Protect newly installed hardwood by covering with cardboard (buy a large roll).
- Read Chapter 15 and apply "Ten Tips You Should Know Before Entering into a Contract".

Sweat Equity

Sweat equity is work you do yourself to save money which becomes equity as long as the work you do increases the value of the property. You will find me saying more than once that you should only perform tasks that you are capable of doing well, within a reasonable time and safely. I love to get involved doing as much physical work as possible. In many cases I worked beside someone who was an expert in their field. That was possible because of my trade contacts, but not for all trades such as mechanical. I assisted the electrician with the installation of the pot light cans and poly which did not involve any wiring. I worked with my carpenter friend for the demolition, the framing and some of the finishing. I was also the cleanup man at the end of each day. It helps to have your own tools. Tools enabled me to make a deal to work with a hardwood flooring carpenter. Drywall involved hiring a crew as well as the plumbing rough-in and finish. I did the priming and painting but not the spray finish on the doors, casings, baseboards and railings. My son who is a certified journeyman tile-setter did all the tile and travertine. Acting as the general contractor and doing all the planning, shopping, contracting and scheduling is also a part of sweat equity. Being the project manager means you have the advantage of using your own trade contacts which can often save you money. What work you do all depends on your background and situation. You might decide to do all the planning work then hire a renovation contractor and do nothing at all as far as the demolition and construction, or you might do just the cleanup work after each trade. Whatever work you do will be based on your trade experience, your tools, available time, the tradespeople you know and those you hire.

Work You Might Do Yourself (sweat equity) to Reposition a Home for Profit

- Plan, design, estimate, contract and schedule for repositioning or major/minor renovations.
- Shop for new items, cabinets, appliances, flooring, light fixtures, plumbing fixtures, tiles, finishing materials (see Cost Summary for Renovation).
- Clean or remove old carpet/linoleum.
- Prepare subfloor for new tile adding a layer of plywood (impact drill, glue and flooring screws).
- Remove drywall, cut top corner, cut horizontal along middle, make a hole, wiggle drywall until screws pop, pull from wall (use a utility knife), do not touch electrical. Using a reciprocating saw, cut nails and wood framing, break free the electrical from the top plate using the back of your hammer to hit the top plate next to the hole, break the wood and shake the wires loose leaving the electrical hanging for the electrician to remove. When demolishing, wear protective clothing and take extra precaution measures for asbestos removal (asbestos was common in flooring tiles, ceiling texture and drywall joint compounds) installed prior to 1990. For your safety or when in doubt about the presence of asbestos, hire an experienced restoration contractor to safely remediate the old building materials.
- Demolish wood framing using a sawzall tool to cut wood and nails, remove to land fill, clean up.
- After carpenters complete any new framing and drywall is installed and completed, prime new drywall, prepare existing walls by filling holes, sanding and priming spots before applying two coats of paint to all walls.
- Prepare for final brush, roll, spray painting i.e mask and paper off areas where cutting in or trim work is required and/or off-spaying can occur.
- Install new cabinets (carpentry skills needed) or refinish old cabinets, sand, stain or paint.
- Install new laminate flooring, hardwood or refinish old hardwood.
- Add landscaping items to enhance the curb appeal of the front yard.
- Cut grass, remove weeds, trim walks, trim bushes/hedges, open areas to expose windows and add light.
- Consider exterior changes to enhance the curb appeal to front of home.
- Improve the front door appearance with updated trim and locks.
- Paint trim, soffit and fascia for a fresh, clean look.
- Paint window trims, add window grills and interior window blinds.
- Paint and repair damaged siding, stucco, bricks or other visible areas.
- Add stone, shutters, and flower pots?
- Power wash concrete steps/walk and repair any large concrete cracks, use concrete paint.
- Hire a furnace cleaner, clean furnace area, top of water heater, replace furnace filter, humidifier filter, empty built in vacuum canister.

Renovation Construction Sequence

1. Plans on paper, drawings, sketches, kitchen layout. You need professional drawings! A napkin is not good enough!
2. Begin the process of shopping for appliances, cabinets, door handles, countertops, new windows if required, tile, hardwood, and other flooring, paint colors (put your color board together), light fixtures and plumbing fixtures.
3. Meet with Plumber, Electrician, Carpenter at site to discuss planned changes, make note of bearing walls (discuss electrical panel changes, room for new breakers, upgrading service).
4. Shut off main water and most electrical breakers leaving some power on for tools, lights and heat.
5. Remove baseboards first and then remove old carpets, linoleum and other flooring.
6. Remove all doors, casings and electrical plates.
7. Using a utility knife, cut and remove drywall from walls and ceilings. Cut top corner and horizontally across the middle of the wall, make a hole and wiggle out large pieces of drywall, toss in bin.
8. Do not disturb any electrical or cut near any wires.
9. Using a reciprocating saw, cut top plate on each side of electrical wire going through the top plate. Knock wood out next to wire with back side of a hammer. Wires are now exposed and loose for electrician to deal with.
10. Remove studs, pry up and remove bottom plate, corner pieces with studs and drywall, bang nails flat, toss in garbage bin.
11. Remove old counter tops. Remove old cabinets and vanities using an impact driver with a robertson or phillips bit.
12. Remove old underlay (k3 board) using a pry bar, hammer and drill to remove screws.
13. Determine thickness of new underlay and tile to ensure level with other flooring.
14. Add new *plywood* underlay (do not use particle board) to prepare subfloor for new tile (tools: impact driver, flooring screws, glue, table saw, skill saw).
15. Some electrical might be saved and some removed at this time.
16. New framing: each stud cut and placed using impact drill and 3-inch #8 Robertson wood screws. Careful to avoid any electrical still in place. Tools required: levels (2,4,6 foot), large and small square, miter saw, impact driver with Robertson bits, 3-inch #8 wood screws, tape measure, hammer and pencils.
17. Install large tub, if needed, before bathroom walls are completed.
18. Complete all rough-in heating, plumbing and electrical in this order (electrical last).
19. Install pot light boxes put in place using poly pans if facing exterior and then wire.
20. Complete other wiring, cable TV, phone, internet, security, intercom rough-in
21. Confirm the Plumber and Electrician have ordered their inspections.
22. Install backing for towel bars, toilet paper holders, blinds, TV wall support, etc.
23. Complete any changes to the heating ducts and vents.

24. Install a built-in vacuum or rough-in.
25. Frame around a jet tub or large soaker tub, other framing before drywall.
26. Complete exterior changes, install any new windows, siding, roofing, garage door and new side-mounted opener.
27. Insulate, acoustical sealant and use 6 mil poly.
28. Install drywall board, tape and sand.
29. Texture all ceilings with a knock down procedure (avoid the popcorn style).
30. Prime walls (primer for new drywall can be 1/2 tint to wall color).
31. Apply first coat of paint on all walls (and ceilings if they are to be painted).
32. Install cabinets, vanities, countertops (refer to designing a new kitchen).
33. Clean and remove garbage every day.
34. Arrange for hardwood to be delivered at least two weeks before installation.
35. Install doors, door & window casings, moldings, built-in shelving, wainscoting.
36. Install railings then apply stain and finish coat.
37. Install flooring, hardwood and tile (protect new hardwood using a 4-foot roll of cardboard and the boxes the hardwood came in).
38. Tile bathrooms, kitchen back splash, shower, tub surround, etc.
39. Install plumbing fixtures (sinks, toilets, taps), hook up dishwasher (plumber and electrician).
40. Install light fixtures, microwave, cook top, wall ovens, other electrical including panel work.
41. Install baseboards after hardwood and before carpet (allow 3/8 - 1/2 inch gap from floor to bottom of baseboard depending on thickness of underlay and carpet pile)
42. Fill holes, sand, apply masking tape and paper to prep for spraying finish paint (lacquer).
43. Apply spray paint, lacquer.
44. Install a decorative matching wood panel in front of large (framed in) tub/jet tub, attach with magnets for ease of removing. Stain or other finish to match the bathroom vanities. (consider granite or other alternatives for the front panel if one is required)
45. Add final coat of paint (total 2 coats) in addition to the primer.
46. Install custom closet material, pre-finished melamine or other custom made.
47. Install shower door, mirrors, bathroom accessories (towel bars, paper holders).
48. Install electrical switch plates.
49. Install remaining appliances, fridge, washer and dryer.
50. Install new front door locks.
51. Order and install new blinds.

Things to be Aware of that Cost the Most

- New roof (consider purchase to include improvements and avoid paying for this item)
- Changing all the windows which also may require new casings and painting
- Major mechanical, heating, plumbing or electrical changes to meet current codes
- Structural changes or correcting major design flaws
- Changing the entire kitchen including appliances, adding premium granite countertops
- Water damage areas, mold removal, grow operation remediation
- Finishing the basement (more advantageous to do if home has a walkout basement or open design with high ceilings and large windows)
- Older homes (approx. prior to 1960) with lead paint and requiring asbestos abatement (old tile flooring, mud, insulation, drywall and stipple or popcorn ceiling prior to 1986, lathe and plaster, mechanical seal/wrap, etc.)
- Hiring the wrong contractor as shoddy work costs twice as much (see contracting tips)

Renovating a New Kitchen for Profit

Have you ever spent a full day in the kitchen. I'm sure your answer is yes and if not yourself I'm pretty sure someone in your family certainly has. My home plan designer says "the kitchen is the heart of the home". When he designs a new home he starts with the kitchen, takes advantage of sunlight and any view to place the kitchen in the best location then builds the other rooms around the kitchen. When I instruct classes on building a new home I always ask participants to pretend they are working in the kitchen. Move items from the stove to the sink and then to the dishwasher. Pretend to remove items from the dishwasher and place them in the cabinets. Now check how many steps that took. Hopefully just a pivot maneuver or one short step. If you have to walk across the room to the cutlery drawer that's not a good design.

The choices seem endless when it comes to planning a new kitchen. You will likely want to design something superior to what a track builder would offer. I have visited many show homes and my opinion of many kitchens leaves me thinking that some architectural designers have never cooked a meal. One row of pull-out drawers doesn't fit well with my idea of a dream kitchen. Many designs are disappointing. My assumption is it's a combination of the cost factor and the designer not having the space and budget to place emphasis on a large functional kitchen. If you are renovating, it's probably because you have one of those kitchens or an old design that no longer fits your lifestyle and it's now time for your own custom plan.

Considering this book is about "buying, renovating, building and selling for profit" it should be noted that there is a high mark up on kitchens at the retail level. Personally, I don't like to pay retail. I get a contractors pricing by shopping, researching and negotiating with the supplier or manufacturer. Cabinet making in many cities is a reasonably large competitive trade where you should be able to find a deal somewhere. I signed on as a dealer with a manufacturer to receive a 50% discount off cabinets and this single idea saved $21,000.00 on just one kitchen.

A Kitchen Renovation - 1001 choices

There are many things to consider when renovating for a new kitchen and it's important to spend time planning the space as well as all the features. It's a big job because like many things today, you will need to make more decisions with every year that passes. Use paper (also helpful to use graph paper) to draw out a top view of your available space and add in the measurements. There are programs available but I like to draw it out on paper first using a measurement scale of 1/2 inch = 1 foot. The first thing to do is place on paper all the major appliances and the sink. Cabinetry can be incorporated into the design after the appliances are positioned close to where you want them. Take into account the working triangle.

Obviously, individual preferences will vary. We have come along way with kitchen designs, modern small appliances and television cooking shows. We built our own home five times and each time we learned more about kitchen designs and what works best for our lifestyle. The designs and features that we built changed with each new kitchen.

You can hire a professional kitchen salesperson who has the kitchen software to design it for you. This service is often available through big box stores and cabinet dealers. The problem is, you may not get the drawings unless you purchase the cabinets. It's best to have your own design so you can easily compare prices. When acting as the renovator, it's important to know all the ways to save money. Chapter 14 and 15 show you techniques on estimating and contracting to help you save money when buying your cabinets and other items.

If you are planning to build your own home, ask your designer to start with the kitchen and approve the draft floor plan/design before going further with your plans. You may want to plan for adequate space for an island and design a walk-in pantry. With a renovation, the space can be restricted. The pantry in the renovation example is a cabinet style design which utilizes far less floor space. If you are building a new home you can go all out with your design. You can view many options on the Houzz.com website and others.

The design which is included in the following pages represents a renovation from a u-shaped kitchen to a modern open concept with a large island. To get you off to a quick start making kitchen decisions, review the points below followed by the checklist of tips for designing a new kitchen for a renovation or for new construction. These points are aimed at helping you design an awesome kitchen which will add value to your home, provide efficiency catered to your personal needs and create an enjoyable space to work in.

Appliances

One of your first decisions is your selection of appliances. You need the specifications which include the measurements so you can incorporate your choice of appliances into your available kitchen space. For our renovation we chose a Viking six burner electric cooktop and double wall ovens. It was our choice not to go with a gas range or gas cooktop although I know it's considered best for providing instant heat. The double wall ovens gave us a feature many other homes do not have. Your appliance choices will directly impact the cabinet boxes and the design therefore, it is critical to select your appliances first.

The Island

Older homes obviously have older kitchen designs. The U-shape kitchen was very popular as was the galley or longitudinal style. Today's kitchens are central to everyday living and special-occasion entertaining, often doing double duty as family rooms, offices and media centers. This is accomplished with the presence of an island (or peninsula) as a working and gathering place. When it comes to islands, the bigger, the better. The island provides a working surface. It often becomes the gathering place at a house party providing a place for serving food and drinks. The kitchen is no longer just for the cook. It's become very popular as an entertaining area as food now plays a larger role when it comes to entertainment.

Large islands in many homes often have more than one level. In larger homes some even have more than one type of surface (granite, tile, concrete, hardwood block, etc.). The flat island is the most popular because it allows for a larger working surface. The designs and shapes available are as endless as your imagination (e.g rectangular in any size, half circle shape, L-shape). Some kitchens even go as far as having two islands. When they first became popular, many designs incorporated a raised eating bar along the back. One of the benefits of having two levels was to gain some wall area to bring electrical to the counter. This would be achieved by installing a half wall along the back of the island. Electrical outlets can also be located in cabinets on one level islands with some prior planning. This is a more common practice today.

For our last renovation, we were able to incorporate a full slab of premium granite for the island. This was accomplished by removing the old U-shaped kitchen, incorporating the nook area into the kitchen area as well as adding 72 square feet. The new kitchen was three to four times larger with many modern features including island cabinetry, new stainless steel appliances and granite counter tops.

The two island versions illustrated in this chapter are flat one level designs with the idea of maximizing cabinetry under a near full slab of granite. The top on the larger island measured 8.5 feet x 5.5 feet. This allowed for a dishwasher, a large double sink and a bank of drawers along one side. I added a 3-inch spacer for a two-plug electrical receptacle on each end. The solid spacer behind the sink and drawer cabinets gave some additional support for the 1200 pound granite counter top. Behind the sink and dishwasher cabinets are two very large pull-out cabinets (boxes) 2 feet x 4 feet which are accessible from the ends of the island. These two large pull-outs are perfect for garbage, recyclables or storing tupperware and other bulky items. The width of the island measured 24 inches plus a 3-inch spacer as well as another 24 inches for the large pull-out cabinets for a total measurement of 51 inches. This design also allowed for a 12-inch granite top overhang along the back for the eating bar. I used a solid 1.25 inch slab of premium granite and kept the edge profile simple. By choosing a premium granite slab, the extra cost of adding a contoured edge profile would not *contribute* to increasing the value.

Counter tops can make the kitchen look great so it's important to put some thought into the product and design. It's certainly a personal choice and there are a countless number of choices today for materials, designs, colors and edge/profile finishes. Choose one that will compliment your cabinetry and flooring and be a future selling feature in your home.

Storage

Many kitchens fail in this area especially with cabinet storage and a lack of pull-out drawers, often called pot drawers. Maybe the name "pot drawers" is because many kitchens only have one row of them. One reason is the cost difference. A set of 4 pull-out drawers requires the construction of five boxes whereas one drawer and two bottom doors and a shelf only requires two boxes to be built. It's all about saving money and when you build hundreds of homes these small amounts add up to thousands of dollars.

It is common for builders to incorporate a walk-in pantry for storage which will save money due to the reduction of cabinets. A 4-foot by 4-foot pantry could have eight feet of shelving times five rows providing forty lineal feet of shelf space. All that's required is inexpensive framing, drywall, shelving and a door. Then came the larger walk-through pantries affording even greater storage space and providing an additional passage way to/from the kitchen. Other ideas are incorporating a small room for storage or a storage/laundry room.

When renovating an older kitchen, the ability to incorporate a walk-in pantry may not be possible. A 4x4 pantry takes up 16 square feet of floor space whereas a wall pantry would use less than half this area for the same storage. The wall pantry in the example consists of three tall cabinets having six doors. Each of the three cabinets has 4 pull-out drawers in the bottom half and shelving in the top half. When renovating a kitchen consider the wall pantry cabinet to save floor space and add storage.

Cabinets

The kitchen example shown in this chapter, for illustration purposes, has 14 pull-out drawers. The sink cabinet requires some size consideration if it's going to be holding a garborator, a dishwashing drip rack, cleaning supplies, a compost bucket, a soap dispenser and possibly a water purification system. The illustrated sink cabinet is 39 inches wide and has two flip down front compartments for scrub buds and other cleaning items.

Cabinets for your renovation can be custom ordered any size but manufacturers also have standard sizes. The diagrams show the 39 inch sink cabinet, two 36 inch cabinets, two 30 inch cabinets, a 24 inch for the dishwasher and 9 inch pull out cabinets for spices and other items. The island has two feature 24 inch x 47 inch deep pull-out cabinets for recycling and garbage on one end and tupperware storage at the other end. Design your kitchen based on how you cook, how you entertain, the appliances you use, (working triangle layout) and the storage you require for both the items you have and the food you need to store.

For the kitchen, as well as other rooms, *try to visualize a complete room*. When choosing colors always start with the most expensive items first like the millwork (kitchen cabinets), then the appliances and then the flooring and/or granite, etc. Select the less expensive items last such as backsplash, fixtures and paint. Paint is the least expensive item but has a big impact visually.

When you have completed the selection process, the entire kitchen should be laid out to scale on paper either by yourself, if it's a simple and easy design, or by a kitchen designer using kitchen design software. The software designs show three dimensional views incorporating all the boxes and every detail including the locations of any filler pieces.

Electrical

I remember asking the Architect during the construction of a large custom home, "why are there only three electrical boxes in the kitchen?". He replied, "why do you need more than three?". I was stunned by this comment coming from an architect but then again many architects often design commercial projects. I went on to name off a number of small kitchen appliances. The look on his face was one of shock because he designed a kitchen with few walls and now he needed to find locations for electrical outlets. A small kitchen should have more than three plugs, the kitchen in the illustration has twelve.

We use one receptacle on the island for the tablet and one on the other side of the island for things like the electric carving knife and the electric cookware. I use one counter plug on the end of the counter for my cell phone. We also use a toaster, kettle, blender, coffee machine plus other small kitchen appliances from time to time. We located the electrical switch for the garborator in the cabinet under the sink for both safety and a clutter-free countertop.

Lighting

Your kitchen design should incorporate several combinations of lighting to accommodate for general, mood and task related needs. The example kitchen has LED pot lights providing two lighting combinations, island pendent lighting, under-mount cabinet lighting, cooktop hood lighting and lighting under the microwave. All lighting is used at various times throughout the day, depending on the need for brightness. Under-mount cabinet lighting can be achieved with the addition of a valance along the bottom of the cabinet or a preferred method is the manufacturer raises the bottom shelf an inch and adds a face piece allowing the cabinet doors to come down and hide the lighting. It's a cleaner look as there is no visible valance. The electrician should use a double set of plugs (4 plugs) along the wall where plugs go. One or both of these plug sets can house the switch for the under-mount lighting.

Decide what work you are comfortable doing yourself if anything at all. If you have no carpentry skills or tools then your focus will be on hiring the right person and supporting that person as best as possible by providing access to everything needed to complete a job including plans, specifications, a set of keys, etc. Meet as often as necessary to discuss all aspects of the job as well as demolition and removal of old cabinets and other items.

I worked closely with a certified journeyman carpenter who was knowledgeable in renovations, cabinetry, shelving, demolition, staining and lacquering. Together we were able to complete a full renovation. I hired an electrician, plumbers and other trades for drywall, granite countertops, a new roof, new garage door and gas fireplaces. My oldest son is a journeyman tilesetter who installed all the tile floors, backsplashes, tile wainscoting, tub surrounds and steam shower. We did the painting and I worked five days helping the hardwood flooring installer. Sweat equity would include the savings from this labor plus the savings by being the contractor. Everyone will have their own plan. You need to decide what your plan is to get the job done right the first time.

Use the following checklist for planning your new kitchen.

Designing a New Kitchen for Profit - Checklist

1. Choose to improve the existing kitchen or build an entire new kitchen.
2. Define the space to be used for the entire new kitchen. Draw a plan to scale. Consider areas where you can add space, such as opening up the nook area as part of the kitchen, incorporating the space from adjacent rooms or adding an addition. Consider an efficient working distance along the working triangle between the sink/dishwasher, oven or cooktop and the refrigerator. Pretend you are preparing a meal and cleaning up putting dishes in the dishwasher and then in the cupboards.
3. Measure height from subfloor to ceiling and plan size of upper cabinets (add up 4.5 inch toe kick, 30 in. base cabinet, 1.5 inch granite top, 18 inch back splash, 39 inch upper cabinet and 4 inch crown molding = 97 inches or 8.08 feet). Make size adjustments to cabinet uppers, crown molding and back splash to ensure the correct fit.
4. The 4.5-inch toe kick will be reduced to 4 inches after the tile is installed.
5. Consider storage space, pantry walk-in or cabinetry. A Cabinet pantry uses less floor area and might work better in a renovation.
6. Choose the appliances and get size specifications, including clearances.
7. Place appliances on the diagram, including the kitchen sink.
8. Determine the size and layout of all boxes. Standard widths are 24, 30 and 36 which can save money over choosing custom sizes (consider size of sink).
9. Consider where spacers are needed or could enhance the design.
10. Select the interior cabinet color, the most common colors are either white melamine or maple color.
11. Choose door style and exterior stain/finished color. Select location of pot/pull-out drawers.
12. Determine the size and layout of the island or peninsula. The trend is toward a large island with seating capacity (example, an island with a full slab of granite for the countertop). Some new plans achieve this by eliminating the nook.
13. Plan location for garbage, recycling and returns (bottles).
14. Choose style of cabinet handles and features such as hood fan, build-outs, spice rack, cookie sheet rack, appliance garage, undermount lighting design (valance or drop door design), crown moulding, island support brackets, wine rack, glass doors, open shelving, type of slides (soft self-close) etc.
15. Determine location of all electrical plugs, including making provisions for island plugs (consider 5 or 6 locations with 2 to 4 plugs).
16. Select sink and taps with extras (spray, soap dispenser, garburator button).

17. Determine other lighting. It is best to consider several combinations such as undermount, hood fan, microwave, pendants and pot lights with one or more lighting combinations plus dimmers.
18. Choose backsplash material and light fixtures.
19. Consider flooring material and color, kitchen in the example has a 24x24 light grey porcelain tile.
20. Consider extra items such as a toe kick vacuum outlet, pop up electrical outlets, pull-out cabinets and other features.

Installation Sequence

It's best to have a professional kitchen designer provide a layout for your kitchen using the appropriate software. I was able to do my own layout because the space did not have any start to finish measurements along the walls and no corner cabinets. When you have a U-shape kitchen or corners with cabinets continuing in both directions, you are likely to need filler strips and make site adjustments. The more complex, the greater the need for a professional computer design drawing as well as a professional installer. As an owner/builder, I would consider tackling a small kitchen in a rental or basement suite or even a recreational property. For my own home, the cabinet supplier provided the final drawings and I worked with a professional carpenter where I was able to pick up a few installation tips.

Installation Sequence List

- Cabinets are delivered and placed into an adjacent room.
- Install base and toe kicks along the floor. Toe kicks are 4 inches from finished floor to bottom of base cabinets. The base material, which looks like a ladder, is often cut into 4-3/4-inch strips taking into consideration 3/4-inch for flooring material. Precut MDF board in 4-3/4 inch strips might be supplied by the cabinet manufacturer, however 5/8 or 3/4-inch plywood is a better product for building the base.
- Establish the high point on the floor and shim the base (toe kicks) to make level.
- Level toe kicks using a long level and shim where required as the subfloor may not be 100% level.
- Set the bottom boxes into place temporarily to check fit and determine locations of fillers, if required.
- Ensure all rough-in electrical, heating, etc. is in place and clearly marked.
- Verify the sizes and location of all appliances and rough-in electrical, plumbing and gas line (for a gas range).
- Check each cabinet for appropriate size and determine the location on the wall and whether they are upper or lower cabinets. Perform a dry fit with the base cabinets to check position and fit.

- Using a stud finder, mark the locations of wall studs. Check ceiling for level in both directions.
- Measure the room height and check the height required for upper cabinets adding an extra measurement for the crown moulding to be installed on top of the cabinets. Finished floor to top of base cabinets should be somewhere between 52 to 53 inches. Distance from the finished counter to bottom of upper cabinets should be set to 18 inches.
- Starting at one end, install the upper cabinets first. Remove front doors for ease of installation.
- Measure down from the ceiling to establish the bottom of the cabinets. Draw a level horizontal line.
- Measure stud locations on the wall, transfer the measurement onto the back of the cabinets.
- Pre-drill holes before installing.
- Align with a level while securing the cabinet to the wall using an impact driver drill and 3 inch #10 screws, robertson bit.
- Check level both vertically and horizontally. Slide shims between wall and back of cabinets to level where required.
- Pre-drill holes again before installing screws to hold adjoining cabinets with the appropriate size screws.
- Measure from the highest point on the floor or the top of the level base up the wall to the height of the top of the base cabinets.
- Using a six foot level, draw a level horizontal line along the wall where the base cabinets are to be installed.
- Screw cabinets to the wall installing shims as needed along the back to maintain level and support the screws where any gaps between the wall and the cabinet exists.
- Install drawers, door fronts and decorative panels.
- Using a template, very carefully pre-drill and install door and drawer handles.

The next nine pages show an example of a kitchen before and after renovation including actual design prints which can be used to assist you in getting started with planning your new kitchen or renovation.

A Kitchen Renovation - Before and After

Before

After

New design shows a spacious open kitchen with a large island utilizing a full slab of granite. This area incorporated the old kitchen, nook, walkway and a 6 ft x 12 ft open space from the entrance on the floor below.

Designing Your Kitchen (example of a layout)

Top View

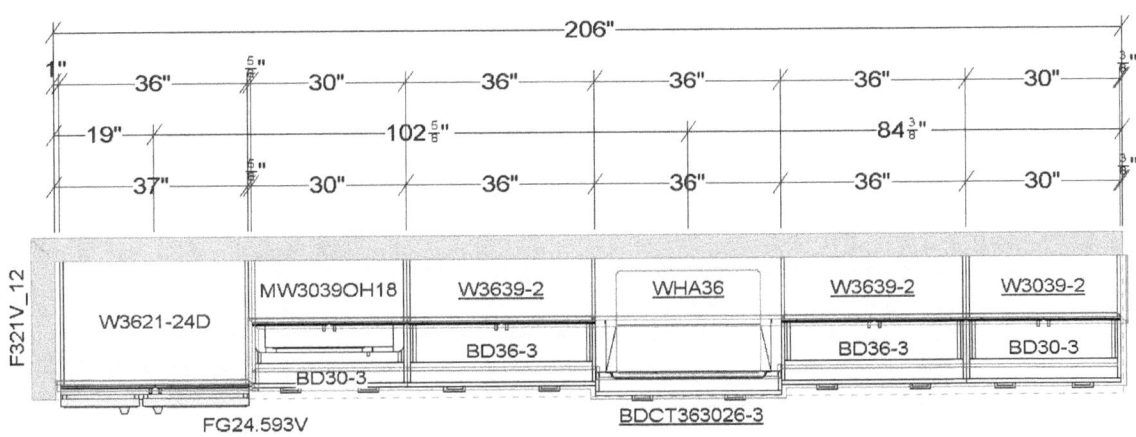

Front View

Top View of two Island Designs

Island supporting a large slab of granite with two 15 inch x 30 inch drawers on each end and dead space behind the sink

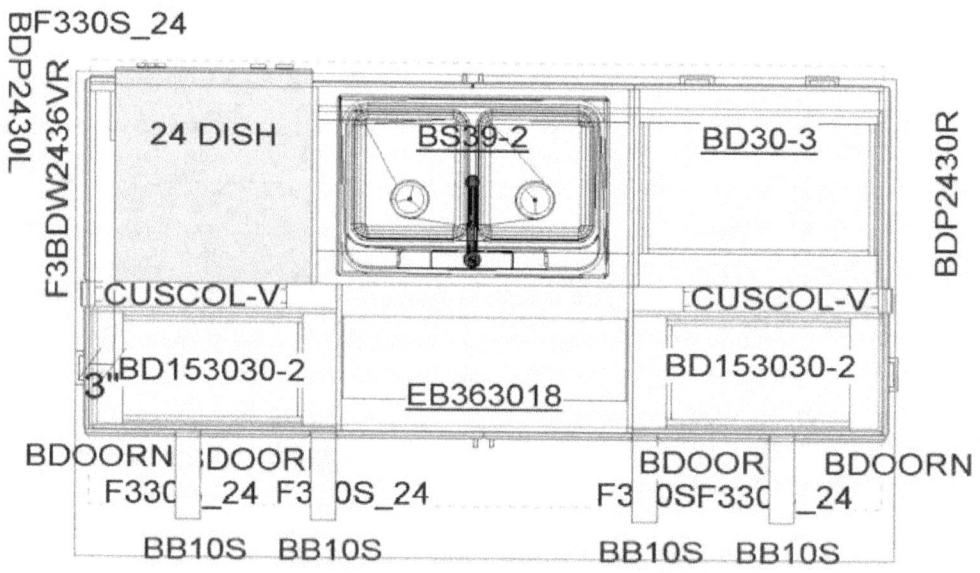

Island plan with 2 large pull-outs 24 inch x 47 inch

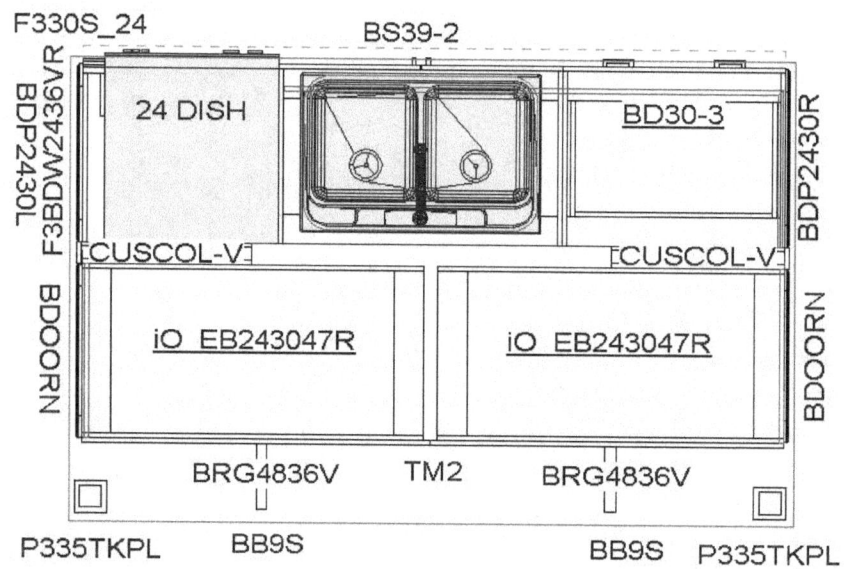

Approx. size of top is 66 x 100 inches

Front view of an Island

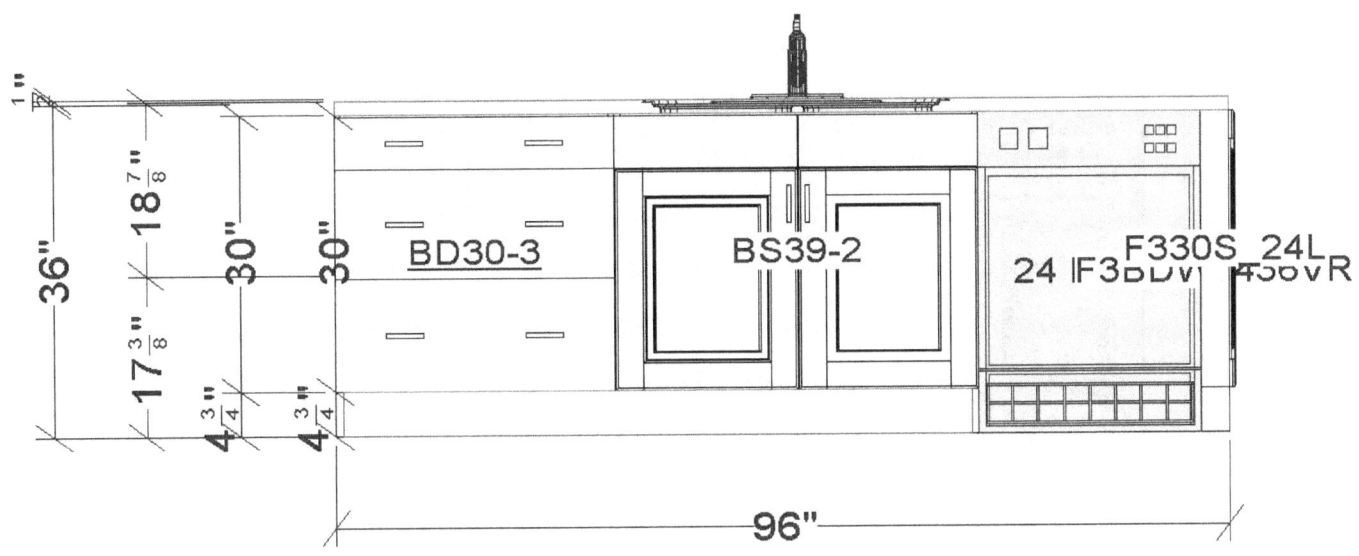

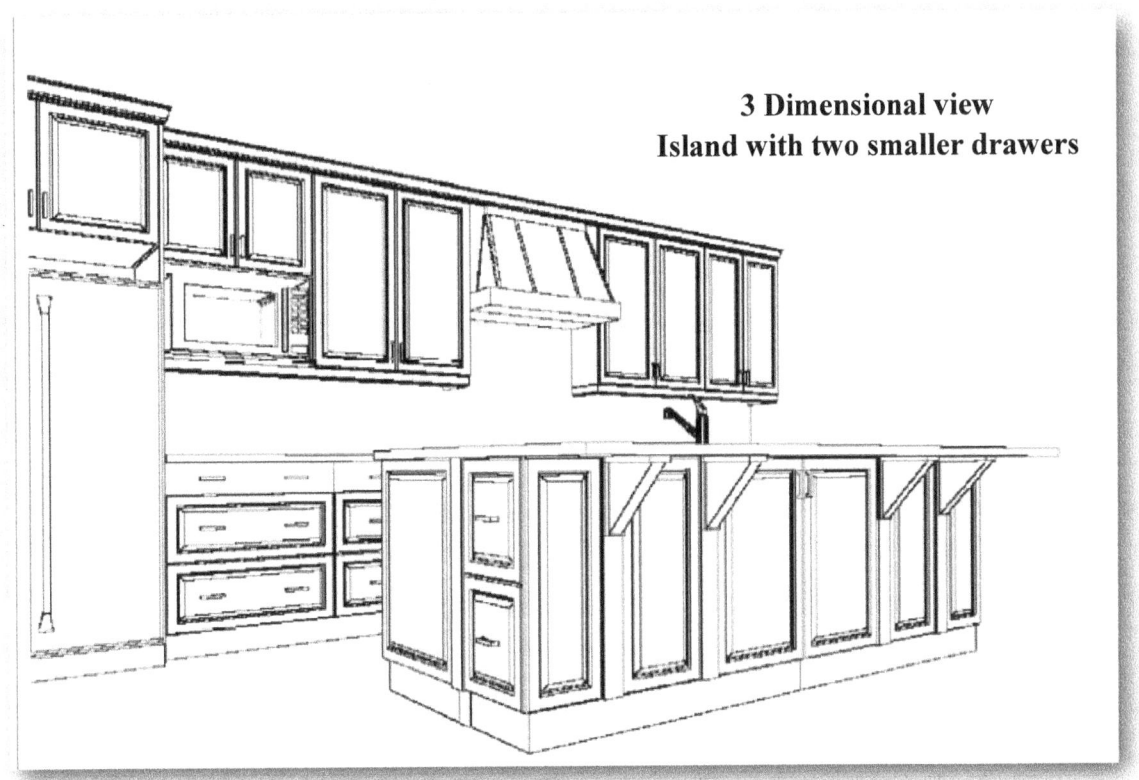

**3 Dimensional view
Island with two smaller drawers**

3 Dimensional view Island with large pull out drawers

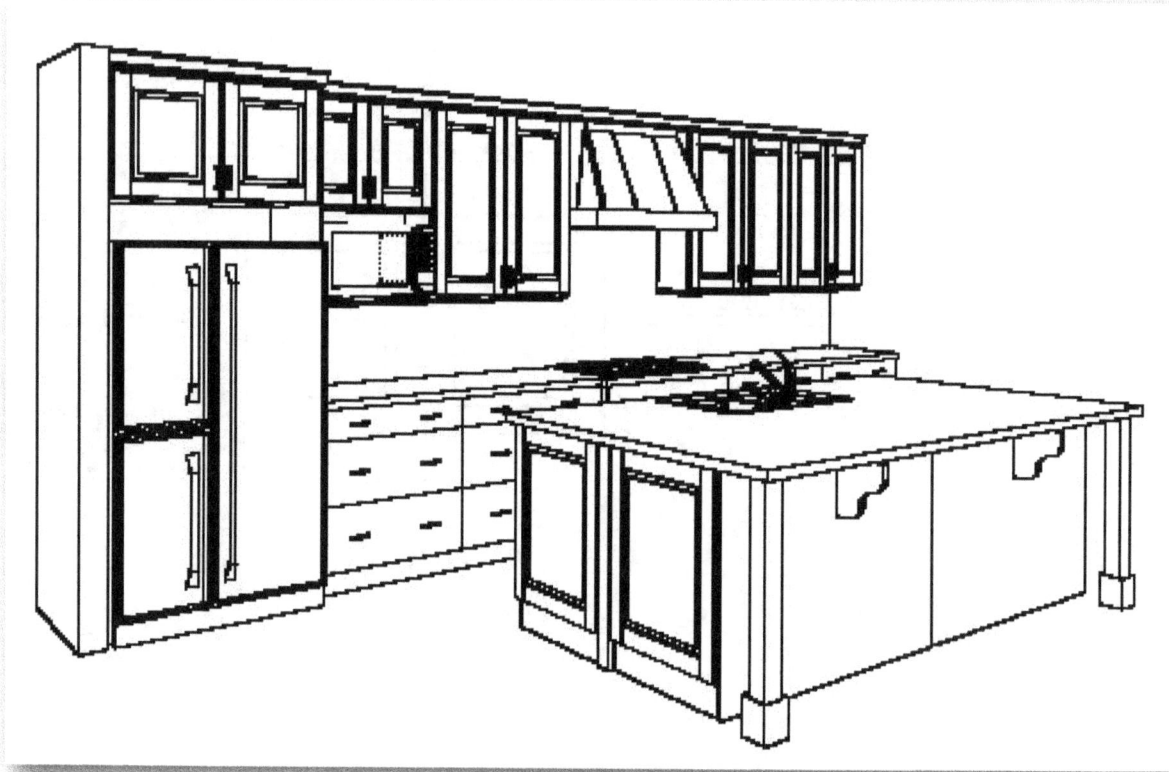

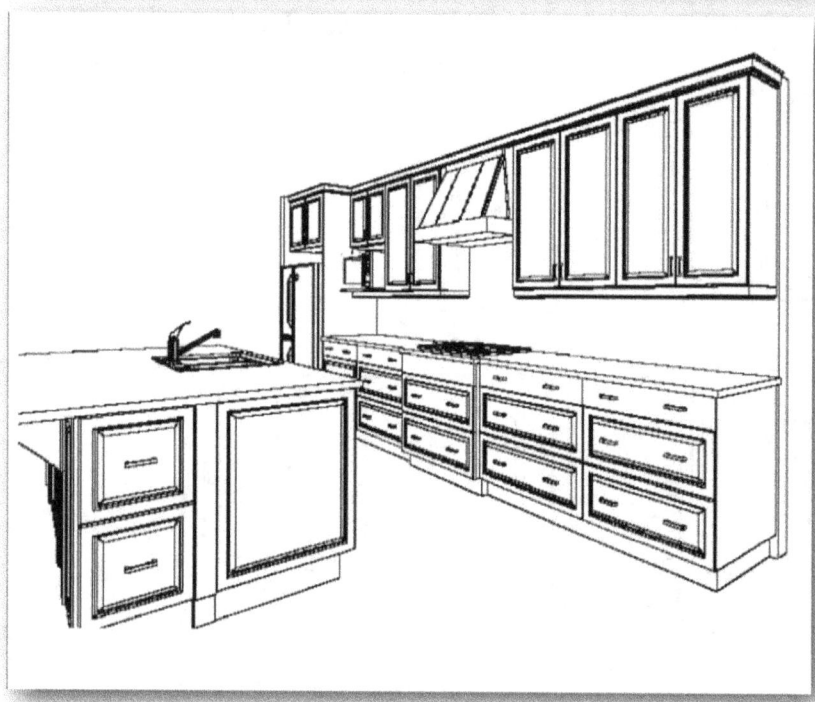

3 Dimensional view of wall cabinets with pull-out drawers

Example of a Cook Top Cabinet and Range Hood

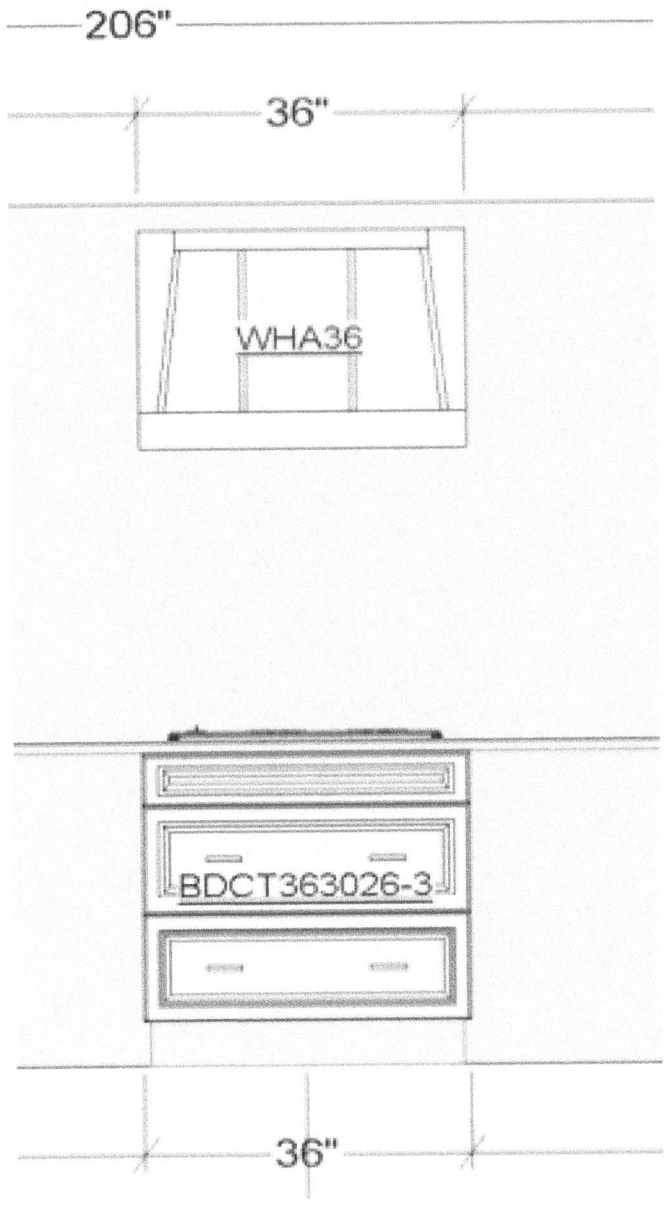

Actual width of the range hood increased to 42 inches for a 36 inch stove top.

A 3 inch spacer was added to each side of the 36 inch cook top.

The 3 inch spacer was inserted on a 45° angle and added to pull the cook top forward giving it more width and accent as a feature.

The counter top followed the cabinets providing some design to the long countertop.

Example of a cabinet with side pull-outs designed to fit the available space surrounding a double wall oven appliance.

Top View

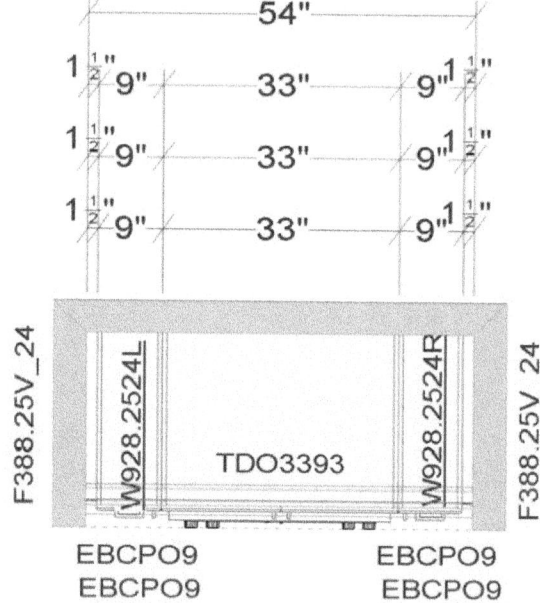

A custom cabinet wall pantry with pull out drawers on lower half.

As much storage as a walk-in pantry with less wasted floor space!

An ideal way to add storage space with a kitchen renovation.

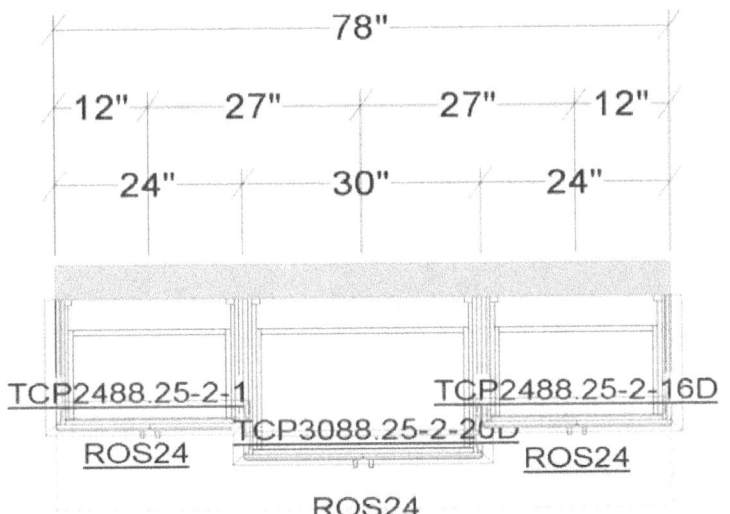

Top view of pantry designed for a renovation

There are many quotes on doing a job right the first time. "If you don't have time to do it right, when will you have time to do it over?". "If you are going to do something, do it right the first time." These are two quotes that are good reminders when renovating. I said earlier that it costs twice as much to fix a shoddy job and that's true with everything you do. It's especially important to follow proper procedures when installing a tile shower or a steam shower. You may think it's just a matter of slapping tiles on a wall but there's a whole lot more to it than that.

I'm including this short section because I made the mistake once by hiring my bricklayer to install the shower base and tiles. He said he knew how to do it and I accepted his word without having specifications on the work. The shower lasted two years and it had to be removed. Now my shower is completed to withstand a hand grenade. Well not quite but my older son who is a Journeyman Tilesetter, owner of "October Stone and Tile" and a Tile Instructor at the local college, builds them right the first time. Here are some points for specification and installation of a tile shower. Additional construction checklists for a new home are covered in Chapter 19, "Construction Tips and Checklists For Profit".

Shower Construction Checklist

- Meet on site with your tile-setter to establish the design and construction of the shower including the layout, mitering, tile trim, grout color, shelving, bench construction, base, drain, curb and doorway
- Framing must be square and plumb
- Shower curb or bench is best not framed with wood members (other options such as pre-fabricated foam block or cement form is preferred)
- For a thick-bed mortar sloped basin (troweled sand concrete mix), a PVC shower pan liner must be installed underneath mortar bed to a proper drain assembly and to code
- Liner should be folded in corners, continue up the wall and not be cut or pierced in order to create a leakproof barrier
- Other pre-made shower basins and waterproofing systems can be used rather than a thick bed mortar base
- Use a recommended backer board product for shower walls (drywall is NOT recommended, glass matt backer board is ideal for a tub surround enclosure and cement or concrete backer board is ideal for a steam shower)
- Use proper fasteners (screws or manufacturer recommended fasteners)
- Backer board seams, joints and corners should be taped with a fibre mesh and troweled with a thin mixed mortar
- For a walk-in or steam shower application, waterproofing membrane must be applied prior to tile installation
- Walls and basin should be prepped with either a paint-on waterproofing or trowel-on fabric sheeting (follow manufacturers instructions and recommendations)
- For natural stone and full walk-in shower installations a thinset mortar must be used to install tile (there are many types of mortar, check on the best type for the job)

- For frequently used shower areas and steam showers, epoxy grout is best.
- Natural stone should be sealed with recommended sealer
- Grout can be sealed but not necessary
- All inside shower corners should be siliconed after application and after grout has been completed
- Glass company (expert in shower doors) to pre-measure, build and install a tempered glass shower door or other as per owner's specifications

Renovation Cost Summary Form

The renovation cost summary list was one of the important lists that was discussed in Chapter 2, "Using Lists to Save Time, Effort and Money". This list can provide you with several uses. It can help you summarize your costs to give you a working budget. It can also be used to provide you with an awareness of the list of items for estimating or for hiring a contractor or project manager. It can help you get a handle on the costs by identifying the specific costs for materials and labor. If new financing is required, this cost summary list shows the lender where money is being spent and shows the appraiser the additional value being added to the property which can enable you to qualify for funding.

Renovations often go over budget, more so than new home construction. The reason is they are subject to a greater potential for unforeseen and unplanned items. The renovator must remove and demolish old construction before new work can begin. All kinds of things can happen such as finding mice, asbestos, rotten wood and incorrect electrical installations to mention a few. Also, change orders are more frequent as owners make decisions affecting product choices and installation.

The renovation cost summary list will help you keep track of your costs providing you with a starting list for creating your initial budget. After completing each item, fill in the amount you spent in the actual cost column and keep a running total of the difference over or under budget. Doing this step will keep you aware of how you are doing as far as staying within your original estimate.

Lists for the construction of a new home are covered in future chapters. If your renovation is substantial and you will be applying for mortgage financing, adding page 2 from the Cost Summary and Loan Calculation form in Chapter 17 will help you with this process.

Renovation Cost Summary Form

	Estimate	Actual Cost
Obtaining a copy of the blueprints from the City		
Designer Fees		
Permits (if required)		
Demolition Costs		
Land Fill (dump fees), Bin Fees		
Building Materials, lumber, 2x4's		
Windows		
Garage Door and Opener		
Drywall (material and labor, including ceilings)		
Plumbing (rough-in, finish and fixtures)		
Bathroom Fans (purchase and installation)		
Bathroom Tile (material and labor)		
Bathroom Accessories (towel bar, paper holder, etc.)		
Heating (sheet metal and changes to ductwork)		
Electrical (material and labor)		
Other Electrical (panel brought to code, hot tub, etc.)		
Electrical Fixtures (supplied by electrician or owner)		
Connections (cable TV, internet, phone, etc.)		
Alarm System (reconnected or installed)		
Roofing (repairs, vent for cook top, other)		
Fireplaces (gas inserts supply and install)		
Exterior work (siding repairs where windows were changed)		

Renovation Cost Summary Form

	Estimate	Actual Cost
Finishing Materials (closets, doors, casings, baseboards)		
Finishing Labor (install doors, casings, baseboards)		
Hardware (door handles, locks)		
Cabinets and Bathroom Vanities (including hardware)		
Labor (cabinets, hardware)		
Granite or other counter top (material and installation)		
Hardwood Flooring (material and labor)		
Tile Flooring (material and labor)		
Broadloom, Carpet (material and installation)		
Paint (material including stain, lacquer and supplies)		
Paint (ceiling material and labor, spray painting)		
Paint (labor for brush and roll painting)		
Paint (labor for spray stain and lacquer finishing)		
Appliances (kitchen and laundry rooms)		
Vacuum System (material and installation)		
Shower (door, mirrors)		
Blinds, Curtains (for windows)		
Moving expenses		
Financing Carrying Costs, Insurance		
General Contractor		
Miscellaneous		
TOTAL		

Drawings

At the beginning of this chapter I mentioned that a napkin isn't good enough, you need professional drawings. Be prepared to spend some money here off the get go. The reason drawings cost so much is they are worth it! They form an integral part of the legal agreement. When planning your renovation, getting professional plans on paper will get you started on the right track. With drawings in hand you are ready to go out shopping and obtain estimates for all work. You are also positioned to enter into discussions with contractors or builders who can take over the renovation.

Hire a Professional

Never attempt to do work you are unqualified to do. Some trades work is best left for the pros who can do the work professionally and quickly. I'm aware of many examples where individuals took on framing and roofing and other tasks only to realize it took twice as long and they struggled to finish it. It costs more to redo bad work than to have it done professionally the first time. This is true for all construction trades but especially when safety is a factor. Legislation governing trade certification should always be checked so you know what trades are compulsory certification trades requiring a journeyperson to complete the work. This does not mean a homeowner can't obtain the permits and do it himself but it does mean you should know these requirements beforehand. Typically the trades where public safety is a factor require some sort of qualification or certification. These would include the electrical, plumbing, sheet metal, gas-fitter and all HVAC trades.

Buy it or Rent It ?

The rule of thumb here is if you are going to use it once then rent it. If you are going to use it over and over again then buy it. Some examples of tools you would buy include small power and hand tools such as impact driver, chop saw or mitre saw, sawzall, skill saw, hammer, tape measure, level, speed square, drywall square and knife, pry bars and stud finder. Some examples of tools you might rent include a floor sander, jack hammer, power nailer, drywall gun and landscaping tools.

Action Exercises:

1. Determine what work you can do yourself and who you can rely on for help.
2. Locate the land fill site and inquire on costs and rules for demolition items.
3. Create a trades and suppliers list and start looking at supply companies to compare the products they have to offer and at what cost.
4. Print or create a copy of the Cost Summary for Renovations List.
5. Make a list of specifications for your new kitchen.
6. Research available Government programs or available tax credits for renovating.
7. Compare construction and liability insurance options.
8. Read chapters on Estimating and Contracting for Profit.

Chapter 13

Improving Curb Appeal for Profit

*"It is not necessary to do extraordinary things
to get extraordinary results."*
Warren Buffet

In Chapter 2 we discussed principles of real estate appraisal and recognized that curb appeal is an important component when determining value. From a buyer's viewpoint, the home has to meet certain expectations to even warrant a viewing. It's common for a buyer to drive by first before setting up a showing. You may have heard the saying "you only have one chance to make a good first impression". This applies to you when the time comes to sell your home for profit. Every home we have bought and sold we have put some consideration into improving the curb appeal or maintaining the front view in a good state of repair. The results led to quicker sales and in some cases a substantial rate of return for dollars spent.

I remember something that happened while working as a bank loans officer. A letter was circulated to our branch about an idea for reducing appraisal fees because the bank would often waive the fee as a way of attracting the client's mortgage business. The letter revealed a plan to request the appraiser just to perform a drive by, take an instant photo with a polaroid camera and write on the back of the photo the estimated value of the property. It was an idea devised by bank executives having the belief that an approximate appraised value could be made from a combination of knowing values within an area and just viewing the front elevation. This letter caught my attention and it gave me the insight to what I refer to now as "Curb Value". When we built our first home it was critical to choose a plan that had an attractive curb appeal as this would have a direct influence on the future appraised value. In the end, the bank idea of a drive-by appraisal did not work. The learning experience made me realize it is important for profit to dedicate a small chapter just on this subject.

Start with the End in Mind

Consider how much money you can save by building your own home. You would have to do a few things right because the money you save is totally dependent on the future resale or appraised value less the total construction costs. I know a few examples of families who spent six months to a year planning and building their own home then realizing no financial gain because their design and ideas were not considered valuable by the marketplace. Their design did not incorporate the artistic components to create a desirable curb appeal.

In one case, the owner/builder was a carpenter and he contributed a lot of labor, including some nice interior finishing. Unfortunately, when he added the green siding to the the tall square two story home, it looked like a grain elevator. Another owner/builder took a popular bi-level design and turned it sideways so it would fit on his lot. What was he thinking? He put all this effort into building a home that resembled the end of a garage or a trailer home having no door on the front elevation facing the street.

Another couple, both airline pilots, spent $20,000.00 on blueprints to have a very energy efficient home designed. When the home was completed, the value was far less than their total construction costs and one of the main reasons was the fact the designer put all thought into energy and very little into curb appeal. Energy efficiency is important but needs to be in harmony with an attractive curb appeal and floor plan.

Start with having the front elevation drawn out on paper or a computer program depending on who does your design. This applies to renovating the curb appeal and would be a first step. The best plan is to have a plan! If you start making changes without having a plan chances are you could be wasting money by possibly making the wrong changes. It's very easy and inexpensive to make all your changes on paper. The secret is to begin with keeping the end in mind and putting it on paper first.

The Right Architectural Draftsperson

In the example illustrated in this chapter, I took a photo of the front of a 1200 square foot bungalow and sent it to my draftsman for his thoughts on redesigning. The sketch which he provided illustrates work by a talented and creative person who is skilled in construction as well as drafting and design. The new design provided enough detail for me to list all the specifications required to coordinate the work as well as identify the trades and suppliers I needed to contract. Had I not sought the professional service of someone with greater knowledge and creativity, I would not have any plan to follow.

The cost of having the front elevation sketched to show the improvements was nominal in comparison to the materials and labor to do the work making this a worthwhile first step. The right draftsperson does not need to be an architect but does need to be creative, have a talent for design and understand construction materials. Hiring an architectural draftsperson for drafting a complete set of working drawings for a new home is discussed in future chapters.

The front elevation should have several items color coordinated to complete the exterior finish and to give the home character. Examples of items viewed from a front elevation include landscaping, front door, garage door, door moldings, windows, trim, grills, battens, gables, a second color for siding, soffit, fascia and eaves, stone, added roof lines, shingles, railings and posts, stairs, porches, lights, locks, mailbox and address numbers. I'm sure you can add more items to this list once you start looking at the exteriors of new homes.

Landscaping

You can tell the proud homeowners by the way they care for the front of their property. The lawn, walkways, trees, shrubs and other appropriate greenery, the way things are displayed like a small court yard sitting area, all play a part of the big visual of curb appeal. This segment of property maintenance is sometimes overlooked and left uncared for. I often see homes for sale that have lawns full of weeds or yards destroyed by dogs and wonder why owners would not take more care in maintaining their investment, especially when they plan to sell. If what you see is what you get then this first impression is not a good one. Keep landscaping in mind when renovating to improve curb appeal.

My designer asked me if I was going to be changing the shingles on the roof. He went on to explain the gable on the front was built in the 1950's when there was little design put to plans. It would be simple to re-frame using stick framing with 2x6 pieces and plywood or orientated strand board (OSB). He asked if I could get a framing crew in for a day to re-frame the front gable and my reply was "yes, I could do this work if I could co-ordinate it with the roofers installing the new roof". The roofers ended up tearing off the front shingles first to allow the framing crew to work on building the new gable. By the end of the same day the roofers were back to the front section applying building paper and shingles over the new plywood. This was a day where I made sure I was there to help out and ensure everyone had the right materials. I ordered pizza for the trades and thanked them for working together and for their co-ordinated efforts.

The before and after photos provide a good visual of the difference. The cost to make all these improvements was just over $10,000.00. The return on investment was more than double the expense. Here is a list of the changes made to the front elevation to complete the plan provided by the designer.

The Plan Changes on Paper

- Re-roof with new (dual black) shingles
- frame new roof gables
- new front door and locks
- add 8 inch smart board trim around front door to make it look bigger and stand out
- new mailbox
- pot lights under soffit
- acrylic stucco over top of old stucco
- add stucco boxes under existing windows and coins on corners
- add vinyl sign tape for illustrating the look of having window grills
- add painted cedar shingles to the gable end
- add cultured stone across front
- add flower pots on step
- improve lawn by removing weed, cutting and fertilizing
- power wash walkway and front steps

Before, the Plan on Paper and After

Adding Curb Appeal to Your Design Checklist

Things to Avoid or Consider Altering for Profit

- Steep walk to front door
- More than 3 or 4 steps up to the front door
- Flat looking front (no character, poor curb appeal)
- Small windows (less light)
- No overhang over the front door
- Older plans with dated designs when building a new home
- Narrow walkway and steps
- Building beside something that will drag your value down

Items to Consider when Renovating or Building New

- Peaks and rooflines, roofing material, especially when visible from street
- Garage with extra room (if possible)
- Front door with appropriate width
- Adding stone
- Jogs on front elevation to avoid a flat looking design
- Terraced walk to avoid too many steps or steps that are too steep
- Installing quality front steps using right materials and design
- Larger windows on front (possibly add grills)
- Trim around front door and windows
- Modern earth tone colors
- Lighting along front (under eaves)
- Use smart board or other trim/cladding to add to appearance and relief to blank walls
- Quality front door and high security locks
- Landscaping, placement of trees, shrubs, grading
- Adding a courtyard area (patio with outdoor table, chairs) close to the front door

Today you can google any topic and spend hours searching sites. There are countless design ideas for improving curb appeal. Spend some time and money on this valuable improvement and seek expert advice. Get a plan with all the changes to products, select the appropriate color scheme then determine the best sequence for scheduling trades to make the required changes. You might need a short critical path to have the changes made in a specific order. The chapter on scheduling construction provides some explanation to critical path and scheduling work. A good idea is to show the before photo and the new design to those doing the work and ask them what preparations need to be completed and finished before they show up to do their work. There are countless ways to add curb appeal by dressing up windows with trim and improving walkways and entrances. Below you can see the improved look of a window and a walkway designed to enhance curb appeal.

An illustration of the use of Smart Board for Window Trim, the addition of Window Grills and Cultured Stone to Enhance Curb Appeal

An illustration of a Terraced Walkway, Designed to Enhance Curb Appeal

Action Exercises:

1. Determine if the property you are looking to buy has potential for making improvements to the curb appeal?
2. Determine if the property is a gold mine or land mine (too costly to make the improvements).
3. Take a photo of the front elevation, get it printed and sent it to a talented design person for making improvements on paper.
4. Using the photo and the new design, estimate the cost of the improvements by visiting the required trades and suppliers.
5. Seek advice from trades when needed. Examples include; installing new stucco over old stucco, steps and procedures (correct cement type, installing mesh, etc.) for installing cultured stone, technique for installing window grills on the front windows, procedures for installing trim or smart board around doors and windows, paint and stain colors.
6. Investigate products like shutters, door locks, mail box, lights, cladding and other materials you may need to complete the new plan.

Chapter 14

Estimating for Profit

*A Little Progress Each Day
Adds Up to Big Results*

    This chapter will cover, in layman's terms, what is important to know to perform the estimating function for residential construction. Your role as an estimator will pertain to both renovating and building new. You have three options, act as your own renovator/builder, hire a project manager or project coordinator or third, contract with a renovation company or builder who will do the estimating and subcontracting. Under the first two options you would complete the selection of products and also perform the estimating function. The information to follow is designed to set you up with tools and tips to help you complete the estimating for your renovation or new build. When you are finished you will have a two-page summary of your estimates which is the "Cost Summary and Loan Calculation Form" for a new home or the "Renovation Checklist" from Chapter 12 "Renovating for Profit". These lists were also mentioned in Chapter 2, "Using Lists to Save Time, Effort and Money".

    Whenever money is involved, whether you are applying for financing or dealing with the contracting and disbursing payments to contractors and suppliers, the procurement process of obtaining bids and estimating the cost of the project is an important role. In a larger commercial setting the procurement process is often via a tendering or competitive bidding process. This process is used to ensure the buyer receives goods, services or work at the best price and also for finding those suppliers and trades interested in bidding. For your renovation or new build, the builder (either yourself or one you hire) would perform this function by contacting and inviting suppliers and trades to provide an estimate. Do this the right way and you will be estimating for profit.

    Building homes during a time when margins were very low made it critical to know all my construction costs prior to signing a contract, as well as, during construction right to completion. I remember losing jobs to other builders who came in lower than my costs. I did my homework. Those who didn't went out of business. Things were so tight at one point that if I included a contingency factor I would lose the contract and client to another custom builder. Some builders would perform part of the labor themselves and still make a living but with little to no profit on a job. This made it very difficult to compete as a custom builder. That was then, today a builder (you) can make a handsome profit if you do your due diligence in the role of estimating. Remember to apply items that support the "Principle of Contribution" discussed in Chapter 3. To make all this relevant to you, I'll share a number of tips and things you should know to perform the estimating function. It's really not difficult to do yourself. If you like to shop for your own home building materials you will enjoy getting out and about talking to suppliers. This chapter explains some things you can do to prepare in advance to save time, effort and money. Your objective is to complete these three simple steps. Everything else that is discussed is just identifying important things to know and do to help you complete these three steps. I like to use the KISS principle here, keep it short and simple!

Three Simple Steps

Step 1 Preparation

Step 2 Obtain Estimates

Step 3 Complete the Estimating Checklist and Cost Summary

To properly prepare, you require plans and specifications. You must have some idea of what products will be used outside and inside. For my last renovation, I was able to obtain a copy of the original blueprints from the city. The home was built in 1979 and in 1978 the city planning department started inventorying a set of plans when building permits were issued for all new homes. This was a tremendous help because I could see the cross sections and bearing points. I knew which walls could be removed and which walls were bearing and must not be removed. It provided a top floor plan to a scale of 1/4 inch = 1 foot which was used for calculating floor areas for estimating hardwood flooring and planning the new kitchen, bathrooms and bedrooms. The old process of printing architectural drawings using a contact print process transmitted on a blue background layer brought into existence the term "Blueprints". This reference to working drawings is still common today even though printing architectural drawings have changed to using large printers and modern ink cartridges.

I was able to take the blueprints to a designer to discuss the renovation plans. Using velum paper to overlay the blueprint he was able to re-draw areas eliminating hallways, draw a rough outline for the new kitchen, provide ideas on the ensuite and other minor structural changes. We were fortunate that the home was built with 14-inch web floor trusses. The designer showed how we could close in the two story open foyer area using 6-inch Timberstrand material (resembles a 2 inch wide microlam beam) placed on 12-inch centers and still have a 9-inch depth for a ceiling design feature in the front foyer. Closing in the floor added an additional 72 square feet to the kitchen above on the second floor of this hillside bungalow.

None of this would be possible without a plan on paper. The first step in preparing is to have a plan on paper for your renovation or complete working drawings for building a new home. Plans are necessary for estimating material quantities and showing trades the scope of work. For renovations, drawings provide a visual of the before and after view. For new home construction, drawings are used by the framing crew to reference every construction detail. Working drawings play a critical part in estimating and construction. New construction plans will have some material specifications which you should study and be aware of when talking to suppliers.

Today, with modern technology, sections of plans can be scanned and sent via e-mail. I consider doing this when asked by the trade or supplier but it's still not my preferred method. I know from dealing with many trades, there's something to be said about working with paper that makes it seem more real. Maybe it's just my age but I know trades work with their hands not computers and many prefer to see it on paper rather than look at a screen. It also provides them with a copy of the plan and estimate that they can keep on their desk where they see it.

If you are wondering why it's taking weeks to get a reply maybe it's because your e-mail request for a price is hidden in an e-mail. The insinuating perception you could be creating in the mind of the tradesperson is you couldn't spend a dollar on plans and you are sending this e-mail out to the world to get the lowest price possible. Remember the attitude discussion in Chapter 1, walk a mile in their shoes. You get to know people on a personal level whenever you can meet them eye to eye. I also want the opportunity to discuss and sell my ideas and needs.

Use Lots of Plans

I think the point now is very clear that good plans are a must for pricing and you want enough copies for all the trades and suppliers to save yourself time, effort and money. Plans are just pieces of paper and copies are inexpensive yet a valuable tool for you to obtain all your costs quicker than if you had just a few copies. Estimators will use plans and make calculations on the drawings. To prove this point just go to a lumber supplier who sells to builders and meet with the estimator. Look around and you will see rolls of blueprints of jobs they are working on performing material quantity take-off's to determine material lists and prices for clients.

When I give out plans I don't expect to get them back. I don't want them back! Imagine running around the city to collect a $10.00 set of plans from an electrician so you can deliver them to another electrician. It would cost more in gas! Your time is worth more than $10.00. Not only that, when you decide to go with an electrician he will say "I need a set of drawings". I think you get the point that paper becomes a tool and using lots of it makes good sense. You save time, effort and money because these copies allow you to obtain more estimates more quickly.

When pricing items for the main floor such as flooring, tiles and kitchen cabinets only the main floor plan is required. When building a new home you should get roughly 20 full sets of plans and an additional 10 pages of just the main floor plan. For the estimating role, many trades can use plans copied onto 11 x 17 paper which saves printing large sheets. Ask what they require and send them the way they prefer to receive them. For example, when re-roofing and existing home, the roofing estimator may use a program called "Eagle-eye" to view and measure the top of the home via Google. Not all details can be seen from this program so plans fill in the gaps and help you obtain a better, more accurate estimate. You can use a courier service but once again, whenever possible, my preference has always been to meet trades face to face. More discussion is provided on this topic in the next chapter "Contracting for Profit."

Importance of Good Specifications

Specifications identify the products and details for the scope of work required. Clear specifications are important. The shower installation procedures in Chapter 12 "renovating for Profit" provide one good example. If you are planning a steam shower then proper installation of specific wallboards, use of grout, tile and sealants and other materials are all part of what's needed to obtain a proper estimate. The specifications for a new kitchen would include the door style, species of wood, exterior color, interior material and color (e.g. white, maple or other melamine or birch plywood), type of slides, base material, height of the toe kick, moldings, any installation instructions (example #10 screws), style of handles and so on.

The more detailed the specifications, the easier for the contractor/tradesperson to provide an accurate price. Fewer unknowns help lower required contingency factors. When you are building a new home, it's comforting knowing you have included everything in your budget and you will have enough funds to complete your project. Bankers often frown on individuals wanting to build their own homes because they remember those who ran out of money before their homes were completed. I remember a story where this happened to one family and the bank had to float them a separate loan to finish the construction.

Using Estimating Software - or Not?

I would not recommend buying estimating software for one home renovation or building your own home. By the time you understand how to use it, I would be done the estimating. Obviously this does not apply to a larger builder or track builder who builds many homes. It also does not apply to the lumber estimator who may use a system for completing a material quantity take-off from your drawings. Remember the KISS principle. All you need to do is complete an estimating checklist like the one provided in this chapter. You might want to add and delete some items and transfer the list to an Excel spread sheet for a paperless version which automatically does the calculations for you. Using software or not is your option, but it's not necessary to spend time buying software and afterwards spending more time learning how to use it.

The Material Quantity Take-off

For a large renovation or building a new home, a lumber take-off is a listing of all the different lengths, widths, types and grades of lumber needed to complete the project. You would only do this yourself if you have the construction (framing) background and training. Some items are easy to calculate and formulas are used for many areas. For example, the perimeter of the building establishes the number of exterior studs required. Also, the total floor (square footage) surface determines the number of sheets of plywood required as there are 32 square feet to one sheet of plywood. For some renovations like a basement development you can do this yourself but for large renovations or a new build, get help from a professional source.

There are a couple methods I use for obtaining the lumber estimate. One method is to just request the lumber supplier to do the take-off. They may do it for free or sometimes charge a nominal fee which is often waived when you purchase the lumber package.

Another option which I prefer to use is to obtain an independent material take-off from an independent expert who is not selling the lumber. This method allows me to get price quotes from a few different suppliers making it easier for me to compare. It also provides me with an unbiased opinion where I'm comfortable the quantities won't be short. Some lumber yards when providing an estimate will want to show the lowest price because some customers just look at the bottom line. To present a low price means less materials quoted. They may not include an allowance for waste or a contingency factor. It could mean being short materials during construction. If this happens you are still going to order the extra pieces from the same company where you set up the account so it's no loss to the lumber yard. However, it becomes more work and more troublesome for you, the builder.

A third approach is to first request a contractors price on a list of items which you plan to use for your major renovation or new home. This list will allow you to compare lumber suppliers and locate the one who is willing to provide the best contractors price. The one providing the best price on the largest number of items is the one you go to for the material quantity take-off.

When building a new custom home I always show the take-off to the framer and ask him to check a few of the quantities for accuracy. Your carpenter, I refer to as the framer (or yourself) can easily check the sheets of plywood or OSB (oriented strand board) the subfloor against the floor square footage. You have to allow a couple of extra sheets for wastage. The electrician might also use one in the basement for the electrical panel.

For a new home, the roof truss supplier often provides floor trusses. This firm will supply you with an accurate truss layout, an accurate quantity and a price for floor and roof trusses. They may provide the flooring material (e.g. plywood or OSB) so check with them and confirm what they supply.

Stairs are another item I leave out because I order them from a construction stair manufacturer. Their representative visits the home once the subfloor is installed to measure the opening and the height. The information is fed into the computer providing the exact rise and run. The measurements are read from the plant where they are built with equipment that routers the stringers and properly glues and nails it together to construct steps that are solid and correctly customized for the opening and height.

For both floor trusses and stairs, I advise the lumber supplier to leave these two items off the material quantity lumber take-off to avoid duplication. You should check the material take-off to see that plywood is included. One thing I do is meet with the floor truss supplier to discuss the options for flooring. Discussion will cover the type and size of floor truss, the spacing, plywood or OSB and some consultation on roof trusses and any beams that will be supplied.

The following page shows a short list for obtaining lumber prices used to locate a supplier offering the best price. This method could be used prior to requesting a complete quantity take-off and a full price.

Lumber List of Materials

Option 1

Based on your plans, provide the suppliers with a list of the main items for comparing prices.

Example:
Make a short list of a few major items pertaining to lumber and subfloor design.

2 x 6 # 1 construction grade spruce studs 9 foot   Quantity _____ Price $ _____

2 x 4 # 1 construction grade spruce studs 9 foot   Quantity _____ $_____

2 x 4 # 1 construction grade spruce studs 8 foot   Quantity _____ $_____

4 x 8 sheets of 3/4 inch OSB   Quantity _____ $_____

4 x 8 sheets of 3/8 inch OSB   Quantity _____ $_____

4 x 8 sheets of 1/2 inch Plywood   Quantity _____ $_____

4 x 8 sheets of 1/2 inch OSB   Quantity _____ $_____

2 x 10 #1 construction grade fir joists   Quantity _____ $_____

2 x 12 #1 construction grade fir joists   Quantity _____ $_____

Note, floor trusses and roof trusses will be priced when you obtain estimates for roof trusses.

Obtain a complete materials list from the supplier who is offering the best contractor price based on the list you created.

Option 2

Obtain a materials list from an independent source not supplying the lumber.
Check with your architect or designer who may be able to provide a reference.
Use the material list to obtain three quotes on lumber.

Establish Yourself as a Contractor

The simplest way to get contractor's prices is to set yourself up as a contractor. I know one tile supplier that offers a 40% discount off the listed retail prices for all contractors. This is a substantial savings and necessary to save or make money when acting as your own builder. The quick and easy way is to create a business name. I advise my students to just use their own name followed by the word "contracting" as in "John Doe Contracting" or "John's Renovating and Construction". One of my students used "Homes by Matthew", you can guess what his name was.

Set up a separate checking account to control your costs. It's quite inexpensive to apply for a registered trade name. The registered name gives you the benefit of proving you have a legitimate contracting business in case you are ever asked. It also allows you to have checks made with the business name. Another helpful tip is getting a small batch of business cards printed with your company name, address, phone and e-mail. This saves considerable time when introducing yourself to suppliers and trades and also informs them you are in the contracting business. The perception you want to portray is not one of a retail customer.

Establish accounts with the big box stores who offer contractor pricing. Be prepared to complete the credit applications and you will likely also get a credit card which means the retailer will conduct a credit check. This is a quick procedure but plan to spend 30 minutes at the counter when you go there.

For large projects you will benefit by establishing a line of credit with a major lumber supplier, a concrete company, a wholesale paint supplier, a flooring supplier, a window manufacturer and any other companies that you intend to use that may require prior information to add you to their database of contractors. A line of credit can often give you 30 days before you have to pay and in some cases you can extend this credit to 45 or even 60 days.

Always ask for and take advantage of cash discounts offered if you pay early. An example of a cash discount is 2% off if paid within 15 days of the invoice date.

Sometimes when I felt that a new tradesperson was a bit reluctant to deal with me I would do my selling spiel on them. It goes like this; "My house is sold, I have approved financing and I can pay sooner than most builders who want long lines of credit. I'm not building a spec home and I do not have a limited liability company, therefore there is less risk with me" ....now negotiate a discount!

You do not need to buy a truck. You can have material delivered on site. Even if it costs for courier fees it's still far cheaper than buying a truck or trailer. Hire a company to place a garbage container on site and instruct trades to use it. You do not need to haul garbage away. This is well worth the cost but I realize exceptions exist and you might already have the truck and availability to do some of this work.

It's always necessary to have a contingency factor. This is especially important when renovating where you are most likely to have unknown costs. Often when you tear out walls and ceilings you expose something that requires additional removal or repair. You don't have this when building a new home but it's also necessary as some unexpected costs will occur. The bank also likes to see you have a built-in contingency factor for their security.

Buying Plumbing Fixtures

I found it better to have the plumber supply all the fixtures. There are exceptions such as a specialty tub or selecting the kitchen sink and faucet. The reason is the plumber has an account at the wholesalers and buys at a lower discount than what you would obtain as a contractor going to the same place or from one of the big box stores. There are always exceptions especially when those big box stores run their specials but otherwise it's difficult for you to get a better price than the plumber who sometimes buys fixtures by the case. I proved this on one large renovation where my cost for purchasing just the fixtures was not much less than the plumber's cost to purchase plus install the same list of fixtures. It is also much simpler to deal with one source when feasible. The plumber is then responsible for all the fixtures supplied in the event of damage before installation or if pieces are missing.

I remember one plumber being upset with the taps he was supplied by an owner/builder because they were an unfamiliar and uncommon european style. There were pieces missing from the boxes. He was extremely frustrated and as a result he charged considerably more for the time it took to install the taps.

For pricing plumbing, select all faucets, sinks, toilets and tubs first and include these specifications in your request for pricing. You can get some suggestions from your plumber, visit the big box stores, or go to a fixture supplier like Kohler to choose the items. Remove any fixtures you bought separately and give the list to the plumber. Your plumber will buy at his discount and add a small markup. If he does not supply the fixtures he will charge more on the installation. Remember the win/win and allow your plumber to earn a portion on what he supplies.

Buying Windows and Doors

When it comes to a manufactured product like windows, there are dozens of companies out there eager to get your business. You can buy direct from the manufacturer but they will likely not undercut their dealers which makes buying from a dealer an option. Considering prices vary significantly with windows, it's important to remember the principle of contribution. The quality of product you buy should reflect the value of the homes in the area. There are some manufacturers of extremely high-end products costing thousands per item. Some builders of larger custom homes would easily spend $10,000.00 on a front door while this same amount could pay for all the windows on a smaller track-built home, duplex, town-home or condo. How much you can pay for windows is like asking the question "how long is a piece of string?".

The best strategy to locate the right company offering the right price would be to send out a bid offer to all the suppliers in your area. This is accomplished by creating a window schedule with some specifications and sending it out as an e-mail attachment. It's easy to do this task and it will give you a good idea of price ranges. If you are replacing windows on a renovation you would just use the outside measurements minus at least a full 1/8 inch. This is to ensure they fit into the existing opening. The installer will caulk around the opening and fill in the gaps. For new construction you would use the measurements on the architectural drawing.

Example of Creating a Window Schedule for Estimating
(draw a picture of your windows and include measurements and specifications)

4.0 x 3.6 S.U. (V)
one side vented

Quantity - 2

6.0 x 6.8
Garden door

Grills

6.0 x 5.5 SU (V)

24 inch transom window

Total 7 ft tall, grills on top

5.0 x 4.0 S.U (V)

Quantity - 2

Casement, one side vented

Some window manufactures might require eight weeks lead time which might not fit your renovation schedule. This is because windows are custom made to order. When the window firm, either a manufacturer or a supplier, receives your request for a quote via e-mail or other means, the impression is you are shopping price and the only way they will see you as a customer is to offer you their best contractor price. Your strategy is to remain distant until you can compare prices. For the front door I just specify one design knowing later I can select the front door from a catalogue or have one custom made. After you complete this step you would plan to visit one or two suppliers to review each window and firm up all the details.

You can expect to get a phone call from a sales representative asking you questions and wanting you to visit their showroom. I would hold back until after all prices come in then choose the one or two suppliers where the windows fit the budget. During this process you will find manufacturers who will not want to follow through because they see you are shopping price and they know their product is higher priced. On the other hand, if you were shopping for high-end windows then you would likely be eliminating those suppliers with the lowest prices.

Your first page would have your name and address with a description of what the request is for and when the windows would be required. You would also mention the wall depth which is usually either 2x4 or 2x6 construction. If you were adding extra rigid insulation on the outside then this needs to be accounted for in the jam width when the windows are manufactured. Include the specifications such as sealed unit or the opening style either slider, casement or awning. Mention any special features that you want like heat shield if the windows are south facing, argon gas for energy efficiency, low-e coating for increasing the "R" value, triple glazed for 'R' value if in a northern climate, window grids (grills), or other features. You don't need to be 100% accurate at this stage because this step is done only to locate the right firm to supply your windows. Do some homework first because the pay-back when you spend money on some of these extra features is very long or none at all. In cold climates (northern States and all of Canada) it's best to get triple glazed windows to avoid icing on the inside. This item is worth the additional cost.

Buying Flooring

Look for those companies that have inventory on the floor, inventory they would like to move and have the right quantity for your project. Often the location of suppliers to the construction industry can be found in commercial/industrial areas, away from the retail stores.
They are in warehouse style buildings which are less costly to rent and have significantly less overhead so considering them for specialty suppliers for lumber, hardwood, carpet, tile, fireplaces and cabinets can be very beneficial. Visiting new construction areas is one good method for locating tradespeople. Using the internet is certainly another option but getting a good reference from a reputable source is one of the best ways to find qualified tradespeople.

The big box stores such as Home Depot, Lowes and Costco stores need to move a tremendous amount of inventory. I suggest checking these stores because there are occasions where they have purchased train loads of an item and the price is at a point where even the wholesaler can't match it.

Headings for New Construction - Checklist

- Survey, elevation check and certificate
- Compaction test (Engineer fee)
- Excavation, backfill, trenching
- Demolition, removal, dumping charges
- Concrete, footings, walls, basement floor, garage floor, volume and price/cubic meter
- Cribbing labor (for concrete basements footings and walls)
- Tar, weeping tile, gravel
- Lumber - examples plywood, studs
- Roof and floor trusses
- Stairs, other wood steps for framing and hand rails
- Framing labor
- Windows, doors and garage door
- Exterior siding, soffit, fascia and eaves (material and labor)
- Roofing material and labor
- Plumbing, include fixtures
- Heating and/or air conditioning
- Electrical (service, rough-in, panel, install fixtures and finish)
- Insulation and poly vapor barrier
- Drywall, material, labor and textured ceilings
- Kitchen cabinets, vanities, supply and install or supply only
- Painting, prime and paint walls, staining, lacquering material and labor
- Countertops, granite, other, supply and install
- Finishing materials and labor (doors, casings, baseboards, shelving, hardware)
- Railings, material and labor to install
- Hardwood/Engineered flooring or other, material and labor priced separate
- Tile for flooring and bathrooms, material and labor priced separate
- Exterior steps, walkways, grading, lawns, trees and other landscaping
- Light fixtures, blinds
- Moving expenses

Estimating can be a lot of work so you will want to follow all the tips and shortcuts in this chapter. I like to combine work whenever possible to reduce some estimates and for ease of scheduling. A good example would be a concrete firm that also provides the gravel, prepares, places and finishes their work and may even do the damp-proofing or weatherproofing. More on this topic is covered in the Chapter 18, Scheduling for Profit.

Estimate or Contract

Estimates you receive can take many forms including writing on a napkin or even a tradesperson giving you a verbal price. I have examples of estimates I show students that are written on invoice stationary that only state "I will frame your house for XXXX dollars per square foot". There is nothing wrong with this because all you are asking for "at this time" is a price. You may not choose to use this company, therefore, a detailed estimate is not necessary at this stage. Some estimates will be very detailed in a contract form itemizing the materials supplied, labour and other costs. Consider estimates simply as price quotes. Contracts are more detailed and discussed in the next chapter on "Contracting for Profit".

Completing the Estimating Checklist and Cost Summary

The third step is to complete the Estimating Checklist and the Cost Summary. You will need to obtain quotes or tenders on all the major items and judge the remainder yourself. While dealing with the major suppliers and trades, ask questions which will help you determine the cost of the extra items. For example, you receive a quote on all your cabinets and the supplier suggests adding in a $500.00 allowance for hardware. With some items you just need to make calls, ask questions and then plug in the figures. It will take experience to be 100% accurate, another good reason for having a contingency factor.

Once each section in the Estimating Checklist is complete, the subtotal is transferred to the cost summary pages, the last two pages of the list. It's important to use this detailed list to ensure all the major costs are included in the final count. For example; the electrician may not quote the outside service because he is unaware of the distance from the house to the source. If these extra amounts are not included, you could run substantially over budget. It's a comfort feeling knowing you have an accurate budget for mortgage purposes. If you underestimate and spend too much you will not save any money, hence no profit. To avoid this you must have knowledge of all costs associated with the project before contracting. Complete every line that's applicable and edit any area to customize the lists to suit your personal needs.

When it comes to building your own home, you will be almost half done before you start construction. Some owner-builders will spend a year getting working drawings and estimates for a project that takes three to six months to complete. The more work you do up front in this area, the easier time you will have later when it comes to contracting and scheduling construction. The more you do this work yourself, the easier and quicker it becomes as less research will be required. The formula "knowledge x experience = confidence" applies here, so both knowledge and experience are needed to become an expert in estimating.

Estimating Checklist for New Home Construction

PREPARATION

Check	1. Working drawings, blueprints, survey, etc.	Amount
	Architect, draftsperson, plan copies	
	Insurance	
	Site plan, real property plan or plot plan	
	Estimate fees for material quantity take-off	
	Survey stakeout, Survey certificate (or real property report)	
	Footing elevation check and reset survey pins if required	
	Engineer soil bearing test, soil type test (if required)	
	Finished grade check (if required)	
	Other	
	Subtotal	

FOUNDATION

Check	2. Excavation, backfill, trenching, grading	Amount
	Remove topsoil (if required)	
	Excavation	
	Trenching for water, sewer and electrical	
	Move-in equipment	
	Haul away excess dirt	
	Backfill, Bring site to rough grade	
	Bring site to finish grade, Deliver and spread topsoil	
	Landscaping (materials, decorative rock, trees etc.)	
	Other	
	Subtotal	

Check	3. a) Basement	Amount
	Footing forms, lumber for footings, and top of walls	
	Rebar (reinforcing steel bars)	
	Concrete for footings, telepost pads, posts	
	Concrete walls	
	Pump charge, charge for delivery and placing concrete	
	Concrete additives, calcium (winter construction) color, etc.	
	Other	
	Subtotal	$

© David Pocock All rights reserved. The contents or parts thereof, may not be reproduced, for any reason, without permission from the author.

Check	3. a) Basement (continued)	Amount
	Dampproofing, foundation waterproofing	
	Weeping tile around foundation walls, labor charge to install	
	Washed gravel for covering weeping tile	
	Other	
	Subtotal	$

Check	3. b) Alternative basement construction (wood or forms)	Amount
	Engineered drawings or engineered stamp	
	Forming footings for walls or slab on grade	
	Concrete and reinforcing (if designed with concrete)	
	Washed gravel delivered and placed	
	Compacting gravel	
	Preserved wood basement materials or insulated concrete form	
	Subfloor materials	
	Weeping tile, extra gravel, sump box, pump (if required)	
	Framing labor to construct basement	
	Other	
	Subtotal	$

Check	4. Basement labor	Amount
	Crib footings, Crib walls (installing basement beams)	
	Supervise the pouring of concrete	
	Install subfloor (if required by cribbing contractor)	
	Other	
	Subtotal	$

Check	5. Basement floor	Amount
	Basement gravel (should be clean 3/4 inch rock)	
	Preparation, placing gravel, leveling, tamping, etc.	
	Concrete for basement floor	
	Finishing Labor	
	Pit run or gravel fill for garage	
	Preparation for garage floor	
	Concrete and finishing for garage floor	
	Other	
	Subtotal	$

STRUCTURE

Check	6. Framing materials (sections from material quantity take-off)	Amount
	Main Subfloor	
	Glue, nails, insulation stops, other materials	
	Lumber for interior and exterior walls	
	Second story subfloor	
	Lumber for second story interior and exterior walls	
	Roof trusses (supplied by a roof truss manufacturer or supplier)	
	Roof materials, plywood or OSB board, sheathing	
	Pre-manufactured stairs and other stair material	
	Garage walls, garage roof	
	Basement framing materials	
	Decks, railings, stairs, bolts, finishing nails, screws, etc.	
	Other	
	Subtotal	$

Check	7. Framing labor	Amount
	Contract from framing carpenters (check items listed below)	
	Subfloor	
	Main structure	
	Garage	
	Deck(s)	
	Basement framing	
	Stairs, install manufactured steps, build steps in garage	
	Extra items, fireplace hearth, (check contract for list of extras)	
	Other	
	Subtotal	$

Check	8. Doors and windows	Amount
	Basement windows	
	Doors and windows	
	Window extras (grills, delivery, increased "R" value, etc.)	
	Garage door supplied and installed	
	Garage door opener	
	Skylights, storm doors, custom front door, etc.	
	Other	
	Subtotal	$

Check	9. Roofing	Amount
	Roofing estimate, labor or materials and labor	
	Roofing materials (shingles, tiles, metal, shakes, rubber)	
	Accessories (flashing, drip edge, nails)	
	Accessories (vents, building paper or other under sheathing)	
	Other	
	Subtotal	$

Check	10. Siding or stucco, stone, brick	Amount
	Siding estimate, labor or materials and labor	
	Siding materials	
	Trim boards, trim for windows and doors	
	Staining (painting) siding and trim	
	Stucco (paper, wire, scratch coat, finish coat)	
	Masonry, brick, stone, material	
	Masonry labor	
	Parging (finishing on exterior basement walls)	
	Other	
	Subtotal	$

Check	11. Fascia, soffits and eavestroughs	Amount
	Soffit material	
	Fascia material	
	Labor	
	Eavestrough (material and installation)	
	Other	
	Subtotal	$

MECHANICAL

Check	12. Plumbing	Amount
	Plumbing contract (including fixtures and installation)	
	Fixtures supplied by builder	
	Gas line connection	
	Water and sewer connections	
	Well and septic system (if required in a rural area)	
	Other	
	Subtotal	$

Check	13. Heating	Amount
	Heating contract	
	Heating extras, air cleaner, humidifier, air exchanger, solar	
	Other	
	Subtotal	$

Check	14. Electrical	Amount
	Electrical contract	
	Electrical permits	
	Temporary power supply (if required)	
	Service from main line to house	
	Fixtures (other than those included in fixtures # 20 below)	
	Electrical trench (if not included in # 2 above)	
	Other	
	Subtotal	$

FINISHING

Check	15. Insulation and vapor barrier	Amount
	Wall Insulation - main structure	
	Basement wall insulation (include any rigid or foam insulation)	
	Garage insulation	
	Roof Insulation, batt or blown-in	
	Caulking, materials and labor	
	Poly vapor barrier supply and installation	
	Other	
	Subtotal	$

Check	16. Drywall	Amount
	Drywall (gypsum board), wallboard contract	
	Drywall material	
	Boarding labor	
	Taping and sanding	
	Texturing ceilings	
	Garage drywall material and labor	
	Basement drywall material and labor	
	Other	
	Subtotal	$

FINISHING - CONTINUED

Check	17. Kitchen Cabinets, bath vanities, counter tops	Amount
	Materials, cabinets, vanities contract	
	Laundry room cabinets, bar, office or other cabinetry	
	Countertops, granite, arborite or other material	
	Installation of cabinets and counter tops including hardware	
	Other built-in cabinets, shelving, medicine cabinets	
	Kitchen extras, soft close hardware, moldings, etc.	
	Other	
	Subtotal	$

Check	18. Flooring, floor coverings	Amount
	Hardwood or laminate flooring materials	
	Labor to install flooring	
	Broadloom, underpad, metal strips, linoleum, supply and install	
	Floor tiles, porcelain tiles, travertine, slate, marble	
	Other	
	Subtotal	$

Check	19. Ceramic tiles, other stone, bathroom accessories	Amount
	Bath tiles - material for bathrooms, kitchen backsplash	
	Tile installation labor	
	Mirrors, shower door	
	Bathroom accessories (towel bars, paper holders, etc.)	
	Other tile or stone work	
	Other	
	Subtotal	$

Check	20. Electrical fixtures	Amount
	Light fixtures and bulbs (include fans, door chimes, pot lights)	
	Installation if separate from the electrical contract	
	Extra indirect lighting, wiring and plugs	
	Electrical permits and inspection if not included in the contract	
	Other	
	Subtotal	$

Check	21. Painting	Amount
	Painting contract, brush and roll, primer and finish 2 coats	
	Prime and paint exterior (if not included in contract)	
	Prime and paint exterior trim	
	Prime and paint interior and exterior (materials only)	
	Thinner, brushes, rollers, sand paper, filler, other accessories	
	Painting interior trim, spray staining, materials and labor	
	Contract for lacquering and staining	
	Painting front door, garage door, basement floor, steps	
	Other	
	Subtotal	$

Check	22. Interior finishing	Amount
	Finishing materials, (baseboards, casings, mouldings)	
	Interior doors, bi-fold, by-pass, pocket door, french door, etc.	
	Shelving, tile or carpet underlay material	
	Extras, book cases, built-in closets, ceiling trim	
	Finishing labor	
	Finishing around fireplace	
	Hardware installation, handles, door locks, closet rods, etc.	
	Bathroom mirrors supply and install, shower door	
	Other	
	Subtotal	$

Check	23. Exterior masonry, stone, brick, parging	Amount
	Material and labor (not included in #10 above)	
	Other	
	Subtotal	$

Check	24. Steps, sidewalks, driveway, supplied and installed	Amount
	Steps, front and back	
	Railings, deck covering	
	Sidewalks, placed and finished, retaining wall, other specified	
	Driveway, concrete or other prepped, placed and finished	
	Gravel for driveway, reinforcing wire, rebar, other supports	
	Other	
	Subtotal	$

Check	25. Extra items - include applicable extras	Amount
	Damage or security deposit paid to land developer	
	Financing land, accrued interest	
	Land taxes, other land costs	
	Mortgage application and appraisal fees	
	Construction insurance	
	New home warranty costs (if applicable)	
	Tool Rentals, gravel vibrator, jackhammer, water pump, etc.	
	Heating and power utility costs during construction	
	Appliances, fridge, oven, dishwasher, cooktop	
	Appliances, laundry, garborator, microwave	
	Fireplace, mantel, hearth, finishing face, labor to install	
	Built-in or rough-in vacuum system	
	Specialty ceilings i.e. beam, tray, coffered, panel, medallion, custom plaster, etc.	
	Decorating, wallpaper or other decorating	
	Blinds, curtains, and other window coverings	
	Worker's compensation (if trades not covered)	
	Decks, patio, fence, sod, trees, shrubs, other landscaping	
	Garbage removal and dumping fees	
	Basement development, material and labor	
	Tools, skill saw, impact driver drill, hammer, wheel barrel, etc.	
	Other construction costs	
	Subtotal	$

Check	26. Services and permits	Amount
	Building permit, development permit, other permits	
	Water meter	
	Natural gas application	
	Natural gas trenching, and installation of service	
	Other trenching, plumbing, electrical not included above	
	Electrical permit (see # 14 above)	
	Sand fill over services if backfill material is not useable	
	Winter allowance for trenching and excavation	
	Communication installations, internet, TV, phone, security	
	Septic system, tile bed, water well (if required)	
	Other	
	Subtotal	$

Check	27. Builder's costs (if required)	Amount
	Salesperson commissions, salaries	
	Costs to builder, project manager and other management costs	
	Site supervision, wages and other benefits	
	Displays and advertising	
	Auto, travel, gas, mileage, maintenance, insurance	
	Office and administrative, salaries, rent, utilities	
	Office, printing, stationary, legal, accounting	
	Insurance, licenses, dues, warranties	
	Bank charges, interest, business taxes	
	Other	
	Subtotal	$

Check	28. Legal and interest costs	Amount
	Legal fees	
	Land financing interest	
	Mortgage draw interest	
	Interim financing interest	
	Service charges	
	Credit financing interest	
	Other	
	Subtotal	$

ESTIMATING SUMMARY		Amount
Estimated total construction costs - total 1 to 28 above		$
First floor area		
Second floor area		
Other developed areas		
Total area developed		
Add contingency factor		
Estimated costs per square foot of construction		$

COST SUMMARY AND LOAN CALCULATION (page1)

Builders Names (s) _____

Preparation
- Blueprints, site plan, survey, engineering etc.   (1) $_____

Foundation
- Excavation, backfill, trenching, grading, loam   (2) $_____
- Basement material, forms, concrete, weeping tile
  waterproofing or damp proofing   (3) $_____
- Basement Labour, cribbing concrete, ICF, other   (4) $_____
- Basement Floor, gravel, concrete and finish   (5) $_____

Structure
- Framing materials, floor and roof trusses, stairs   (6) $_____
- Framing Labour   (7) $_____
- Doors and Windows, garage door, opener   (8) $_____
- Roofing material and labour   (9) $_____
- Siding, stucco, stone, trim   (10) $_____
- Fascia, soffits and eavestrough   (11) $_____

Mechanical
- Plumbing   (12) $_____
- HVAC (heating/air conditioning)   (13) $_____
- Electrical   (14) $_____

Finishing (all items are a summary of material and labour)
- Insulation, caulking, poly vapor barrier   (15) $_____
- Drywall (board, install, taping, sanding, ceiling   (16) $_____
- Kitchen Cabinets, vanities, counter tops   (17) $_____
- Floor Coverings, carpet, hardwood, tile, install   (18) $_____
- Ceramic Tiles, other bathroom items & accessories   (19) $_____
- Electrical fixtures, all lights, bulbs, extra wiring   (20) $_____
- Painting, primer, paint, stain, lacquer, brushes   (21) $_____
- Interior Finishing, doors, casings, railings, closets   (22) $_____
- Exterior masonry, stone, brick, parging   (23) $_____
- Steps, sidewalks, garage pad, driveway   (24) $_____
- Extras (appliances, fireplace, vacuum, landscaping,
  blinds, other)   (25) $_____
- Services and permits   (26) $_____
- Builders costs, general contractor, project mgmt.   (27) $_____

CONSTRUCTION COSTS $_____

COST SUMMARY AND LOAN CALCULATION (page2)

CONSTRUCTION COSTS		$_____
Contingency Factor		$_____
Home Warranty		$_____
Land (incl. interest, taxes, security deposit)		$_____
TOTAL (finished home and land)		$_____
Legal and interest costs	(28)	$_____
(SUB TOTAL)		$_____
Mortgage Insurance fee, appraisal fee		$_____
Other		$_____
TOTAL CONSTRUCTION COSTS		
Less: Downpayment (deposits paid, items purchased, cash, other)		$_____
TOTAL LOAN / MORTGAGE REQUIRED		$_____

Transfer the subtotal amounts from sections 1-28 in the Estimating Checklist to the Cost Summary and Loan Calculation Form. This completes the final step in estimating the cost of your new home. Later in "Financing a New Home for Profit" you will receive instructions on completing page two of the "Cost Summary and Loan Calculation Form" for using sweat equity for part of your downpayment.

Qualifications of an Estimator

To do a good job of estimating you should work towards gaining;
1. The ability to read plans and measure if you are estimating quantities and lengths.
2. Some general knowledge of construction materials, methods and trade terminology.
3. The ability to see the project being built in your mind (reference chapter on Scheduling for Profit).
4. A conscientious attitude, ability to deal with others, ask questions and add numbers.

Better to be "Looking AT It" than to be "Looking For It"

A final reminder when ordering material, you need to be aware of wastage. For example, a 12 x 12 room with a 2 foot x 8 ft closet requires 144 square feet plus 16 square feet for a total of 160 square feet of flooring material. Now add 10% for waste equalling 176 square feet of flooring materials. I would round this up to 180 square feet knowing that *it's better to be looking at it than looking for it*. When tradespeople run out of material, the work stops and they leave until you order more. Maybe they start a different job and don't return for a few days which is reason enough to have a little extra so you don't run short. Quite often the unused material can be returned for a refund.

When it comes to tile or hardwood flooring, dye lots can be a little different. If you run out of product you might not find a perfect match. This is another good reason to double check all measurements and always order extra.

Action Exercises:

1. Obtain or create working drawings for estimating your project (e.g. a renovation or a kitchen design for a new kitchen).
2. Refer to the Chapter 16 "Designing a New Home for Profit" prior to obtaining drawings for a new home.
3. Refer to the Chapter 12 "Renovating for Profit" for a list of items to estimate.
4. Create a detailed specification list for each item to be purchased or installed.
5. Obtain references, source suppliers and locate trades or alternatively source contractors or builders at this time.
6. Obtain estimates by visiting, faxing, e-mailing or phoning.
7. Complete the Estimating Checklist in this chapter or the Renovation Cost Summary form in Chapter 12.
8. Summarize all items onto the Cost Summary and Loan Calculation Form.

Chapter 15

Contracting for Profit

"Good contracts make good friends."

*"I have 6 honest learned friends that taught me all I knew.
Their names were what, where, when, which, how and who."*
Brian Tracy

Now that you are competent in estimating for profit, it's time to use what we know to either hire or become a bonafide contractor. That's one who is honest, obeys the laws, and negotiates in good faith. This chapter covers a list of things you should know and do before you enter into a contract and a contract check list for saving time and avoiding potential pitfalls.

In most cases, when an owner-builder or owner-renovator receives an estimate, the work is done on that estimate and no other contract is formed. Too often, not enough information is specified in writing which leads to problems down the road. Problems can be stressful and costly and those bad contracts are often the cause. They can delay projects, cost extra in legal fees, cause construction liens being placed on title and having to deal with shoddy workmanship. On the other hand, the opposite happens when both parties have a clear understanding of the scope of work, terms and conditions.

One method is to form a separate contract, but this results in some additional work when you are contracting with up to 20 suppliers and trades. For some trades, when the estimate is not acceptable as a contract, it's a good idea to use your own contract form. When I accept estimates I then say, "lets use my contract form as it has a little more information". The time to ensure the contract has all the right details included is when you negotiate the acceptance. A list of what contracts should contain is included in this chapter under the contracting summary checklist.

Another alternative is to ensure all the required details are specified in the estimate. The estimate can be modified or rewritten to suit your purpose. When the estimate is accepted and signed by both parties, it becomes the contract. You can attach an additional sheet of conditions and terms and have both copies signed by both parties at the time the estimate is accepted. The contracting summary provides a sample list of terms and conditions.

During or after obtaining estimates you should engage in some conversation and questions which will aid in the research of sorting and investigating the trades and suppliers you might contract with. These questions are provided in a list for ease of referencing under the first tip in the next section titled "Ten Tips You Should Know Before Entering into a Contract". When you use this knowledge and put these ten tips into practice, you will have the confidence of an experienced contractor.

Ten Tips You Should Know Before Entering into a Contract

Research Qualifications, Certification and References

Are they reputable? How long have they been in business or the industry? Any complaints with the Better Business Bureau? Many good Tradespeople work 100% on referrals. They don't need to advertise because their customers do it for them. As a general rule of thumb, ask around and you may get a good referral from an already satisfied customer. Some questions to ask the contractor or tradesperson are:

- Are you certified ? Most trades take 3 to 4 years training and experience to gain a Journeyperson Certificate. Completing an apprenticeship means having completed time on the job training, technical training and passing exams. Some trades such as Electrical, Plumbing, Sheet Metal and Gas Fitter have compulsory requirements for apprenticeship participation and certification. In most other construction trades (Roofer, Carpenter, Bricklayer, Drywall or Lather, Painter, Tilesetter) apprenticeship certification is optional. Holders of Journeyman or Journeyperson Certificates usually carry their small wallet size certificate in their wallet. You can ask if they are certified in the trade and if they can show you their pocket card.

- Can you provide me with a couple of references?

- How long have you been in business or doing this kind of work?

- Who will be working on the job and what are their qualifications?

- Do you live or work in this area? Use local trades and suppliers when possible! Once I hired an electrician for a new home construction who lived in an adjacent town 30 kilometers away. He wanted to complete his contract with 3 site visits; rough-in, finish and fixtures. It was more difficult to co-ordinate. I would have preferred a few more site visits. In comparison, I did a complete renovation on a home about the same size and the local electrician I hired visited the site more than 60 times. I was fortunate that this person did not charge extra for travel time and additional visits. I would recommend that you discuss the number of site visits in their estimate and what, if any, additional charges there will be for travel to your site. The rule of thumb here is "Hire Local Whenever Possible".

Three Quotes

This was mentioned in the Chapter 14 "Estimating For Profit" and is worth noting again. A rule of thumb that is common in construction estimating is "get three quotes" or "get a minimum of three quotes". This is especially important if you have no references and little experience with the subject trade or supplier.

The formula "confidence = knowledge x experience" is true when hiring tradespeople. The knowledge and experience gained from a reputable referral source can give you confidence to hire someone good and you might only need to obtain one quote. The more experience you have the fewer estimates you will require. Eventually you reach a point where you use the same trades over and over because they are reliable and do good work. This is one of the advantages of hiring a professional general contractor or project manager. The right general contractor would already have a team of favorite trades and suppliers, people he can trust and know their quality of work. I was a general contractor for a number of custom homes. During this time I was very fortunate to have conscientious tradesmen who worked well together. Many of them would get to know each other from seeing them again on several of my job sites. They knew what was expected from them and they often surprised me by doing work in advance of having to ask them.

One time I called the cement firm to arrange for the preparation and pouring of concrete for the driveway. The preparation included some bobcat work, forming and placing of rebar. The fellow from the concrete firm asked me when I needed it and I told him it's ready now. He said jokingly, "it would sure be nice to have a few days notice". Later that afternoon I found out they had already visited the site and completed the preparation work. He never told me they were monitoring the job site. It was very enjoyable dealing with people who could add humor to their work. They don't work in an office where you can associate with a group and enjoy those mini office conversations. You are their office!

You get three quotes or a satisfactory number of quotes, not just to find a better price but also to locate those trades having the skill and character that you are seeking. The three quotes is a rule of thumb. You can call it "the rule of thumb for the dumb" because until you start researching, you really do not know anything about anybody. When you shop for a new couch you go to more than one store before making a purchase. It's the same thing here. When you shop for an Electrician or a Plumber or a General Contractor, you go to more than one before you make your decision.

There were times when I knew from the initial meeting that they were the right contractor. There were also times when I knew I needed to get another quote because my spider sense was telling me they were probably not right for the job. Again, price was only one factor and often the lowest price is not the best price. I would keep searching for a supplier, contractor or tradesperson until I had not only a fair price but also a person who could work with my client, the new home owner, and someone I would be comfortable with. The three quote rule of thumb for me was not a hard and fast rule I followed. On one contract to supply materials and labor, I got eleven quotes before I was satisfied with the people, the product and the price.

When you obtain several quotes you know who is offering you contractors prices and who isn't. However, the decision to get three quotes is your call and should be based on many factors which may include; price, terms, quality, references, availability, buying power, overhead, specializing in that kind or work or supply, time to complete, guarantees or warranties, how long in business, are they a member of the Better Business Bureau, reputation from references, workmanship, easy to contact, on time and good character.

Specifications

Specifications are for estimating and carry over to contracting. It is important to specify the same thing when pricing so you are comparing apples to apples. Some specifications are simple like the product name and number for the porcelain tile to be installed. However, for tiling a shower, more detail is needed, like the color for grout, pattern, set up, preparation, time to complete, clean up, garbage removal, type and color of thin-set on certain tiles, type of trim, sealing or not, installation of the back board (if required), shampoo and soap holders (if required), installation of a shower bench and so on. As you can see, these items also form part of the contract in the form of specifications to ensure you are getting quoted what you are planning to have done.

Specifications for a new kitchen should include diagrams, measurements, door style, wood species, drawer style, color, details of range hood, spice rack and other speciality or custom cabinets, details of under-mount lighting and other lighting and electrical plugs, slides, handles, moldings, material for toe kicks, installation, details of appliances to be fitted including the hood fan, garborator, microwave and any options or special items plus particulars regarding the material for countertops and the edge profile along with sink cut-out or under-mount details.

Estimate or Contract

I was approached by a neighbor to have my roof re-shingled. He said he would supply and install the dual black shingles, supply and install a metal flashing drip edge, install the 3 foot ice and water protection around the perimeter, paper the entire roof with heavy building paper, add additional vents, install flashing in the valleys, remove the existing shingles and pay for a large garbage bin to have the garbage removed. He was also going to coordinate with the framers who were installing a new gable on the front of the home in order to improve the curb appeal. Since he was a neighbor this was a cash price.

Whether you are dealing with a neighbor, a relative or friend, it's critical to avoid any future problems by knowing you are both working from the same page or set of circumstances. I said, "John, lets just put this down on paper so we are both on the same page". Good contracts make good friends or they help keep them as friends. I copied the roofing contract from my book "Build or Renovate Your Own Home" and we wrote in the details of the work to be completed along with the price. It just so happened that soon after we started John asked for some money to cover the materials which were delivered.

I paid him and had him sign on the contract next to the amount paid with the words "received $1,000.00". This happened again, two more times, before the job was complete. Now it was time for the final payment. John didn't know the final amount but I did because I had it on paper. When he received the balance, I wrote the amount paid and the words "paid in full" next to his signature.

I can only imagine the list of potential money problems having only a verbal contract for this one small job. As I mentioned before, often the estimate is detailed enough to become the contract when accepted. But when an incomplete estimate becomes the contract, problems can occur because some items were not negotiated or put to paper prior to starting work or prior to starting the contract. Treat these estimates as price quotes only and they can even be verbal. The contract is completed after you agree on price and it should include the following:

- The deadline date, the current date and the start date
- company name and names of both parties and addresses plus the work site address
- an estimate as to how long the job will take
- lead time required
- full description of the work to be done
- full description of the materials supplied including specifications
- the method and terms of payments
- statements or clauses pertaining to insurance, WCB coverage, permits, building codes, damages, clean up and removal of garbage, holdbacks and any other responsibilities
- signatures of both parties

Good contracts do make good friends! A good contract will keep you on the safe side of potential money issues because you dealt with it up front. Also you have some protection against poor quality and a host of other potential issues that can arise. You can say that a good contract is like having an insurance policy because of the protection you have built into the contract.

Availability

What does the owl say in the deep woods? Who? Who? Who? Once I hired a finishing carpenter because he showed me his vast portfolio of quality work in his photo album. After signing the contract I never saw him again at the job site. Instead, his son showed up and it was obvious his son was not the tradesperson who did the work that his father showed with his photo album. I learned to always ask "who is doing the work?". I would like a little information to know they have the tools, the skills, the manpower is available and I would like to know they are not just intending to subcontract this job out to an unknown third party.

When tradespeople get too busy, the price naturally goes up. When they are too busy and don't have time for the job it may end up being reflected by them throwing out a really high quote. Suppliers will do the same when they are too swamped to handle more work. Go get more estimates and you will see that eventually you will get a respectful price from someone who has the available time to perform the work.

Downpayment or Deposits

I know several people who have lost thousands of dollars because they didn't know the do's and don'ts pertaining to paying deposits. Generally, you never give a deposit on work in advance of it being done. There are some exceptions and they are for custom manufactured items to get to production. In these cases your deposit is given to a reputable manufacturer who is established with buildings, inventory, employees, etc. Therefore, you would only give deposits to a truss manufacturer, window manufacturer, cabinet manufacturer, stair and railing manufacturer or similar company when you are asking them to use building materials to make something which is custom ordered for your new home or renovation.

Never give deposits to trades who have not started any work. Once I hired an individual to supply and install the drywall. The drywall was about $10,000.00 which was a large bill for the contractor to carry. I simply removed this from the equation by paying this money to the supply company immediately following delivery of the drywall.

When times are busy, some individuals (I won't call these people tradespeople) will ask for deposits and then renege on the work, or do a poor job, or not complete the work, not show up, demand more money, etc. It often begins with the act of asking for a deposit prior to doing any work. This should be your red flag. To avoid getting ripped off, know the company and people you are giving any deposit to. The rule of thumb, with a few exceptions, is to never give a deposit.

When do you pay?

There have been cases where a sub-trade abandoned a job when it was only partially done. It was possible the job was too big for them, they estimated too low or maybe they were offered more money to work somewhere else. In any event, they would have probably received a partial payment equal to the work they have already completed.

Any partial payment should either reflect the contract "example 60% upon completion of rough-in plumbing" or it should be substantially less than the work in place if the work is not complete. There should be a large enough incentive for your workers to complete the job they were hired to do. The builder's holdback would cover for any minor deficiencies remaining when the job is determined to be substantially complete.

On a new home construction, a payment to a framing crew could be made following completion of the framing inspection. It is after this time when the homeowner/builder would be receiving an advance of mortgage funds from a construction draw mortgage pertaining to the lock-up stage. An interim payment or an advance payment is not recommended. It could leave you at risk of losing your framing crew (or other trade) to another job. I made sure that any advance during the construction period was a small goodwill advance to help the sub-trade meet payroll, cover some expenses or cover living costs. On large projects, advances are certainly necessary and should be negotiated at intervals related to time and/or work completed. The Golden Rule with contracting is "he who holds the gold, rules!". In other words, do not pay your bills too soon but pay them on time.

No mistake, I do like to pay quickly and not nickel and dime them because I know they will want to do work for me again. They are very appreciative when they get paid quickly so it's important not to hold payment when payment is due. Another good "rule of thumb" to be safe when making an advance payment to a trade is; always receive a written receipt, do not fully pay until 100% complete and inspections (if necessary) have passed.

Holdback

Every State/Province has passed legislation pertaining to holdbacks and liens. In could be called the "Builders' Lien Act". A provision under the act allows the builder to hold back money (e.g. 10 % for 30 days) from the time the job is determined to be substantially complete.

The allowed holdback is provided by law which means it is your legal right. It does not need to be mentioned in the contract because it is law. The holdback period allows you time to see if any liens were placed on your title by suppliers or other tradespeople who may not have been paid by the contractor you hired. When you are dealing with tradespeople who subcontract out work or have suppliers to pay for materials, it is more important under these contracts to hold funds for your protection.

When financing is involved, your lawyer will do a title search before advancing funds to check for liens. If a lien was placed on your title, it is a prior charge which must be dealt with or funds must be set aside equal to the value of the lien. A large lien could easily halt construction because it could tie up mortgage funds needed to complete the project.

Mark "Paid in Full"

Pretend that you and your contractor are standing in front of Judge Judy. You have the piece of paper, a contract that has the words "paid in full" written next to the contractor's signature. It is likely you would win judgement. You should always prepare for the worst case.

To avoid someone from coming back and saying they didn't get paid, write those words "paid in full" or "fully paid" on the contract or last invoice or last check. You can write it on the bottom of the contract after the job is done and have them sign it when you pay them. If there is a holdback, then write the amount paid and have them initial or sign next to the amount that was paid. It is always best to pay by check to have a record of payment. If you pay by cash it is even more important to have an invoice or a contract to record the amount paid and their signature next to the amount that was paid.

In any cash project it is very important for both parties to be on the same page which means having a written agreement to go by. Consider the phrase "I had six honest learned friends that taught me all I knew, their names were what, where, when, which, how and who". Say to your tradesperson, "I just want to put this on paper so I know we are both on the same page". A good rule of thumb is to avoid paying by cash! If you do pay electronically or by cash, during the transaction, pay only at the same time that you get a signed receipt for the amount paid. This confirmation of payment receipt is your only proof of payment. You must obtain this during the time you hand over the money regardless of who they are, relative, friend or other.

Awareness of Legislation

I have mentioned compulsory trades and liens but there are laws also in place regarding deposits and cancellation of contracts. For more information on dealing with these subjects visit the government consumer protection websites for your jurisdiction.

All trades should have a license. When they are operating without a license they can't be bonded and you have little recourse as a consumer. You will find contractors who don't have or want to be licensed and yet still do excellent work. To minimize any risk, check with previous customers but also make certain that those who are required to be licensed are.

The same applies to certification. A trade certificate shows a tradesperson has achieved a certain standard of qualification. It does not imply they are an expert as their fours years to certification might not have given them the experience needed to be an expert in their field. However, certification is one good indicator which proves a tradesperson has attended training and passed all the exams. In a trade that has compulsory certification, where it is mandatory to be certified for the public's safety, the trade certificate is often referred to as their license. A business license and a trade certificate are two different items and you should know if they have either of them.

Builder's or Mechanic's Lien

A construction lien gives builders, contractors, subcontractors and suppliers a legal recourse to get paid for their work as well as materials purchased and supplied to a project. A lien is one remedy to resolve payment problems. You avoid liens by having good clear contracts and maintaining a good rapport with trades at all times. Knowing how and when to schedule contributes to running a smooth project and this is covered in a future chapter. Use everything in your means to avoid a lien situation because a lien represents a charge filed at a court house and registered at the land titles office to show a charge on title. When a mortgage advance is made, the lien must be covered, funds paid into court or it can be a situation where a lien prevents further advances until it's resolved.

As soon as a situation arises, a conflict, a problem dealing with payment, or other which could involve a lien being placed on your property, you should deal with it immediately. Set up a meeting at the site or other location and negotiate a fair resolution, if it's possible. I've never experienced a lien being placed on one of my properties. I've also never let the threat of a lien bother me. On one project a tradesperson said, "I'm just going to lien your property". I was not intimidated or threatened by a lien and you should not be either. My reply was, "go ahead, my lawyer looks after all my liens". The truth is, if a lien was placed, my lawyer would need to take care of it. Sometimes the courts are so busy that it can take a year before your case is heard. I've seen this situation twice where it took two to four years to resolve. The end result was costly for both parties. Legal fees being roughly $450.00/hour is another good reason to avoid liens whenever possible.

On the positive side, knowing about liens and what could happen provides us the knowledge to be sure to include the things we need to know and do before we contract in order to avoid liens. These items are captured in a list for ease of reference at the end of this chapter.

Lien Waiver

During my time as a home builder, I never used a lien waiver. The reason is because I was not aware of it. Fortunately, I never had the need as I did my homework researching trades and developed trusting relationships. That's not to say it's a bad idea because it's one document that could provide some protection especially when there are work or quality/payment issues or when dealing with unknown third parties such as sub-trades hired by other contractors. Under these circumstances, when you pay contractors, get a lien waiver that waives their right to file a lien on your property relative to that portion of their fee.

Complete Contract

One objective is to mitigate risk whenever you enter in a contract for service. Having all the details in your contracts can save you time, money and headaches later on when work is being performed. I remember one time when I hired a framing crew for our new home. The estimated time to complete the contract was two weeks. After a few days I noticed half the crew was gone. It appeared they took on another job and split the crew to work on both homes at the same time. The pace of work would take them far beyond the two weeks agreed upon. This delay was going to cost extra in interest charges and require myself to pay rent, where we were living, for an additional month. The contract stipulated a timeline for work to be completed once it started. Having this agreed upon in a contract I was able to review and explain the circumstances to the framing contractor. I said, "hey fellows our agreement was for two weeks. If you take a month that's going to cost me thousands of dollars. Are you prepared to renegotiate the contract because this is not what was agreed?". After explaining the penalties and that I would need to charge to compensate for the job taking an unreasonable amount of extra time, they agreed to return the full crew to finish the framing. You never know when you might need to refer to the contract terms, specifications and scope of work to resolve an issue.

When you are dealing with family and friends for work, work that you would normally contract out, you should also both agree by signing a contract! It's just as important that you are on the same thinking path, you make the agreement official and there will be no misunderstandings. There are far too many things that can be misinterpreted when you are dealing with construction contracting. Never put yourself in an uncomfortable position when you are dealing with close friends or relatives. On the other hand, you would not sign a contract where a friend is coming over to help you out cleaning, installing laminate, building a fence or other. The big difference here is they are volunteering to help you while you are working. The work being performed is not something substantial where your friend/relative is responsible for the entire job.

The following list of items provides a guideline for obtaining all contracts with trade employers. The estimate you receive will often form the contract when it's accepted. However, if the estimate does not contain all the contractual information, then you should either add in the missing information to the estimate or write up a separate contract that covers everything.

Contracting Summary Checklist

Research the Market

- It pays to compare estimates
- Companies have different overhead costs and buying power
- Qualifications of the person/people doing the work
- Quality of their work
- Payment Terms
- Time it will take to finish the work
- Guarantees that are offered
- Get at least three estimates for each major job unless you have prior knowledge about the trade
- Know what you are looking for and ask for the same thing (use specifications)
- Make use of the estimating department (for lumber at a lumber store)
- Consider an independent material quantity take-off

Check Qualifications and Reputation

- How long have they been in business?
- What is the background of the company?
- What is their reputation from referrals?
- Did they stick with it?
- How was their workmanship?
- Did they have to keep phoning for service?
- Check with the Better Business Bureau.
- What are their Qualifications? Certified in the trade or not?
- How many years of experience?
- Will they guarantee their work in writing?
- Are they doing a job now?
- Do they have a business license?
- What safety standards or procedures (if any) will be followed?

Obtaining an Estimate or a Contract

- The estimate forms the basis of the contract
- Could be a separate contract
- All details to be included
- Signed and Dated by both parties

Insurance and Worker's Compensation

- Obtain a copy of their contractors license, trade certificate if required, insurance certificate and worker's compensation certificate

Contracting Summary pg. 2

Contracts should include:

- The deadline date
- The current date
- Name and address of the company/contractor
- Name and address of the builder
- Job-site address
- Lead time to start
- Estimated time to complete
- Full description of the work to be done
- Full description of the materials to be used and their quality. New items and model numbers
- Description of warranties
- The total price and how long the price is in effect
- The method and terms of payment
    Example 50% after rough in electrical, 50% after completion
    Example 60% following rough-in plumbing and 40% after final
- A statement that the contractor has the necessary insurance to protect the homeowner from liability that may arise from his work (obtain a copy of the insurance certificate)
- A statement that workers compensation will be the responsibility of the contractor
- Obtain their WCB (Workers Compensation Board) number or a copy of the worker's compensation certificate.
- A statement that all necessary permits will be obtained and that all the work will be done in strict accordance with the Building Codes and the specifications in the plans and those attached as a schedule to the contract
- A statement that the contractor will be responsible for cleaning up and removing their own waste from the job-site upon completion of work
- Signatures of the builder and the contractor including the date
- Extra room for other discussions
- A termination clause

Making Payments

This may sound like a broken record but know that whenever I mention something twice it's because it is important. Typically, to learn well and remember something, it's necessary to hear it more than one time and hear it in a different way. Remember back when you studied for school exams, you had to review the material several times before the exam. So here it is again one more time. Always receive a written receipt and have the sub-trade sign or initial beside the words "paid in full". This is your proof of payment and it's very important to have some proof that payment has been made. When you pay by check you have the cancelled check for proof but also having it in writing on the invoice, signed and marked "paid in full" leaves no question that full payment was made. My brother-in-law gave me this tip when he went through a lawsuit that took two years to settle. The main contractor he hired for work when he built his own home was the contractor from hell who overcharged, charged him for materials sent to other job sites and claimed he wasn't paid. Following his two year battle and attending court, he advised me to tell all my students to always write "paid in full" on the invoice and have the tradesperson sign it to ensure they understand it's a final payment and there is no possibility of coming back for more money.

Case Example Liens, Payments and Holdbacks

Under the legislation and acts pertaining to liens you will find information pertaining to allowable holdbacks. A holdback, a small percentage of the total contract, can be withheld for a specified period. To understand these provisions, it is best explained by using a case example. Joe's Drywall was hired to drywall your home. The contract states he is to receive payment upon completion. For some reason you decide to delay paying Joe. Joe has a certain amount of time after substantial completion of his contract to register a lien against your property. The act protects Joe by allowing him an interest in the property as security for payment.

Now reverse the situation. How does the Lien Act protect you? Suppose you hire Joe's Drywall and Joe in turn hires a boarder to install, a taper to tape and mud walls, a sander to finish the walls and a ceiling company to finish the ceiling. To go one step further, assume one or more of these trades also subcontracted their portion as they were too busy to do it themselves. You have no contact with these third parties and likewise no knowledge of how or when they are to be paid. They have a right to full payment for service and under legislation have a specified amount of time after the work is complete to place a lien against your title.

In the case above, you would hold back the amount (10% or other as the act states) from Joe's Drywall for a specified period of time. This amount becomes the lien fund which limits your liability by holding back an amount that could be used to pay those subcontractors who placed a lien against your property for non-payment from Joe. I'll mention again, it's important to check your local regulations because the percentage of contract price, time periods and laws vary between states and provinces.

The process of someone collecting on a lien can be cumbersome in itself. It first involves filing a statement of claim at the courthouse and registering the claim on title at the land titles office followed by attending court and then taking the steps necessary to collect on the lien.

You certainly want to do your contracting in a professional way that avoids all this troublesome activity. The following questions and answers help to provide a better understanding of liens.

Q. What is a lien?
A. A lien is a charge registering an interest in the lands as security for payment.
Q. How can I search my title?
A. A title search can be performed easily by identifying yourself and paying a small fee at the land titles office. You can also hire your lawyer to do the checking for you. The lawyer will search title prior to advancing mortgage funds to ensure no liens exist. This protects the bank because a lien represents a prior charge against tittle.
Q. I'm worried my tradesperson may not pay his supplier. What precautions can I take?
A. Pay the supplier directly removing this portion from your contract or make the check out jointly to the supplier and tradesperson.
Q. What should I do if a lien is placed against my property?
A. Contact your lawyer. The amount of the lien or holdback will be placed into court. The charge will remain against your title until it's resolved. The judge will decide whether or not the lien is valid.
Q. Can a lien halt construction?
A. Only if you are borrowing money on a draw mortgage and the lien is large enough that it prevents you from receiving further mortgage draws. When you run out of funds, your construction will stop until the lien is settled.
Q. Must I inform a tradesperson in advance that I will be holding back a portion of the contract?
A. Not normally as it's covered through legislation. It is your legal right and it does not need to be in the contract. Every contractor should be aware of this. It is advisable, however, that you inform them of your policy regarding payments. Otherwise, when paying, send your payment stating that the holdback will be paid after a title search has been conducted on a certain date. The contractor will have received most of the payment. He will not file a lien against your property knowing that this is your policy for payments. The only person who would is a third party who has not been paid by your contractor.
Q. Is it necessary to hold back funds in every contract?
A. No. You are generally safe to pay the whole amount when there are no third parties involved or you are certain the company is in good standing and has paid all third parties. If the job is one requiring an inspection then final payment should be after a satisfactory inspection. Another precautionary step is you can request a signed statutory declaration confirming all sub-trades and suppliers have been paid.
Q. When the payments are scheduled, do I hold back a portion of each payment?
A. The holdback must be calculated on the entire contract price.
It can be taken off the last payment or the percentage can be taken from each scheduled payment.

Q. When is the contract complete? What if there is one little thing left to do?
A. The legislation should specify that "completion of contract" means substantial performance, not necessarily total performance of the contract. An example would be a homeowner who is able to take possession of a newly built home even though there are a few deficiencies or items that remain to be completed. The home would be deemed substantially complete.
Q. What policy should I follow regarding changes or additional costs after a contract is signed?
A. Contract changes must be in writing. Both parties sign a "change order" form.
Q. What other protection do I have as a consumer?
A Other legislation may exist preventing unfair business practices which aid consumers in recovering losses or protect them against transactions where products are being misrepresented.

Tip. When dealing with trades who subcontract to third parties it's a good plan to hold back the allowable percentage. This is your right according to the Act (legislation) and therefore does not need to be entered into the contract. Always ask the question, "who is doing the work?". Protect yourself in the event sub-contractors do not receive payment for work done on your property. When dealing directly with the tradesperson who is doing the work, it's your decision whether to hold back money or not.

Specifications for Building a New Home

How much does it cost per square foot to build a home? That question is like asking how long is a piece of string? Costs will fluctuate depending on specifications. We already mentioned how important specifications are to a contract. As soon as you are armed with good plans and specifications, you are in a position to start estimating as the owner-builder or the alternative option to contract with a builder, a renovation contractor or a project manager. When contracting out work, the plans, specifications and payment schedule all form part of the contract and can be referred to as schedule A and B and C. The specifications identify all the materials that are to be used. They can also specify other details like how work must be performed. For a complete new home these specifications need to reflect what's being supplied for the hundreds of thousands of dollars being spent. Many specifications should be right on the working drawings while others are listed in the individual trades contracts, which you obtain only if you are the builder. For plumbing, as an example, you would select all the fixtures and provide this list to the plumber who would purchase all the fixtures from a plumbing wholesaler. The list of fixtures would form part of your specifications and contract for plumbing.

The following examples of specifications were used for hiring a builder to complete a custom home. They provide you with a starting point for determining specifications for your new home. You would certainly create your own detailed lists according to your plans and personal needs.

Sample Specifications for a New Home

Concrete, Damproofing and Weeping Tile

- Note: Special requirements such as concrete will be determined by a soil bearing or a soil type report at time of excavation
- Footings are 20 MPA type 10 concrete - 20" x 8" concrete piles under garage floor depending on fill required and soil compaction
- Concrete piles for decks and walk-out patio as required
- Frost protection footings and walls for walk-out basement
- Foundation walls are 20 MPA type 10 concrete with double row 10 mm rebar continuous, according to plans
- Telepost pads are 20 MPA type 10 concrete on 36" x 36" as per plan
- Floor slab is 4" 20 MPA type 10 concrete over 6 mil poly and 6" washed rock with 10 mil rebar on a 24" grid
- Garage pad is 4", 20 MPA concrete type 10 concrete over 6 mil poly and 6" pit gravel with type 10 rebar on a 24" grid
- Damproofing is tabbing snap tie holes and one coat of asphalt emulsion (tar) on exterior of foundation walls from footings to the marked grade level
- Weeping tile is continuous at base of footings covered with 6" washed gravel installed to sump box or storm sewer (dry well) as required
- Front step to be supplied by others
- Walkway to be poured concrete formed and properly prepared and poured over a gravel bed
- Builder to determine the edging and finish styles prior to work being performed
- Concrete steps and wall for walk-out entry
- Parging is from the grade level to the underside of siding

Framing

- Note: House is to be framed according to the blueprints, plans, specifications and the national building code
- Floor joists are 11-7/8" I beam trusses at 16" O.C. as per engineered floor plan
- Floor plywood is 3/4 inch tongue and groove fir plywood glued with PL 400 glue and nailed
- Microlam beams as required by engineered floor plans
- Underlay is 3/8" spruce plywood under tiled areas
- Exterior walls 2" x 6" kiln dried spruce at 16" O.C. with 3/8" OSB sheathing
- Garage walls and bonus room 2" x 6" spruce studs at 16" O.C. with 3/8" OSB sheathing
- Interior walls including exterior basement walls 2" x 4" kiln dried spruce studs at 16" on center
- Engineered roof trusses at 24" O.C. with 1/2" OSB sheathing
- Interior stairs are pre-manufactured closed riser type with 1" plywood treads routered, nailed and glued
- Garage steps, decks, fireplace hearth, tub surround, pocket door and other framing as per plan
- Window and doors to be sealed to framing with tuck tape

Heating, Plumbing and Electrical

Heating, Air Conditioning and Ventilation

- Note: All heating requirements shall meet local and national codes
- Hot water heating with high efficiency boiler with two fan coils
- List of products to be supplied including model numbers
- In-floor heating in underslab basement with radiant floor heating in ensuite tiled floor area
- All grills and registers
- Electronic programmable thermostat
- Outdoor ventilation of dryer, bathroom fans and range hood
- Power humidifier

Plumbing

- Main water line 1" copper pipe from city service to home (or from well to pump)
- Other water lines 3/4" and 1/2"
- One water line to the fridge (if required)
- Vents and drains ABS pipe as per code
- Sanitary sewer 4" line of rigid pipe approved according to code
- Basement has a 3 piece bathroom rough-in, 4" floor drain and all necessary valves and piping, drain and vent pipes
- Gas line from meter to boiler, one gas fireplace line, one BBQ outlet on deck and one line to gas range in kitchen
- Two frost free exterior taps with indoor shut off valves
- Water heater is Rinnai RUC80iN Ultra Series Natural Gas Tankless Water Heater
- Fixtures are single lever Kohler type in all sinks, tubs, showers with brushed chrome finish
- One undermount 9" double stainless steel sink in kitchen and three porcelain undermount sinks in both upper floor bathrooms
- Connection of dishwasher
- Upper floor main bathroom has Kohler 60" x 34" tub/shower with Kohler shower head and single lever faucet
- Ensuite has one Altrek 72" x 42" soaker tub (no jets) with Kohler roman tub filler
- Kohler toilets as per plan
- Ensuite has 60" x 42" tiled shower with Kohler adjustable spray shower head
- Laundry room has stainless steel sink with Moen single lever faucet

Electrical

- Note: All installation as per electrical code and all work to be performed or supervised by a certified electrician
- Temporary power installed during construction
- Underground electrical service to house with 225 amp
- Main panel located in garage with a 225 amp main breaker (location as per plans)
- Sub panel on 100 amp located in basement utility room
- Copper wiring throughout
- All boxes, plugs and switches as per plan with location verification during a walk-through prior to installation
- Lighting in stairs leading to upper floor
- 3 smoke detectors, one on each level, installed and hard wired to circuit box
- 220 volt oven and dryer outlets
- Wiring for exterior lamps and 4 weatherproof outdoor outlets
- Decora switches and plugs as per plan
- All bathrooms have GFI outlets
- Wiring for dishwasher and garborator
- 5 cable and 4 telephone outlets, locations determined during walk-through
- Internet wiring to these locations
- Broan 90 CFM bathroom fans in all bathrooms
- Vapor hats on all exterior wall outlets
- Hookup of exterior vented hood fan
- Plugs for garage door opener and door light
- Installation of all owners light fixtures

Roofing

- 30 year architectural composite asphalt shingle as per architectural controls
- Style of shingle to be determined by builder
- Black galvanized metal drip edge and step flashing
- Basic waterproofing membrane underlayment (rolled) under all shingles
- Valleys to be flashed and shingles cut for a professional appearance
- Four ridge roof vents
- Removal of all garbage

Exterior
- James Hardie siding with smartboard trims as per plan
- Smartboard clad posts
- 6 inch aluminum fascia and vented soffit
- 5 inch continuous rolled aluminum eavestroughs and down spouts
- Stone veneer detail on front exterior and garage as per plan

Insulation
- R 40 loose fill fiberglass in house attic
- R 40 batts over sloped pitch areas
- R 20 Rockwool (Roxul) insulation in exterior walls
- R 12 batts full height batt insulation in basement
- All walls between house and garage R 20 batt insulation
- All exterior adjoining plates and studs caulked
- 6 ml poly vapor barrier on external walls and ceilings with acoustical sealant

Drywall
- Screw, nail and glue application as necessary
- Install 1/2 inch drywall board on all walls and ceilings
- Ceilings on main floor and garage finished to a paint ready surface
- Garage common wall to have 5/8" drywall for fire rating
- Denshield (concrete) board in ensuite shower area
- Rounded corners in all common areas
- General touch up of deficiencies prior to final paint
- Knockdown Spantex ceiling texture on upper floors

Windows and Doors
- Triple glazed PVC windows with PVC jam extensions for 2 x 6 walls
- All windows are white interior and exterior
- Low E coating applied to glass or argon gas between glass panes for energy efficiency
- Front elevation windows to have 5/8" interior grills as per plan
- Window sizes, and opening style as per plan and window schedule
- Front door, insulated steel, as per owner selection
- Allowance for front door is $_____
- Garage door, insulated raised panel metal garage door with top windows as per plan elevation with side mount garage door opener

Millwork

- 5" MDF baseboards
- 3" MDF casings on all windows and doors installed with mitered corners
- All baseboards and casings around windows and doors finished to a smooth crisp white lacquer painted finish
- White lacquer inset panel slab doors 6'8" and 7'8" as per plan
- French doors with clear inserts as per plan
- Pantry door stained with matching cabinet stain
- Melamine shelving and drawers in ensuite walk-in closet to owners design
- All remaining closets to have 16" single shelves with one or two rods
- 5 shelves in pantry 16" melamine or tight wire shelving as per owner's design
- One custom maple mantle for fireplace
- Stairs from main floor to upper floor have straight maple rail top with steel spindles and maple posts as per pattern and designs chosen
- Hemlock or pine handrail from main floor to basement level
- Exact stain color by owners

Hardware

- Weiser Troy satin nickel on interior door handles
- Entrance doors Weiser Troy satin nickel finish knobs and keyed deadbolts
- Privacy locks on all bedroom and bathroom doors
- Hinges and baseboard doorstops for all doors in satin nickel
- Towel bars, shower rods, hooks and recessed paper holders are satin nickel Taylor or equivalent
- Cold air returns painted metal except on hardwood floors where registers are wood stained to match floors

Tiles and Glass

- Ceramic tile backsplash full height to underneath of kitchen cabinets
- Ceramic Tile to ceiling above tub/shower unit in main bathroom
- Ceramic (porcelain or travertine tile by owner) on floor, walls and ceiling in ensuite shower
- All tile, pattern design, and grout selection by owners
- Shower to have a wall soap and shampoo shelf location
- 1 row of ceramic tile above vanity areas in upper two bathrooms
- 3 rows of tiles above tub area in ensuite
- Full width mirrors over vanity tops in upper two bathrooms
- Tempered glass shower door full height in ensuite

Paint

- One coat of primer sealer ½ tinted to final paint color
- Inspect and touch up prior to application of the final coat
- All areas two coats of high quality latex paint on walls, color as specified by owner
- Interior of closets painted two coats latex
- Other finish stain and lacquering under "interior finishing" section

Flooring

- Brazilian Cherry solid ¾ inch pre-finished hardwood on all main floor areas
- Kitchen, pantry and mudroom to be ceramic tile
- Selection of all tiles and grout color by owner
- Front foyer entrance to be ceramic tile inserted in hardwood
- Upper floor area to have a high quality 50 ounce berber carpet with 1.2 inch rubber underlay
- Main bathroom, ensuite and laundry room to have ceramic tile, selection by owner
- Stairs from main floor to upper floor and from main floor to basement to have high quality berber carpet
- Stair stringers are to be carpeted

Cabinetry

- All kitchen cabinets to be solid cherry raised panel
- Laundry room cabinets above washer and dryer in white shaker style, door design and stain color as specified by owner
- Cabinets for complete kitchen and island as per kitchen layout and specifications
- Cabinet features crown moldings and under-mount lighting
- Drawer slides are all soft self-close
- Cabinet boxes made with 5/8" melamine and all drawers of birch plywood
- Cabinets are custom pre-manufactured and installed by manufacturer
- Hardware to be brushed chrome, style by owner
- Vanity cabinets to be 36 inches tall with four drawers

Countertops

- Kitchen, island and all vanity countertops to be 1-1/4" granite
- Granite slab for kitchen and granite vanity countertops to be selected by owner

Fireplace

- One gas fireplace, make and model by owner
- Installation of fireplace including venting and fresh air intake
- Fireplace facing in stone veneer, owners design choice
- Direct vent or exterior of chase finished same as outside exterior

Extra Items
- Rough-in vacuum (locations as per owner walk-through)
- Light Fixture allowance
- Appliance allowance
- Fireplace allowance
- Two garage door openers
- Back deck as per plan
- Basic security system rough-in

Other
- All necessary permits and surveys
- Septic field as designed (following soil bearing report)

Now you have some idea what to include in your specifications for a renovation or a new home. Your specifications will be quite different as they reflect your choices for products and scope of work. Create your specifications as you select your products during the designing and planning stage. Use the specification for obtaining comparable estimates to help select your tradespeople, contractors and suppliers.

Action Exercises:
1. Contact the City/town to determine permits needed for your project as well as what permits tradespeople require to perform work.
2. Contact the trades authority to find out what trades require certification.
3. Determine if your estimate has all the requirements to become a contract including safety procedures, insurance requirements and payment details.
4. Using the contract list of points, compare this list with a trade estimate that is meant to become a contract for service. Amend the estimate if items are missing to ensure a complete and fair contract or, if not provided with a contract, create a separate contract using the item list in this chapter as a guide.
5. Look up the legislation for your area pertaining to construction liens and contracts for service.
6. If there is any concern, review your contract with a lawyer before proceeding.

Chapter 16

Designing a New Home for Profit

*"A napkin isn't good enough -
You need professional drawings!"*
David Litwiller
Litwiller Renovations and Custom Homes

If you google "build your own home" you will see over 500 million search results. There is no shortage of available information. In fact, there is too much information making it difficult to know where to begin and what to do right to not only build a nice home but also acquire equity when it's complete. The objective of this chapter on "Designing a Home for Profit" is to obtain an understanding of all the concepts and ideas used by expert builders who are profit driven and also take advantage of any custom measures as a benefit of being an owner-builder or by doing the pre-planning yourself then hiring a builder. By following the KISS principle to condense miles of information, an understanding of a few important checklists will put you on the right track for saving thousands and profiting as a builder.

Important Lists for Designing a New Home for Profit
- Checklist for Designing a New Home for Profit
- Designing a new home for profit "What's In" and "What's Out"
- Saving Money (in six areas)
- Checklist of Items that Affect the "Cost Per Square Foot" of Construction
- Development Permit and Building Permit List
- House and Lot Considerations List
- Checklist of Steps to Obtaining Working Drawings for a New Home
- Checklist of Lot Facts
- Qualifications of a Good Architect or Architectural Draftsperson
- What To Bring When You Meet With Your Architect
- Checklist for Planning a New Home (low, medium or high importance)
- Checklist for Evaluating a New Home Plan

I have to assume that even if you are building your own home, one of the reasons is to save or make money. After all the effort and time you put into building your new home, you want to see a reward at the end. The size of that reward will depend on a long list of items that must be taken into consideration starting with the selection of lot and location. Cost wise your savings could be up to 30%. The key words here are "up to 30%" because you can also spend a year planning and months building and have no savings at all.

I once asked a class to tell me the attributes of a home if they were building one for profit. We ended up with a pretty good list. This chapter deals with explaining this list of items, design features and qualities that will enable you to build the right home for your chosen lot. Upon review of this list you will note some topics that were covered in previous chapters.

Checklist for Designing a New Home for Profit

Plans and Lot

- Application of Principles of Appraisal
  - The right location
  - The right plan for the lot
  - Having the plans drawn to take advantage of the lot features
  - Great curb appeal
  - Conforming to the area
  - Using the principle of substitution to your advantage
- The right size, shape and style for profit
- Applying knowledge of cost/square foot of construction to maximize profits
- Following a house planning sequence for designing your home
- Building a modern plan with desired features
- Building over the garage to lower cost/square foot (if design has a second floor)
- Having good plans with smart measurements, detailed cross sections
- Avoiding older stock plans which have more hallways, wasted space, small bathrooms and less open space
- Incorporate a modern kitchen with a large island or peninsula and sitting space

Selection of Products

- Using the right construction methods
- The right construction products for "contribution to value"
- The right selection of interior design items for maximum appraisal
- Obtaining multiple estimates and contractor pricing

Construction

- Spending time planning to save time building
- Building in a shorter time which can depend on the size of project, availability of trades and proper scheduling
- Negotiating lot price, shopping, three estimates, contractor discounts
- Applying sweat equity by being the builder/manager and possibly adding some of your own labor

It could be very difficult to find a plan today from a house plan book or other source that will fit all your requirements and meet with the expectations, needs and wants of today's buyers. Plans have changed considerably over the years and the last thing you want to do is build an outdated design, where the outcome is no profit. To increase profit you want to add as many desirable features as possible.

Designing a New Home for Profit
What's In

- Open concept with a large kitchen open to a living area
- Walk-in or larger walk-through pantry, or adjoining room
- Large island (one level) with seating capacity, dining space
- Stainless steel appliances, dishwasher, larger cooktops, double wall ovens
- Large ensuite, two sinks, two sets of drawers, shower stall, tub
- Nine foot or higher ceilings, pot LED lighting, neutral colors
- Larger, planned and organized furnace and electrical utility area
- Consideration for basement or future development, windows, beams, stairs, utilities
- An entry for an added suite and mechanical rough-in
- Larger windows, larger closet and storage space, larger garage if possible
- A nice front door and entrance area
- Home theatre room, gas fireplace
- Space for a king size bed and other master bedroom furniture, two master bedrooms

What's Out

- Wasted floor space, hallways
- Small kitchens, u-shaped kitchens, islands with a raised eating bar
- Small 1/2 bath off the master bedroom
- Small closets
- Nook eating areas
- Popcorn style textured ceilings
- Narrow hallways and stairs
- Long narrow straight staircases with no turns and no landings
- Older outdated house plans with little open space

In the majority of cases, you will want to have your own plans drafted or make changes to an existing plan to add consideration to current trends and desirable features plus accommodate your own needs. In either case, your next step is to find a good residential architect or an experienced home plan draftsperson. I'll use the words architect, designer and draftsperson in this chapter. They all refer to someone you will hire to create working drawings. The important criteria is not the title but the knowledge and experience with residential construction framing, designing, drafting and building codes.

Saving Money

I built five of the first eight homes I lived in. The first home was a bi-level followed by a two story then a bungalow, another walk-out bungalow and another two story. The possible savings can be huge because the savings can come from these six different areas.

1. Acting as your own general contractor. You are the builder or alternatively you do all the pre-planning and hire a builder or a project manager to take on this role.
2. No real estate commissions on your new home. You may pay a commission that's included in the price of your lot.
3. You can do some work yourself if qualified. This is referred to as sweat equity. If you have a trade background then you can apply your trade to save money.
4. Take advantage of sales and specials. You can save by doing plenty of research and shopping.
5. Build something more attractive than the other homes being constructed in the area. This can add to the appraisal value.
6. Taxes! The money you save by building your own home is tax free.

Understanding Cost Per Square Foot

If you are serious about building for profit you must have some understanding of cost per square foot for construction. When you apply this perspective with principles of appraisal you will be building the right size home, spending your budget wisely with the correct amount being spent in each of the 28 areas that are listed on the cost summary form.

I remember one couple who were planning on building a home just outside the city on an acreage. Their future value would be competing with other homes for sale that were built twenty years earlier and some of these homes would be listed below replacement costs. Their plan was a large two story with every extra you could imagine. The windows were all arched with fancy features. The cost per square foot of construction was far too high when compared to the homes in the area. The result was the appraised value of their plans and specifications was around $200,000.00, less than their total construction costs. They decided not to build and instead found a home to buy. Months of work planning and estimating were wasted because they did not have the intuition pertaining to design, construction costs, the current economy and appraisal.

Review the list of factors that affect cost per square foot to recognize the areas where you can save money while at the same time raise the appraisal value of your home. Know that your savings will be calculated by the difference between your construction costs and the future value. Therefore, your efforts should be to utilize this information to lower construction costs per square foot while at the same time maximizing value using your knowledge of appraisal and all collective information you have gained from this book.

The example of a cost breakdown is to provide an illustration of how monies for each item can be allocated. The percentages will change depending on design and other factors but it's beneficial to have an example to follow and some knowledge of a cost breakdown.

Example of a Cost Breakdown
Illustrating a Percentage of Total Costs Applied to Each Item

Preparation
- Blueprints, site plan, survey, engineering, etc. (1) 2.26%

Foundation
- Excavation, backfill, trenching, grading, loam (2) 2.2%
- Basement material, forms, concrete, weeping tile, waterproofing or damp proofing (3) 3.37%
- Basement Labour, cribbing concrete, ICF, other (4) 3.37
- Basement Floor, gravel, concrete and finish (5) 1.84%

Structure
- Framing materials, floor and roof trusses, stairs (6) 16.15%
- Framing Labour (7) 5.21%
- Doors and Windows, garage door, opener (8) 6.13%
- Roofing material and labour (9) 2.70%
- Siding, stucco, stone, trim (10) 5.52%
- Fascia, soffits and eavestrough (11) 1.53%

Mechanical
- Plumbing (12) 5.82%
- Heating/Air Conditioning (13) 3.07%
- Electrical (14) 4.74%

Finishing (all items are a summary of material and labour)
- Insulation, caulking, poly vapor barrier (15) 2.11%
- Drywall (board, install, taping, sanding, ceiling) (16) 4.0%
- Kitchen Cabinets, vanities, counter tops (17) 4.36%
- Floor Coverings, carpet, hardwood, tile, install (18) 5.83%
- Ceramic Tiles, other bathroom items & accessories (19) 1.22%
- Electrical fixtures, all lights, bulbs, extra wiring (20) 0.74%
- Painting, primer, paint, stain, lacquer, brushes, etc. (21) 3.68%
- Interior Finishing, doors, casings, railings, closets (22) 4.79%
- Exterior masonry, stone, brick, parging (23) 2.45%
- Steps, sidewalks, garage pad, driveway (24) 2.82%
- Extras (appliances, fireplace, vacuum, landscaping, blinds, other) (25) 2.09%
- Services and permits (26) 2.0%
- Builders costs, general contractor, project mgmt. (27) 100.00%

CONSTRUCTION COSTS 100%

If you were planning to build and spend 10% of your budget on windows you may need to cut spending in several other areas to make that fit your budget, otherwise you are spending too much on windows. Similarly, if your framer/carpenter was charging you more than 5.21% of your budget for framing labor then the question is, what areas are being reduced so you can pay the higher amount and still have enough funds to complete your home?

Architects are generally required by their association to charge 3-7% of the cost of construction. A draftsman/home designer is usually in the 1-2% range depending on the years of experience that he/she has drafting homes. Stock plans are the most economical because you pay for copies of existing plans only and no drafting. A fourth option is to modify an existing plan which will require some custom drafting service.

Here's some items which can adversely affect the cost of construction. It's important for you to consider all potential costs in the planning stage to ensure you save money when you build or renovate your own home.

Items that Affect the "Cost Per Square Foot" of Construction

- Method of Construction, slab on grade, full basement or insulated concrete forms (ICF)
- Specifications - structure, quality, finishing
- Services - water, sewer, power, gas, phone, cable
- Acreage land - distance from suppliers and trades, roads, services, well and septic system, landscaping adding or removing fill
- Infill land, city requirements, development permit, demolition, new services
- Size, Shape, Style (square two storey is least expensive)
- Winter Construction - ripping frost, concrete additives, extra time, interest, propane heat
- Lot Particulars - grades, excavating, blasting, landscaping, retaining walls, removing or bringing in fill, soil conditions
- Architectural controls determine building size, exterior materials, etc.
- Design - straight vs spiral stairs, walk in pantry vs extra cabinets, right detail, dimensions on plans having odd or even sizes (more waste material with odd sizes), high ceilings, coffered ceilings, other special features
- Time it takes to build, interest costs
- Availability of trades
- Work you do yourself
- Amount of research, estimating and negotiating, taking advantage of sales, discounts, obtaining contractor's prices
- Warranties, regulations, policies, procedures, safety requirements
- Extra items
- Problems, liens

Lot Selection and House Plans

The characteristics of the lot often determine the best suited style, size, position of garage, location of rooms, size of windows and many other factors. Building out on an acreage would have far fewer restrictions than an infill city lot or a developers lot in a controlled subdivision. Nevertheless, there are still considerations for style, window location, decks, front orientation and other planning items. In consideration of the future appraisal value, the goal should be to design and build something suitable, conforming to the homes in the area, roof lines that are in balance with the neighboring homes and the plan takes advantage of any special features of the lot.

A common example is building a walk-out design on a sloped lot. The designer requires the lot grades when drafting the elevations. Another example is one where an owner-builder built along the side of a treed ravine. The chosen house plan incorporated the living, cooking and eating rooms along the ravine (view) side with the bedrooms along the opposite side. A third example is the style chosen for a home with a spectacular mountain view when looking out the front. The design was a two-story split with the main living and eating areas taking full advantage of the mountain view and evening sunsets.

Lots in city locations have restrictions that need to be met. They differ from in-fills with city and community controls to developers with architectural controls. Here are some examples (rules/regulations/permits) that you need to be aware of before spending money on drawings.

Development Permit and Building Permit List

- Township/city development permit requirement list for a building permit or meeting the rules for infill dwellings in established communities and community approval
- Building permit requirement list, meeting all lot and city rules
- For rural areas, rules and regulations for water wells, septic systems and drainage
- Architectural (developer) controls
- Building restrictions, utility right of way, height, size and other lot restrictions (i.e. corner lots)
- Site plan, side-yards, setbacks, grades, what are the implications/rules
- Location of all utilities, utility right of way, existing or new water and sewer lines needed
- Tree removal or tree disclosure statement (if required for removing trees on the property)
- Application fees

Always investigate these restrictions before spending money buying a building lot and before spending money on drawings. With one of our homes, the developer accepted an option to purchase on the lot, giving us the necessary time to ascertain a suitable site plan. The option was simply a hold on the lot with the first right to purchase should another party also have an interest in buying it. This option required no deposit until the lot was purchased.

The house plan should compliment the building lot. Evaluate the following table of considerations between house characteristics and lot to determine suitability of your plan.

House and Lot Considerations

Lot	House
Walkout or sloped front to back or side to side	Style - Bungalow, 2 story, split, bi-level
District/Location	House Size
Lot Size	Architectural Controls
Sunlight, direction facing?	Windows
View Lots	Roof Lines
Trees	Shape of Building, Utility right of way?
Shape of Lot, Pie, Rectangle	Decks, patio location
Proximity to noise	Driveway
Developer controls	Total Cost
Easements	Location of Garage
Utility right of way	Room Placement
Price	Cost of the house
Drainage and soil conditions	Electrical panel, other services

Great Curb Appeal

It is absolutely necessary to cover this one more time. You know the value of curb appeal from Chapters 11 and 13. There is a process I'll share for ensuring you get plans with great curb appeal. Follow the steps in the sequence below to make certain your front view is the very best. Pictures are like a thousand words, the illustrations that follow will show you exactly what I mean.

Checklist of Steps to Obtaining Working Drawings for a New Home

1. Provide designer with lot particulars, grades, restrictive information, photos of neighboring homes.
2. Complete the requirements checklist in this chapter to save time when you meet with your architect/draftsperson.
3. Discuss your lifestyle, the style of home and your list of requirements.
4. First ask for a preliminary draft of the main floor plan.
5. Request plans to be drawn in imperial measurements because residential framing uses wood which is sold in imperial sizes, 4 x 8 sheets of plywood, 2x4, 2x6, 8, 9, 10 foot lengths etc. Metric drawings are common for commercial projects.
6. Have your designer begin the layout with the kitchen, the heart of the home.
7. Obtain a rough draft of just the main floor plan.
8. STOP HERE! Receive preliminary approval from the developer, architectural co-ordinator, city planning department or other before proceeding any further.
9. Work through the draft floor plan making changes on paper.
10. Obtain a second draft of the main floor plan (continue back and forth until complete).
11. Request a sketch of the front elevation and obtain approval from the developer if required.
12. Re-draw the front elevation, again and again if necessary until looks right (see example).
13. As the client, you accept the front elevation sketch and floor plan design once it's completed to your satisfaction.
14. Give your designer or architect the okay to complete the drawings including all elevations and cross sections plus adding in all the numbering, lettering and other details.

Start by asking your architect/designer if he/she can provide you with a main floor "draft" layout and a "sketch" of the front elevation as part of their service. If he/she cannot draw something you like then there is no point in proceeding further. Either a new drawing would be required or go back to square one and start over with a new floor plan or choose a different draftsperson.

Front Elevation Sketches for a New Home

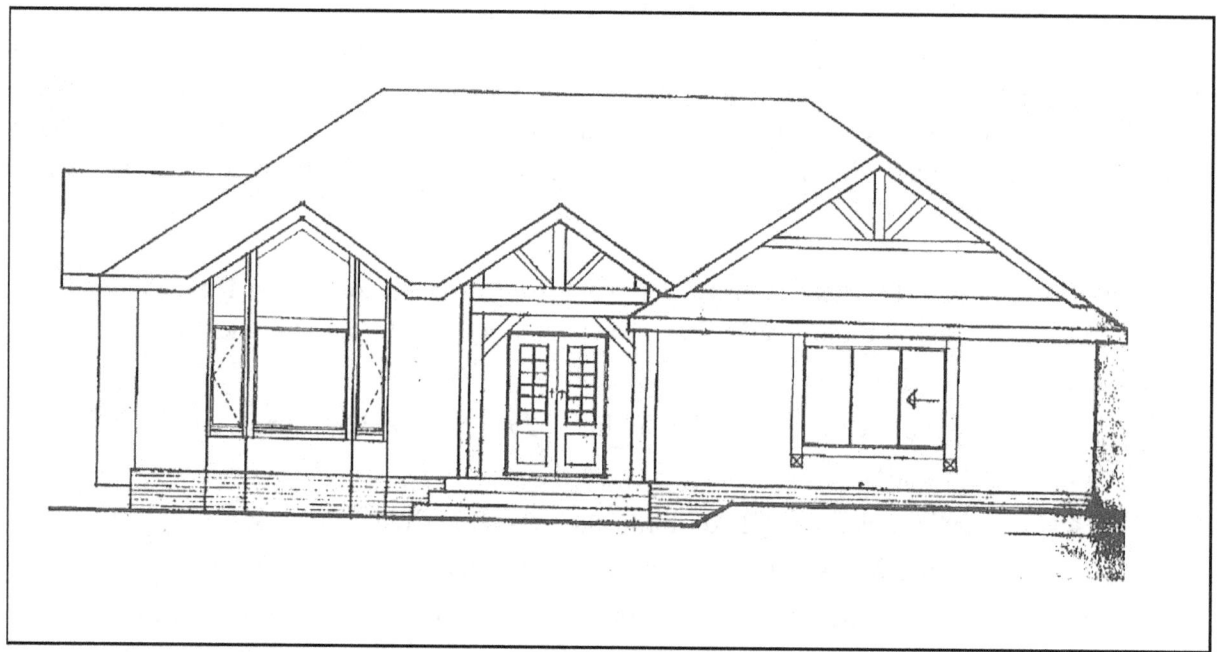

The top elevation was drawn by an Architect for a 2200 sq. foot bungalow.
The home has a double front drive garage protruding on the right side.
This drawing would not work due to no provision for drainage between the garage roof and the front veranda.
The second drawing was done by a talented designer with the goal of improving the appearance and raising the future appraised value for the client. There is a substantial noticeable difference.

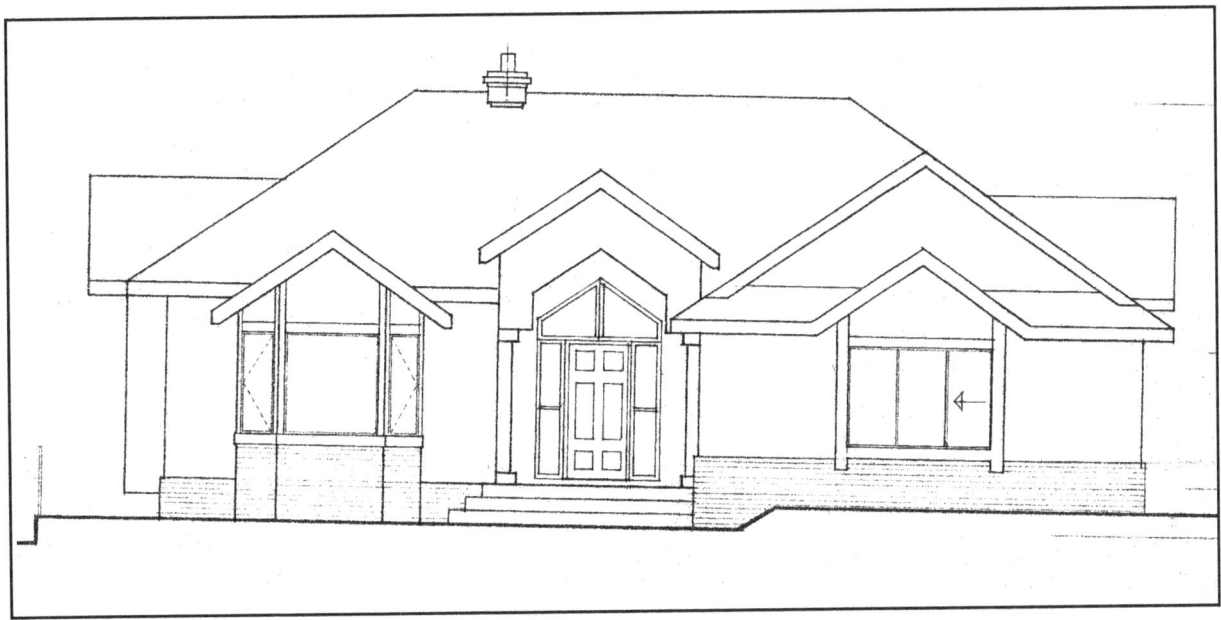

The top drawing was the second drawing completed by an Architect. There is no improvement to the first drawing other than a better design for drainage.

The bottom drawing is the fourth drawing for this home. The arches were replaced with rectangular windows and trim to economize but still maintain an eye appealing look.

The lesson learned is to get a good front elevation. It may take several attempts and more than one designer. Don't just build anything, make sure you have the right curb appeal for profit!

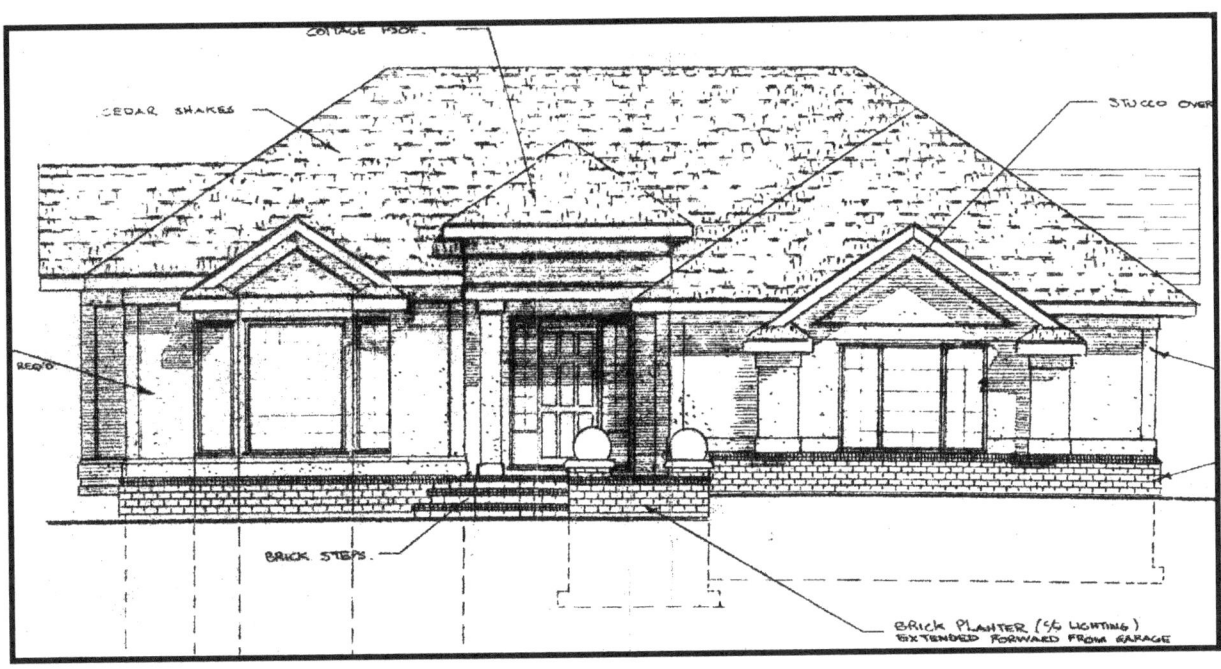

The front elevation should have several items color coordinated to complete the exterior finish and to give the home character. Examples that make up this important elevation are window grills, battens, trim, a second color for siding, soffit, fascia and eaves, stone, added roof line, shingles, garage door, door moldings, front door, railings and posts, stairs, lights and locks.

Here is an illustration of a front elevation for a narrow city lot. It shows development over the garage and the designer/architect planned a combination of materials to enhance curb appeal including roof lines, shingles, siding, windows and doors, trim and stone.

Old designs like the bi-level plan that was shaped like a shoe box are not designs for profit. These illustrations show the front view of newer bi-level plans with development over the garage.

The following questions should be considered carefully before purchasing a building lot.

Checklist of Lot Facts

- Are the other homes in the area well designed and constructed?
- Do the styles of homes in the area complement each other?
- Will you be building within the appraisal values or is there a risk of overbuilding?
- Are satisfactory educational facilities available for your family and for resale?
- Is there a nearby shopping center for groceries and other necessities?
- Are the sewage, water, garbage, snow removal and lighting services satisfactory?
- Is there street sanding in winter and cleaning in spring?
- Are public transportation facilities such as bus routes and train adequate?
- Is any future development planned that would appreciate or depreciate the value of the property?
- What are the city/town restrictions, if any?
- Are there restrictions in the form of construction and architectural details (building size, type of dwelling, colors, exterior products)?
- What are the required side yards and setbacks both front and back?
- Are the soil conditions good for excavation or is there any rock and loam to be removed?
- Was the land used previously? A farmers field is fine ... an old slaughter house or industrial shop may not be so good. Conduct a soil test if you feel it's required.
- Is the lot on virgin soil or did earth movers shape the land? A soil compaction test might be needed to determine the size and type of footings required to support the building.
- Is the lot level or would considerable amounts of soil need to be removed or brought in?
- Would there be the need to build a retaining wall?
- Are there zoning restrictions and existing easements or utility rights of way that could affect design, construction or value?
- Is the neighborhood improving through growth and rising values or are homes depreciating?
- Is the property tax situation stable and reasonable?
- Are the roads paved and services installed? Will the lot have sidewalks?
- Is the street safe or very busy from traffic?
- Does the lot have a desirable shape to suit my ideas for a plan?
- Will the lot support a front drive garage? Is there a location specified by architectural controls?
- Will the finished grade be desirable for appearance and drainage?
- Are there flooding problems in the spring?
- Is there water, air or noise pollution?
- For acreages, is there a well? Is good water available?
- Will there be room for future development?
- Will the lot be affordable using less than 1/3 of my budget?

There may be other questions you can ask depending on your particular needs and for infill or acreage properties. Be sure to run through this checklist before you buy. It's up to you to determine whether or not the property you want is a good buy. The only protection you have is by doing your due diligence on the property before buying. The first step is to analyze what your requirements are and exactly what you need. If this is done first, there should be little chance of being coaxed into something you don't want. You should have a good idea of the type and size of property you want to build on. From this information you can determine the size of the lot. It's also a very important to consider the existing and required property grades.

Your strategy should be to build on the lot as soon as possible to keep interest costs down if the purchase is financed with borrowed money. Land itself is not generally a good investment for profit until a building exists providing revenue or value exists as your own residence. Do your homework before negotiating the land agreement. You will be better informed on all the details and have more information to negotiate with. Compare prices, do a title search at the land registry office to see what existing restrictions exist on the title and get the facts on paper. In a new subdivision, ask the developer if you can look at the development plans and the property report if one exists. Obtain a copy of their standard offer to purchase and read it through carefully then discuss any articles of concern with your lawyer.

Find out if you have to begin construction within a certain time period (e.g. within one year). It is usually to your advantage not to have a building commitment, however, a development with no building commitments may take years to complete. Refer to Chapter 5 "Negotiating for Profit" for tips on buying a building lot.

Selecting Your Floor Plan

Before you begin looking at house plans, you need to understand how to tell a good floor plan from a poor one. An efficient floor plan will separate working, living and sleeping areas. Traffic patterns will allow easy access from one room to the next without having to cross through rooms in the process. the rooms will be functionally designed with respect to others and minimize wasted hallway space. In the last 30 years, with new technology and experience, newer house plans have become more efficient with fewer hallways resulting in roughly 10% less wasted space.

In the planning stage, try not to worry about precise details and do not commit yourself to a single idea too soon. Follow the numbered sequence outlined in this chapter to achieve the right home plan for your needs as well as for profit. This is a very important sequence to help you get the right plan for your lot. Your architect can incorporate the fine details after you select the basic floor-plan layout.

Good drawings will be a big asset when it comes to estimating and construction. Too often this job is hired out to the first available person who has some drafting experience or to the person who is the least expensive. I've taught many classes covering this subject where many times at the end someone would say, "darn, I need to get my plans drawn over again". Building from plans that have insufficient detail, wrong codes and specifications, mistakes and a lack of curb appeal will cost far more than the cost of the good drawings.

For your new home, take the time to find a good architect/architectural draftsperson. The person or firm you hire does not need to be an architect. The key is to find someone who is experienced in residential construction. Architects have training to design commercial buildings, high rises, etc. Because of their complex training and certification they are frequently not price competitive with a draftsperson specializing in residential drawings. Sometimes architects charge a fee determined by a percentage of the expected total project construction costs. One reason for this is the added service of consulting their client on every detail and monitoring the construction from start to finish. Another reason is the clients have the financial resources and want this service whereas an owner-builder who is building for profit would likely not pay the higher fees charged by an architect.

If you intend to use stock plans to construct your home, be sure they are the work of a reputable draftsperson and designed for the climate you are building in.

Package homes where the home is pre-fab and delivered to site have both advantages and disadvantages. The main advantage is having the framing completed (95%) which can help when building at a distance from available trades. Disadvantages are the limitations on design and the added costs associated with the management of hiring a firm to build a package home. The lowest cost is almost always having your home stick built on site.

Qualities of A Good Architect or Architectural Draftsperson

- Provide a free estimate regarding the cost of your plans
- Provide a sketch or layout that you both agree on before any contractual commitment is made
- Have experience or knowledge with framing and residential construction
- Provide insight into interior floor plans and offer recommendations for changes
- Understand the costs associated with alternative construction methods, materials, styles and the economics of design
- Offer advice/discussion on HVAC (heating, ventilating and air conditioning)
- Know the required codes and specification for working drawings
- Know what drawing details are required by building permit departments (cross sections, beam details, etc.)
- Keep work neat and easy to read by others, their client, trades, suppliers
- Provide additional detail where required, will not just assume construction details to be understood by trades (beam construction, truss details, floor joist layout, etc.)

- Work in imperial measurements for residential construction, all wood products are made in imperial measurements
- Draw a site plan
- Double check measurements to reduce the possibilities of costly mistakes during construction

What To Bring When You Meet With Your Designer/Architect

1. A copy of the map showing your lot and legal address (to prepare a site plan)
2. The development plans, if available
3. The requirements checklist in this chapter which is your dream list of everything you want in your new home along with a binder containing a collection of pictures and photos of design items you like (from magazines, internet sites, other homes, etc.)
4. Pictures of the property and adjoining homes
5. Information on grades showing any slope
6. Rules, regulations and any architectural controls for building on the property
7. A list of questions

Every individual/family will have their own desires and your designer/architect will want to spend a considerable amount of time identifying all your needs, likes and dislikes. Your architect will keep these items in mind when designing your new home. To save time, a good idea is to put some thought into these areas and make decisions on items prior to meeting with your draftsperson/architect. Use the following checklist for planning a new home as a resource tool to identify your needs.

Checklist for Planning a New Home (Low, Medium or High Importance)

Requirements of Occupants

Provision for guests, in-laws, others
Provision for pets, dog wash
Profession of owner, home office

Individual Requirements

Formal entertaining
Separate formal dining room
Informal living areas
Outdoor living and eating areas, decks, patios
Supervising the outdoor play area from inside
Nursery
Recreation room, theater room
Hobby area (music, sewing, carpentry, automotive, etc.)
Study, reading area
Laundry area
Screened porch or breezeway

General Design

Bungalow
Bi-level
One and one-half story
Two Story
Split level
Basement, slab on grade and/or crawl space
Number of exterior entrances, basement entry or third level entry
Exterior Style, traditional, colonial, french, tudor, country, etc.
Exterior having a variety of different styles

Roof Styles

Gable, split gable, third gable, continuous gable
Hip roof
Shed roof, double shed (roof over deck or porch)
Flat design
Tudor design, cottage roof
Dutch gable
Combination of styles determined by plan designer

Dress-up Ideas

Trim around windows (smart board)
Shakes on face of gable end
Fascia board design on front elevation
Exterior light fixtures or pot lights in eaves
Stone work, cultured stone or real stone, brick work
Stucco, regular mix or acrylic stucco, stucco relief, other added stucco design work
Siding, wood, composite material, metal, vinyl, other combinations of materials
Shutters on front windows
Window grills
Batten boards, Lattice work
Gable dormers
Pillars
Front porch, steps, railings, walkway to front door
Mail box, house numbers, attic vent
Color co-ordination
Style of roof material visible from front (e.g. dual black roof shingles)

Extra Items

Wood species, quality of interior trim
Style and Quality of plumbing fixtures
Style and quality of light fixtures
Floor covering products
Cabinets: style, quality
Other: fireplace, wood stove, jetted tub, finished basement, bar
Plumbing items, rough-in plumbing, steam shower, water heater size, water softener, hot tub
Window style: casement, awning, slider, vertical slider, patio door, skylights, bow or bay window
Higher 9 or 10 foot ceiling, sloped or vaulted ceiling, full vault, cathedral ceiling area, specialty ceiling
Laundry room: location, laundry shoot
Basement: design, windows, openness, beams, cold storage, usage
Concrete Driveway, paved drive
Built-in vacuum
Appliances: built-in appliance(s), other
Built-in shelving: dining, office, storage, linens, other
Large Tub, steam shower, specialty tub, other

Mechanical Equipment Required

Forced Air heating, type of furnace
Hot water heating, electrical heating, solar heating, other
Passive solar heating
Air to air heat exchanger
Power humidifier, water softener
Air Conditioner
Security, intercom
Washer, dryer, freezer
Exhaust fans
Extra wiring (220 electrical plugs) for workshop, hot tub, etc.
Size of hot water heater

Storage Areas Required

Entrance closet
Bedroom closets
Linen closets
Storage areas, cleaning supplies, laundry room storage
Kitchen storage, pantry, walk-in pantry, separate storage room
Tool storage, toy storage
Gardening equipment
Hobby equipment storage

Kitchen Requirements

The size and desired shape of the kitchen, a general layout
The appliances to be included
The storage area required in or adjacent to the kitchen
Identification of working counter areas
Any special requirements

Dining Requirements

Separate dining room, desired size for furniture
Kitchen stool seating at island or other
Nook seating

Living and Family Room Requirements

Size and locations on site plan, main floor, walk-out basement, second floor
Room for a fireplace, piano, large TV area, library, pool table, other games, fitness equipment, bar, other

Bathroom Requirements

Ensuite: size and fixtures, shower, tub, sinks, cabinets
Main floor bathroom: same as above
Other bathrooms and rough-in plumbing

Utility Room Requirements

Location of washer and dryer, size, style (up/down or side by side)
Room size, shelving, cabinets, storage, ironing
Utility sink/tub, location
Freezer
Other space or utility requirements

Bedroom Requirements

Room for king size bed plus night tables
Walk-in closet space required
Space for bedroom furniture
Built-in closets/drawers/shelving
Other bedroom sizes, closet sizes
Room for study desks, bunk beds

Den/Office Requirements

Space needs for office furniture, desk, chairs, shelving, filing, printer, storage

Once you have your first draft of plans you have something down on paper to work with. To me it's best on paper using a 1/4 inch = 1 foot scale. This allows you to have a clear visual of the space and room measurements. At this stage there would be no numbering and lettering on the floor plan and you would have only the floor plans for the levels, not the elevations and cross sections. This is a working draft to determine if the plan meets your needs. The designer will have put thought into the roof load bearing points as well as the walls for plumbing and HVAC. When you make changes to the main floor plan, the designer will need to consider these bearing points and utility walls when he makes any changes.

You are now ready to use the checklist for evaluation of a new home plan. Run through this list of questions to see if you have captured everything on paper that you want in your home. Highlight any areas that need to be improved and discuss these with you designer during your next meeting. When this is complete, you will be ready to give your designer the okay to finalize all the remaining drawings, cross sections and adding in the details as well as the construction specifications.

Use the following checklist to evaluate your new home plan. This checklist should be reviewed using your first draft set of plans, prior to requesting final drawings.

Checklist for Evaluating a New Home Plan

- Does the plan provide shelter over the front entrance?
- Does the entrance area support the size of home correctly?
- Is there a coat closet in or near the front entrance?
- Will your furniture fit, leaving room to maneuver? Make scale cut-outs ¼ inch = 1 foot and place them on your plan.
- Is there a fireplace and is it positioned so furniture can be arranged nicely?
- Are electrical outlets conveniently located for TV, radio, lamps, cleaning, and other equipment?
- Will heat registers and cold air returns affect furniture placement?
- Is the dining area convenient for serving meals?
- Is there room for daily needs and entertaining?
- Is there convenient access to the patio or backyard?
- Mentally prepare and serve a meal. Will the kitchen be convenient to work in?
- Does the kitchen fit with today's designs for a new modern and efficient kitchen?
- Is there adequate storage space such as an adjacent walk-in pantry or storage room?
- Is there a place to keep and store small kitchen appliances?
- Does the distance between the sink, dishwasher, stove and fridge offer a good, efficient layout?
- Is there a provision for garbage, recyclable material and compost containers?
- Can two people work in the kitchen?
- Is there a minimum of two working counter spaces? Are they large enough?
- Is there provision for a dishwasher and a microwave?
- Will the new appliances fit in the spaces drawn?
- Was space planned behind the washer and dryer for hoses and the dryer vent?
- Are there several planned combinations of lighting?
- Refer to designing a new kitchen for profit for a complete checklist.
- Are the hallways wide enough? Can you eliminate any excess hallway space?
- Is there adequate storage space for clothes, linens and other items.
- Is there planned storage space for your needs?
- Are the stairs too steep? Will there be enough headroom coming down the stairs?
- Are there enough bedrooms and are the sizes sufficient?
- Is the garage the proper width, depth and height to meet your needs?
- Are the bathrooms adequate? Is there an ensuite that meets modern expectations with size and fixtures.
- Will the design be readily accepted in the marketplace?
- Is the curb appeal appealing/attractive?
- Is the plan affordable, when you apply a reasonable current market estimate, using a cost/square foot calculation?

Action Exercises:
1. Complete the checklist for planning a new home.
2. Review all the lists in Chapter 16 for designing a new home for profit.
3. Begin looking for a building lot.
4. Review the lot selection list and house lot consideration table in this chapter before you buy.
5. Meet with a representative at the building/planning department to review all the details pertaining to building a new home. It's a good idea to meet with each department and to do this more than once, until you've received the same information from more than one person.
6. Follow the numbered sequence in the "Checklist of Steps to Obtaining Working Drawings for a New Home" to obtain the best possible drawing/plans for profit.

Chapter 17

Financing the Construction of a New Home for Profit

*"Lack of direction, not lack of time, is the problem.
We all have twenty-four hour days".*
Zig Ziglar
Inspirational, Motivational Speaker

In chapter six on financing for profit you learned about the 5 C's for approval. We scratched the surface on new construction financing including procedures and when to apply. In this chapter you will expand your knowledge of construction mortgages and interim financing. You will learn how to put an impressive proposal together. I'll uncover a secret strategy to apply your own management and sweat labor savings towards the downpayment, a strategy that can help you begin to plan and build equity much sooner than you may have thought.

Building your own home is a great way to build equity. It can also be a source of income which can lead to you doing it again and again. Like many things, the first time is usually the hardest because of all the unknowns. The second time is easier and the third time is a piece of cake. Well, fortunately you have this book to follow which shows you how to do it. I have many friends who built their own homes using far less information than what's covered in this book. Karen and George did it, Heather and Wayne did it, Bill and Barb did it, hundreds of others have done it and you can do it too!

Financing is paramount because anything is possible when you have the money to do it. If you have the resources available you can hire a contractor or builder which is a great advantage. On the other hand, if you need a mortgage to build your own custom home then you will need to put a package together whether you hire a builder or act as your own home contractor. The amount of funds required will determine whether you should apply for a construction mortgage or a line of credit where the mortgage is established at completion. The amount of cash you have on hand for construction will determine how much interim financing will be required.

When you apply for a mortgage, the lender will have an appraiser determine the future market value of your property. This is to ensure the lender's security in relation to the loan amount. It also determines the amount of advances if you require draws to complete the construction. The lender will charge you for the cost of the appraisal and it will be up to the lender whether or not to disclose the report to you. When you apply for your mortgage, ask for a copy of the appraisal report. In some cases, a lenders application fee may be added along with the appraisal fee. Since you will be presenting a professional package which is in essence giving a mortgage to a bank, use your negotiating skills from chapter five and ask the lender if they will be covering the application and appraisal fees. You may not get the answer you are hoping for but this shows the lender your confidence as a builder.

The best way to understand a construction draw mortgage is with a diagram showing advances being made during the period of construction. Some institutions may just offer three advances. You should ask the lending officer how many advances they allow and at what stage of construction. Also ask if an additional advance would be possible if you require it. One bank had a rule of three advances but exceptions would be made if another one or two advances were required to complete the construction. The bank is there to help you but you also must work within their guidelines and be ready to explain and ask for what you need.

One reason a bank might say just three advances is because of the time consuming administrative processing work plus with each advance an appraiser is hired to visit the property to determine the percentage complete. The appraiser would use a guide similar to the Cost Summary Checklist in this chapter and in Chapter 14, Estimating for Profit. The appraiser's guide would show a percentage complete for each item allowing the appraiser to tally up a total percentage of work already completed. To ensure the bank's security by only funding work in progress, this percentage is applied to the total mortgage to determine the amount of money which can be advanced. The bank sends the advance to the lawyer who in turn holds back a lien amount (usually 10%) before forwarding the funds to you. You would deposit these funds into your home building account. The mortgage advance would pay down any interim financing (line of credit or demand loan) used for construction.

The amount of interim financing you require would be determined by the size of the mortgage, the timing of advances and the amount of the lien holdback. The lien holdback is a good indicator because this final mortgage advance comes around 30 to 45 days following completion. It's money held back by the institution to protect their security in the event a lien is placed against the title for non-payment or other reasons. You need enough interim financing to pay all your trades and suppliers before you receive the final advance. Ten percent of the mortgage amount would be a minimum amount for interim financing, however, more is better to ensure you have enough funds for construction. Having more interim financing means you don't have to rely on mortgage draw advances to pay your trades and suppliers. If the interim financing is not a revolving line of credit, you must apply for enough financing to build the home to completion without having to rely on mortgage advances.

Interim financing advances will be determined by bank policy, usually in increments of thousands (e.g. $5,000.00). Call the bank when you begin construction and require money deposited into your account. Maintain good rapport with your bank (loans manager) by keeping them informed on your progress.

I remember one couple who built their own home. They were in the last stage doing finishing work. I said, "hurry up and get it completed so you can move in". They said, "no we will have to begin mortgage payments and so we want to take our time finishing everything". I asked them, "do you think the bank is giving you free money to build? Check your bank statements because you are already making interest payments". Banks charge interest for every advance up to completion which is also the interest adjustment date". This changed their attitude immediately and they completed as soon as they could. The secret is, if you are borrowing money, you don't want to ditsy doodle around especially after receiving several advances. Study the illustration below to visualize how this all works.

Illustration of Advances and Interest on a Construction Mortgage
(based on a 120 day construction schedule)

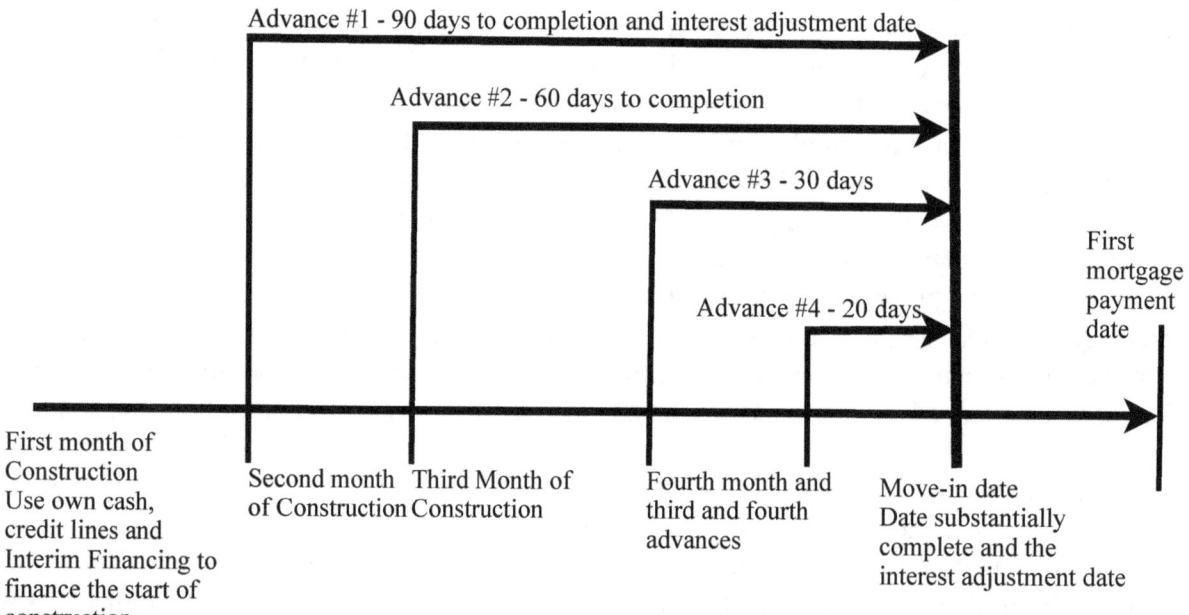

Calculating Interest on Construction Mortgage Advances

You can calculate the accrued interest costs during construction by estimating the time to completion along with the approximate dates and amounts of the expected mortgage draws. All interest will be brought forward to the interest adjustment date. Interest is paid monthly out of your interim financing or house account set up for construction. The diagram provides a visual for calculating the amounts and duration for interest calculations. The amount of advance x rate of interest ÷ 365 = interest cost for one day. Multiply by the projected number of days to estimate the interest cost for each advance. The total of this interest calculation should be included in the cost summary when you go to the bank to apply for a mortgage. If the bank questions you on the amount, you can explain how you did the calculations and estimated the amount.

Mortgage Advances	Amount	Interest Rate	# of days	Amount of Interest
First advance	$_____	_____%	90	$_____
Second advance	$_____	_____%	60	$_____
Third advance	$_____	_____%	30	$_____
Fourth advance	$_____	_____%	20	$_____
TOTAL INTEREST COST				$_____

Advances will require up to a week to process to allow time for the appraisal inspection and transfer of funds to the lawyer who performs the title search, prior to passing the money along to the builder.

One objective when using borrowed funds should be to reduce interest costs to maximize savings. Here's your strategy to save money.

Strategy to Reduce Interest Costs During Construction

- Build in the shortest possible time. This depends on the size, availability of trades, planning and scheduling
- Use all lines of credit with suppliers
- Don't pay too early. Make sure inspections (where required) are done and hold off on payments until all work is deemed substantially complete
- Hold back funds (lien holdback amount) for work not fully completed
- Receive mortgage advances on time and pay down interim financing (demand loan) which is at a higher rate of interest
- Use own cash to start construction
- Complete all deficiencies as soon as possible to obtain all mortgage monies and pay down all interim loans

Knowing what to do and when to do it gives you peace of mind and confidence. This list will help you understand the funding steps taken for the construction of a new home.

Flow of Funds and Basic Procedures for a Construction Draw Mortgage

1. After all financing is approved, begin construction using your own money, lines of credit or an interim financing loan from the bank.
2. Contact the mortgage lender once the subfloor stage is reached (around 16% complete) for the first advance (This is an example, the actual time will depend on the number of draws and when you need money).
3. An appraiser (hired by the mortgage lender or insurer) will inspect the property to determine the percentage complete.
4. The lawyer (acting for lender) receives the first advance which includes any remaining amount owing on the building lot and then sets aside the lien holdback until after the final lien period has been reached according to the lender's instructions.
5. The builder (you) brings the lawyer the survey certificate and proof of the required fire and construction liability insurance, as specified by the lender.
6. The lawyer does a title search for any liens, pays out any balance owing on the land, registers title securing the lender's interest, processes mortgage documents with the owner-builder and advances the first progress advance to the bank.
7. The bank receives money from the lawyer and deposits it into your account to apply directly against any outstanding interim financing loan.
8. Steps are repeated for the next and subsequent mortgage draws.

Presenting Your Application

Talk to your mortgage broker or lender only after you have completed all the information on the summary page and you are ready to talk dollars. Anything beforehand is evidence to a lender that you don't know the process and they will be looking to send you away. From the previous chapter on financing you should already know you qualify for the amount being applied for. It should be just a matter of submitting a complete package or proposal which the lender either approves or not. Presenting a complete package all at once shows the lender you know what's going on and portrays the confidence a lender would expect from a professional builder. In other words, they don't need to worry about all the things you need to know or babysit you during the months of construction. It also puts you in the driver's seat where you can shop around if you need to. You can ask for a better rate, no application fee and for the lender to pick up the appraisal fee. Tony Robbin's once asked a large group attending his seminar, "how do you get everything you want out of life?". He said, "get out your paper and pen and get ready for the answer". After a few seconds he told the audience to write down one word "ASK". It never hurts to ask and often the lender will offer you something for bringing them the mortgage.

Not every lender or mortgage broker will handle construction mortgages. Often it's at one branch where someone who is knowledgeable of the process is assigned to new construction financing. Before presenting your proposal, it's necessary to ask what location and who would be the best person to meet with. The alternative would be meeting wth a mortgage broker who also must be knowledgeable and willing to deal with a new construction mortgage. I've had success using both options.

Tips for Presenting Your Application

- Make an appointment first.
- Only meet when you have a complete package, refer to the Mortgage Application Checklist in this chapter for a list of all documentation and be prepared to bring all the information.
- Prepare a one page summary, refer to the template in this chapter titled "Financing Requirements For:"
- Dress accordingly, first impressions are important. Approach the lender as though you are a business manager.
- Be positive, polite, courteous and optimistic at all times. Show motivation and determination to do what you set out to do.
- Do not say this is your first home when attempting to gain the lender's confidence. When asked if you have done this before, answer by saying you've completed training in every area to be a qualified builder. The lender is more likely to say, "wow, you've done this before", when they see that you are presenting a complete package.

The package you present should be able to fit into a legal file. Do not bring in rolls of working drawings. Drawings might be required later for the appraiser but when you first meet with the lender it's solely to discuss the mortgage and gain approval. I present folded plans only if asked.

Your Mortgage Documents

The pertinent information to present to a lender is identified on the Mortgage Application Checklist for New Home Construction. This information is divided into four sections and organized in the order shown in the checklist. The four sections are; Cover Page, Personal and Financial, Costing and Loan Calculation and House Plan Information. The checklist is not part of your presentation and, as mentioned previously, information that's not listed or asked for by the lender should not be presented.

I once approached a lender with a complete proposal. He didn't know what to do with it. He pulled out an application form and started asking me questions as if I was applying for a car loan. I told him everything is included in the package including the pertinent personal information. I asked him to review the package and reply back to me regarding approval or not. I also asked him to check for the best rate and see if he could waive any application fees.

Then I walked out the door. My position was why would I sit down and spend an hour answering questions dealing with my address, phone number, assets and liabilities when it's already in the package being presented. Besides, I wanted the lender to know that I will be comparing rates and going with the lender that offers the best mortgage and terms.

After you approach one or two lenders and possibly one mortgage broker, you wait for an acceptable offer. This is when you decide who the lender will be and set up a meeting to complete their application. You need to be present to sign the application and authorize a credit check.

A number of templates are included in this chapter to help you put together the items in the checklist. This will help save you time, effort and money as the title of this book indicates. Place the documents in the order illustrated in the Mortgage Application Checklist for New Home Construction. It is best to present the information all at once. If the lender agrees, you can hold off on submitting the folded plans (working drawings) until after you have the mortgage approval.

How to Apply Sweat Equity as Part of the Downpayment

Refer to the "Cost Summary and Loan Calculation" form. You will note item number 27 on page one which states "Builders costs, general contractor, project mgmt." This amount could be zero if you are acting as the builder but that's not what I would do. I would show this amount to be the difference between my total construction costs and the anticipated future market or appraised value. The reason is because when you apply for financing for a new home, which is yet to be built, the approval is often based on the total construction costs. In other words the bank uses a cost approach to value. That seems unfair because if the home was already built the mortgage would be based on the market appraisal. Adding an amount to build up the total construction costs to the expected appraisal value is reasonable. It will help you to finance a higher amount of your total costs. The lender may not want to provide financing for owner-builder costs. If this happens you can say that funds are needed for hiring a project manager or builder. Builders costs are on page one, not page two where the final calculations exist. Having it on page one reduces focus on the addition of sweat equity. The main emphasis for the lender is the page two calculations showing how the total loan adds up. Make sure you also add in a contingency factor whether you think you need it or not. This is something the bank would like to see. Everything explained here assumes you took all the steps in previous chapters to end up with a plan that will appraise much higher than your total costs.

Mortgage Application Checklist for New Home Construction

Cover Page (beneficial for the lender and appraiser to see what you are asking for)
- A summary statement to include the following: House style, size, design features (fireplace, decks, garage, etc.)
  - Lot features
  - Construction start date
  - Estimated market valve
  - Mortgage required
  - Interim financing required

(See the example page titled "Financing Requirements For:")

Personal and Financial
- Mortgage application (lender's forms which can be completed after approval)
- A personal and financial statement (prepared in advance)
- Job letters / 2 pay stubs / proof of self employment income
- Copy of the Land Purchase Agreement
- Copy of the Certificate of Title (available if needed)

Costing and Mortgage Calculation
- Cost Summary and Loan Calculation form (complete the form provided)
- Copies of major estimates from trades and suppliers and/or a contract with a builder/contractor (Estimates are to be provided only if asked by the lender)
- Warranty provider agreement (if required)
  - other - supporting estimates from trades and suppliers (only if asked)
  - other - a contract from a builder or project manager (if required)

House Plan Information (for Lender and Appraiser)
- 8.5 x 11 profile view of the front elevation from house plans
- One set of blueprints - folded to fit into a file (full set(s) of working drawings available on request)
- Site plan and directions to property if required
- Specifications
- Other as required by lender
  - proof of deposits paid
  - proof of insurance (fire, theft, liability)

Financing Requirements
for:

_____

_____

_____

House Style _____

Size _____

Design Features _____

_____

Lot Features _____

Start Date _____

Completion Date _____

Estimated Market Value _____

Mortgage Required _____

Interim Financing _____

COST SUMMARY AND LOAN CALCULATION (page1)

Builders Names (s) _____

Preparation
- Blueprints, site plan, survey, engineering etc. (1) $_____

Foundation
- Excavation, backfill, trenching, grading, loam (2) $_____
- Basement material, forms, concrete, weeping tile waterproofing or damp proofing (3) $_____
- Basement Labour, cribbing concrete, ICF, other (4) $_____
- Basement Floor, gravel, concrete and finish (5) $_____

Structure
- Framing materials, floor and roof trusses, stairs (6) $_____
- Framing Labour (7) $_____
- Doors and Windows, garage door, opener (8) $_____
- Roofing material and labour (9) $_____
- Siding, stucco, stone, trim (10) $_____
- Fascia, soffits and eavestrough (11) $_____

Mechanical
- Plumbing (12) $_____
- Heating (13) $_____
- Electrical (14) $_____

Finishing (all items are a summary of material and labour)
- Insulation, caulking, poly vapor barrier (15) $_____
- Drywall (board, install, taping, sanding, ceiling (16) $_____
- Kitchen Cabinets, vanities, counter tops (17) $_____
- Floor Coverings, carpet, hardwood, tile, install (18) $_____
- Ceramic Tiles, other bathroom items & accessories (19) $_____
- Electrical fixtures, all lights, bulbs, extra wiring (20) $_____
- Painting, primer, paint, stain, lacquer, brushes (21) $_____
- Interior Finishing, doors, casings, railings, closets (22) $_____
- Exterior masonry, stone, brick, parging (23) $_____
- Steps, sidewalks, garage pad, driveway (24) $_____
- Extras (appliances, fireplace, vacuum, landscaping, blinds, other) (25) $_____
- Services and permits (26) $_____
- Builders costs, general contractor, project mgmt. (27) $_____

CONSTRUCTION COSTS $_____

COST SUMMARY AND LOAN CALCULATION (page2)

CONSTRUCTION COSTS $_____

Contingency Factor $_____

Home Warranty _____ $_____

Land (incl. interest, taxes, security deposit) $_____

TOTAL (finished home and land) $_____

Legal and interest costs (28) $_____

           (SUB TOTAL) $_____

Mortgage Insurance fee, appraisal fee $_____

Other $_____

TOTAL CONSTRUCTION COSTS

Less: Downpayment (deposits paid, items purchased, cash, other) $_____

TOTAL LOAN / MORTGAGE REQUIRED $_____

Private Financing

A great alternative if you can arrange it is private financing during construction and bank financing at the end. Private financing can eliminate the appraisal and administration fees associated with the draws. It can prevent having to deal with the restrictive policies of a financial institution. On the downside, finding an investor is not easy and the costs may be exorbitant.

Having access to a personal line of credit to build is ideal but having these resources can also lead to over spending. When building a new home, it's always a good strategy to be on a tight budget.

Recording and Cost Control

Controlling costs and recording information is one critical function of construction management. In the construction of the average home you can issue up to 100 cheques. Without some method of keeping track of those cheques and other expenditures, you can exceed your budget and run out of money. With an accurate record of costs you will be better at making the decisions regarding material specifications, extras, what trades to hire and other expenditures.

You will also be better prepared to go to the bank to discuss your financial needs if you are seeking additional funding. You can easily identify how much you paid the plumber, how much is still due to be paid and what the holdback amount is. You will know after paying each trade and supplier the amount that you are over or under compared to the original estimate. This knowledge, knowing where you stand financially at any given time, gives you the sense of control and the confidence you need to be a builder.

I personally don't like accounting and if you are like me it's easy to procrastinate on this task. By using a simple cost control form it only takes a few minutes every three to four days to maintain a good record system. You can use these headings to create your computer spreadsheet. The index numbers in the first column from 1 to 28 refer to the item numbers shown in the "Cost Summary and Loan Calculation Form". This form is one used for your mortgage application and is also a summary of the estimating checklist from Chapter 14, Estimating for Profit. Using the same index, links the estimating to the recording and cost control enabling you to easily compare your estimated costs to your actual costs which identifies the amount spent over or under the budget estimated amount. By completing this form as you progress you will always know whether you are over or under budget.

Keep your records simple. There is no need to spend hundreds of dollars on specialized accounting software when you are only building one home. There is enough to learn and do without having to learn new software programs. Focus your time and effort to those areas that will bring you profit, don't waste your time and money on accounting software. That's for those who already have it and know how to use it. Everything you need is within these pages.

Index # 1 - 28	Date	Description trade / supplier	Company Name	Cheque No	Tax	Amount Paid Inc. GST	Cumulative Total Paid per index #	Estimated Cost for item (index #)	Lien Holdback	Difference over / under budget

Column groups: Payment Details (Cheque No, Tax, Amount Paid Inc. GST) | Cost (Cumulative Total Paid per index #, Estimated Cost for item (index #)) | Control (Lien Holdback, Difference over / under budget)

Banking Information				Other												
Bank Deposits Mortgage Draws or Interim Financing	**Service Charges and Interest** other bank fees	**Bank Balance** (separate account)	**Misc. items** cash purchases credit card purchases													

In review, a draw mortgage, also called a construction mortgage, is the most common method of receiving mortgage money for the construction of a new home. The process ensures the security of the lender by only advancing funds for work completed. The guidelines, qualifications and documentation required may vary depending on the lender's policy. For example, a lender may ask for a resume for self-build, the name of your solicitor and/or proof of registration in a new home warranty program. It's important to check requirements beforehand to deliver a well prepared, professional presentation.

The information presented in Chapter 16 "Designing a New Home for Profit" is important for financing because a higher appraisal of your plans will improve the loan to value ratio. You are now able to see how there is some relationship between chapters. Once you complete reading all the chapters on building you can add to your resume that you have completed a training course on building a new home. In the next chapter, "Scheduling the Construction of a New Home for Profit", you will learn how to get things done quickly and save interest costs.

Action Exercises:

1. Prepare the House Plan Information for the mortgage application.
2. Complete the Cost Summary and Loan Calculation form after obtaining major estimates or a contract (not signed until financing approved) by a home building contractor.
3. Complete the Personal Information.
4. Prepare a cover page (Financing Requirements For:) to request financing for building a new home.
5. Review Chapter 6, "The Right Financing for Profit" for additional information.

Chapter 18

Scheduling the Construction of a New Home for Profit

"No one lives long enough to learn everything they need to learn starting from scratch. To be successful, we absolutely, positively have to find people who have already paid the price to learn the things that we need to learn to achieve our goals."
Brian Tracy, Author

Right at this moment, producing a job schedule on your device or paper may sound frightening. No need to be anxious, this chapter provides a sample construction sequence which will save you time, effort and money. What is covered in this chapter is work that takes three months or more to complete. What may seem like a lot of information, all up front right now, will convert to you making just a few calls each day during construction.

The objective with this chapter is to gain an understanding of "The Critical Path" sequence for new home construction, review a number of tips and look at those inspections and safety items we need to be aware of. You will learn how to apply the job scheduling sequence to create your own construction schedule.

Let's start once again by using the "KISS" principle (keep it simple stupid). The simple way to look at scheduling the construction of a new home is to do one thing well which is to work from a good list. Here we go again with lists. Why complicate it more than it needs to be? Scheduling, to keep it simple is simply following a well thought through list. The pre-construction and construction sequence lists presented to you in this chapter were developed using information gained from constructing many homes and from teaching hundreds of classes. Many discussions took place with other builders and teachers to create them. These lists are intended for your use to save time, effort and lots of money. There is just one catch, you will need to amend the list to suit the specifics of your project, building requirements, permits, warranties, financing inspections, and trades. The benefit is you have a great list to get you started in this direction.

Once you have completed the building permit and the financing process, follow the key lists pertaining to construction scheduling identified below.

Construction Job Scheduling Key Lists
1. Pre-construction Sequence (21 Steps)
2. Sequence of Construction (Five Stages)
3. Inspection Checklist
4. Safety Checklist

Your job as the project co-ordinator is to edit these lists while following them in order to complete the management functions of planning, organizing, hiring, directing, controlling, co-ordinating, innovating, motivating and representing yourself as a builder. Sounds like a ton of work but all these functions will be performed while you complete the lists. Although it looks like an overwhelming load, remember you are looking at the whole condensed picture right in these few pages. It's work that takes place during several months of construction plus up to a year for the pre-planning list. It's not overwhelming when you break it down to your daily tasks which could be just one or two phone calls. Once again, remember to keep it simple, amend and edit the lists to break them down from a big goal to smaller objectives, priorities and lastly daily tasks.

The Inspection Checklist

The inspection checklist example provided shows a list of inspections compiled from several areas. These include those identified in the building permit, inspections for financing, inspections for a home warranty program and inspections required by mechanical trades such as the Electrical Protection Branch, the Plumbing Inspection Department, Gas Utility Inspectors, the land developer and any other local or regional authority requiring an inspection. When you make an application for a development permit or building permit or both you will receive notice of required inspections when you are approved.

The inspection list is one you should create as you go through the pre-planning stage collecting information, making applications and getting approvals. You can see the list I created in this chapter as an example to follow. The builder, if that's you, is responsible for ensuring all inspections are arranged for and completed. You may not be the person who calls the inspector but you do need to know that the inspection was done and passed. Inspections are often required before going on to complete the next trade task so be aware of them and pay very close attention to getting them all done at the correct time.

The Safety Checklist

I identify this list separately so safety gets the special attention it needs. Construction can be dangerous if safety is not practiced every day with every step of construction. On larger commercial projects the workers start their day with a safety meeting, everyone wears PPE (personal protection equipment) and no-one goes on-site without first undertaking an orientation and knowing the safety rules. The safety checklist for building your own home is a list of good practices by home builders to ensure safe construction.

This is another list that you would amend as needed and use as a working list. Always think safety by asking each contractor "what are the safety issues that need to be considered today?". This applies to both yourself and those working on the site. An appropriate phrase taught by Brian Tracy in his business and sales training is "Prior Proper Planning Prevents Poor Performance".

Planning Your Strategy

Before building my first home, I didn't know what soffits and fascia were. You learn these terms and many others by getting in the trenches and taking action. If you wait until all the lights are on green before you head to town you will never leave home. What I saying here is the Nike slogan, just do it! Follow the GOSPA approach of goals, objectives, strategies, priorities and activities.

As an example, my strategy involved starting construction as soon as the frost was out of the ground, consolidating a few trades where possible to make scheduling easier and completing certain trade related tasks that I was capable of doing quickly. Priorities were defined by following a critical path and a construction schedule list of the proper order of events. Activities were the daily items added to my calendar/planner. I followed my construction sequence in the right order (critical path), made the calls, ordered supplies to be delivered and followed up with everyone involved at that stage. Many days there were only a couple calls needed and that's because a lot of work went into the preplanning.

Everything became much easier with the smart phone allowing you to make calls, use messaging, send e-mails, add items to outlook calendar, add alerts, take notes and send photos. The smart phone really makes a big difference but you still need to have a great list and be vigilant making the necessary phone calls every day during construction.

How do you measure your success as a builder? If time means money then success can be measured by the length of time it takes you to complete your renovation or to construct your home. The shorter the time, the more successful you are because you are more efficient as a planner and organizer. Furthermore, you reduce interest costs by moving in earlier and minimize any further rent payments.

Anyone can build a house in six months or longer but it takes someone with the appreciation of the important function of job scheduling to build a home in less than three months. Your pre-planning period can be much longer. Some owner-builders will spend a year or longer pre-planning their new home. The saying "well begun is half done" really does apply to building a home. Evidence of this can be seen watching the TV show "Extreme Home Makeover" by Ty Pennington. The preparation work to build a home in seven days is mind-boggling. Everything is ordered, shipped, ready to go and hundreds of people are scheduled for a condensed 24/7 schedule for one week. This is not normal or realistic in any way for you acting as a builder or contracting with a builder. A more realistic time frame would be a three to four month schedule for a home that is 1200 to 3,000 square feet and proportionately longer for larger homes. I met one carpenter that was working on a home for two years. The crew had 18 framers all working on the same home. I mention this because the schedule is relative to the size of the project. With every construction project there are factors and criteria to consider which are common as well as specific to each plan.

Among the common factors are the personality traits. Taking action by making calls, communicating to trades and suppliers and doing the little things between trades to keep everything and everyone moving and happy. It helps to be pragmatic, have a "do it now" attitude, deal with issues immediately as they occur with focus on solutions and move forward. When you build a custom home from new plans you should expect a few unknown things to arise. If you expect these unknowns you will not be surprised and you will comfortably move forward by discussing a positive solution. In addition to these personality traits, review the following list of tips for scheduling for profit!

Precise Communication

It's always best, whenever possible, to make the extra effort to meet with your tradespeople eyeball to eyeball, kneecap to kneecap and have a conversation about everything you can think about. Begin by discussing your drawings with your trades. Review the foundation plan with the cribber, the framing details with the carpenter and so on. There are always a few details on the drawings that either party will question. If you want the flooring installed on a 45 degree diagonal then you need to explain this clearly to your flooring carpenter. The same detailed explanation is needed for all trades. The electrician should not need to guess where the plugs and switches go. You would complete a walk through together and identify all locations and discuss all other electrical needs. The tilesetter should know what patterns to use for laying out the floor tiles as well as the shower details for shampoo and soap holding locations. The pattern, the edging, the grout color and sealing all need to be communicated. Be sure to cover payment details to remove any misconceptions that could exist. These pre-construction discussions will avoid many potential misunderstandings and difficulties during construction.

Review the Contract

Review the contract to verify and confirm price, payment terms, the work to be completed and any other specific details important to the contract. This is the time you review Chapter 15, "Contracting For Profit" to make sure all the important clauses are included in your contract. Make any necessary changes before signing the contract. Avoid verbal contracts at all times regardless of how well you know the person and make certain that anything committed verbally is put down on paper. Just say, "lets just add this to the contract so we both have a reference to remind us".

Identify Lead Times

Check with each tradesperson regarding the notice they require before beginning their work and the length of time required to complete the job. This information is valuable for job scheduling and co-ordinating the timely sequence of tasks. The lead time can be requested when you do your estimating by asking how much notice or lead time will be required. For many trades this will be a few days but for some it could be a few weeks or even months.

Be Flexible

Construction has setbacks due to trades unable to meet your start date or time due to their schedule, delivery delays, poor weather, sickness, etc. You must be prepared to accommodate any setbacks. A good project manager will recognize the fact that all tradespeople have their own schedule to follow and accept that making adjustments will be part of the way of doing business. Allow sufficient time to complete each job. If framing takes four to seven days to complete, plan for the maximum. It's always better to gain a day than to have to call several trades and put them off for a day.

Preparation Between Trades

There are some small labor jobs that should be completed quickly between trades in order to reduce construction time. As the renovator/builder (prime contractor) you can choose to do these jobs yourself or hire someone. Some of these labor jobs include cleaning up around the site, sweeping inside the house, some minor framing installing backing, caulking, insulating, painting and some finishing. The secret is to know exactly what work you will be doing and do only the work you are capable of doing within a reasonable amount of time.

Start at the Right Time of the Year

Building in winter where there is frost in the ground definitely costs more. Why spend more money if you don't have to. The following points identify how you might incur extra costs.

- Ripping frost requires more digging with a machine capable of ripping the frozen ground
- Trenching frozen ground for services may require heating the ground along the trench using burning coal.
- Concrete additives for winter heat can add 10% to the cost of concrete for footings and walls
- Heating costs during construction using propane heaters to heat inside the building
- Shorter daylight hours means trades work shorter days increasing the number of construction days
- Construction delays due to severe cold or snow

I found this out the hard way. I remember the plumber calling to inform me that the water and sewer lines needed to go down two feet below the footings for frost protection. Some hand digging was required. I had to rent a jack hammer to cut through the frost, go out in the evening when it was dark and dig in freezing cold weather. It was the first and last time I ever did that. I learned from my mistakes and built when the weather was right.

The best time for me was in the early spring before the rainy season. In a rainy season the excavation can fill up with water, the ground is muddy and construction is delayed. The availability of trades is greater in the off season. To work this to my advantage, I would begin construction just before the frost is all out of the ground to get a jump start ahead of many other builders. The point I'm making here is to incorporate timing into your strategy, avoid the thunderstorms and snow squalls and start when it's to your advantage.

Go Local When Possible

The closer your trades and suppliers are to the job site, the greater the possibility for more frequent visits and less travel expense. That way, when you need them, the site is not too far out of their way to make a visit with little advance notice.

Have a Plan or Job Schedule to Follow

Use the construction sequence (list) in this chapter as a guide. There is far too much information to remember and you can easily miss something important if you don't follow a quality checklist. Your schedule must allow you to make easy adjustments due to any setbacks. Make amendments to this checklist to suit your specific project. When you coordinate activities into your calendar, your schedule will be in the making.

There are alternative job schedules you can use that are not included in this chapter. A bar chart shows the critical path and lengths of time for each trade on site. It looks like a page of graph paper with construction days running along the top and a list of trade tasks down the left side. A bar chart can easily be created using an excel spread sheet. Place an "X" in each square showing the number of construction days for each trade. One benefit of doing this as an exercise is to visually see how trades overlap and days where more than one tradesperson can be scheduled. For example, the framing may start on day 14 and end on day 20. Also on day 20, the heating and plumbing contractors begin their rough-in work, roofing materials are delivered and the roofer begins to install roofing. The bar chart provides a visual of trades overlapping and the critical path which is needed to build in the shortest possible time. There will be days when just one trade is working and it's important not to schedule others. Pouring and finishing a concrete basement floor and spraying lacquer paint are two examples.

Monitor and Follow Up

This is vital to job scheduling and supports maintaining good communication. Check the progress of their work and follow up on required inspections. A good practice is to keep a diary of all communication by making a few notes in your smartphone. These notes will be a record of the day and time you talked and what was discussed. This simple procedure will assist your memory and can be a good reference for future conversations.

You need to know who to call and when to call. Imagine the tilesetter showing up when the painters are working in the same room. How happy is your tile guy going to be. Not very happy if he just wasted hours driving to your property and now he can't work, has to wait or is struggling to work around other tradespeople. It's not imperative you know all this information beforehand. When you communicate to your tradespeople ask them when they would start and when you should call them. The plumber might say, "call me a week before you excavate, then call me again the day of the excavation and trenching". The plumber knows when to add you to his schedule and later confirms the site is ready for installing water and sewer lines under the footing prior to concrete. Add this information to your calendar along with a reminder. It's a good practice to make a written list of tasks the night before. You will sleep better if you do it.

Plan Your Holidays

Plan your holidays at the proper time. You don't want to take them all at the beginning because there is a great deal of work involved at the finishing and move-in stages. Co-ordinate your time off with your work and your construction schedule.

Follow the Critical Path

The critical path refers to the proper order of events. By following the proper order, tradespeople are the most productive, work runs smoothly and you complete the project in the shortest possible time which can save interest costs. The items that are not critical branch off at different stages and can be completed at any time after those key functions in the critical path.

To explain this, I asked my seminar participants, "which mechanical trade could begin their work following the framing? Would it be the electrician, the plumber or the HVAC installer?". I would get a mixture of replies. The answer is both plumbing and heating could start their rough-in immediately, however, it's critical you hold off the electrician until these two trades are done first. Wires can move around plumbing and heating ducts. The last thing you want is a plumbing or heating wall with a number of wires put in first as that would make their job more difficult and wiring could get damaged in the process. You do need a good power supply to schedule two or more trades at one time and this step should be discussed with your electrician.

Hire the Right Carpenters

Certainly you want to hire all the right tradespeople. I single out carpenters because it's the one trade that sees the house from footings to finish. Builders usually subcontract to these groups of carpenters. The cribbers form the footings and walls for concrete. The framers build the subfloor, walls and roof up to the lock-up stage. The finishing carpenters do the interior work installing doors, casings, baseboards, shelving, railings, and other finishing. Some carpenters specialize in installing kitchen cabinets, hardwood flooring, built-in closet shelving or stairs and railings. In addition to all the above, some larger builders will employ back-framers who come in after the framing inspection to fix up any deficiencies and finish minor framing around tubs, fireplaces, basement framing, installation of backing and blocking and other work prior to drywall.

I was fortunate to hire a very qualified journeyman carpenter for a major renovation. He could handle the demolition, new framing, installation of cabinets, installation of doors and casings, removal and installation of new windows, making changes to the stairwell, building and installing bath vanities and installation of built-in shelving. He was also able to do the staining, and white paint lacquering of all the interior finishing materials. I hired other specialty carpenters to install hardwood flooring and new railings and stair treads. Although the cost might appear to be high, hiring the right carpenters to build the home properly and have a professional finished look will pay for itself in the long run. Always ask questions regarding other tasks they can complete. By asking tradespeople questions to confirm their competencies, you may be able to hire fewer tradespeople resulting in saving both time and money.

Before the Framer's Leave

One of the things framers do is install the doors and windows. Make sure these are ordered well in advance and delivered the day prior to installation. You don't want early delivery where they will be sitting around and you don't want them late. While your framing crew is installing these items schedule your plumber and HVAC contractors to arrive on site to start their rough-in work. If you arranged for forced air heating, the HVAC contractor will mark the register locations on the subfloor for the framers to cut out. You planned this right, the framers are still on site and have their skill saws ready to do this task. This is good planning.

I also try to arrange for the drywall firm to do a board count before the framers leave because if there is any missing backing they will advise the framers to add the missing members (2x4's). Similarly the finishing carpenter or supplier (a good reason to have them lined up in advance) visits the home to check all interior door sizes and measure for underlay, baseboards, casings and closets. Any problems with door sizes or walls out of line or plumb can be addressed before the framers move on to another job. Having these trades visit the site before the framers leave saves time and some minor headaches later on.

Save Time Consolidating Trades

Consider this idea only when it's feasible, when it will save you money or time and a few headaches. Some trades are diversified in that they perform or subcontract tasks other than their main focus or by what's implied with their trade name. For instance, a concrete company might also have a crew that does the prep work and supplies gravel for your basement, driveway and walkways. They may also regularly subcontract to a firm to install damproofing and weeping tile. Any money you might save by sourcing this yourself may not be significant to warrant dealing with these small tasks separately. You might even pay more being a one-time customer. By contracting this all to one firm you reduce some scheduling, contracting and payables.

Similar to above, the drywall (gypsum board) contractor might also supply and install or subcontract some of the trade work areas. These might include the caulking, insulating and vapor barrier tasks which precede the drywall installation. After the drywall is installed, taped, mudded and sanded, the contractor might hire a separate ceiling subcontractor to spray and finish the ceiling. They may even have someone to prime all the walls so you are ready for the finishing carpenters to begin their work.

Residential plumbers often have the trade qualifications of Gas "B" which allows them to hook up residential gas lines to the hot water heater which they supply. The excavation company may have a backhoe for trenching, a bobcat for backfill and grading and a truck for hauling in fill or loam and hauling away extra dirt. The roof truss manufacturer is often also a supplier for floor trusses. If this company also supplies lumber to builders then that could save time from having to deal with two separate suppliers, providing they are price competitive. My finishing material supplier, one that deals with builders, puts a complete package together including all interior doors, casings, baseboards, moldings, closet material, door handles and locks, bathroom accessories, flooring underlay (plywood, OSB board, MDF board, masonite) laminates, railings and other materials. Purchasing a finishing package saves time.

The entire package would then be bundled up and delivered inside the home for the finishing carpenters.

Creating Your Personalized Job Schedule

Do a simple calculation of the time it will take to complete your construction. Look at the main sections and determine times based on conversations with the major trades. These are the trades in the critical path who require more than one week on site to complete their work. Allow a contingency for delays, clean up and inspections. Here's an example of how the timing for pre-planning a 16-week "construction" schedule might look. Each stage is further broken down into a detailed sequence of events.

Preplanning

Pre-planning, plans, permits, estimates, financial approvals - 12 months

Weekly Breakdown

Construction Start to Subfloor Stage	2 weeks
Framing to lock-up stage	3 weeks
Lock-up to drywall stage	3 weeks
Interior finishing to painting stage	5 weeks
Painting to move in	3 weeks
Total estimated weeks of construction	**16 weeks**

Your construction schedule will be a working document which, for the purpose of building one home, can simply be your phone calendar where you enter all your daily to-do items. This calendar should primarily identify who to call, what to order and provide any reminders like what to shop for or what sweat labor work you need to do to maintain good flow with all the trades. I prefer a paper list probably because I'm old school and have always done it that way. Whatever method you choose, you absolutely need to create your own custom schedule considering you are building or renovating a one-time custom home. You will have your trade lead times and your trade times for completing work. To make this job simple, I've included a sequence of events which can be followed. What is required now is to make a few edits to suit your specific project then follow the sequence adding dates as you begin making your calls to start construction. You can use these lists straight from this book or begin the process by adding them to your calendar remembering to ask questions and amend the list accordingly.

Following a list is very important so you do not miss any critical steps. In addition to the construction sequence, keep referring to the safety checklist and the sample list of inspections in this chapter. In the next chapter you will receive many construction tips which will provide valuable guidance when dealing with many of the major construction trades.

Construction Job Scheduling Checklist

Pre-Construction Sequence (21 steps)

1. Plans (working drawings) and site plan or plot plan to be completed.
2. Get plans approved (if required in an architecturally controlled subdivision or by a city planning department).
3. Receive "Grade Slip" from land developer or engineers (not applicable on acreages).
4. Development permit approved (if required for an infill property development).
5. Building permit application and approval (make note of required inspections).
6. Financing approved (mortgage and interim financing) and name of lawyer.
7. Set up a separate bank checking account, specifically for the project.
8. Established a line of credit with suppliers (lumber, concrete, windows, cabinets, flooring, finishing).
9. Confirm contracts with most trades and suppliers, ask and make notes of lead times.
10. Confirm workman's compensation (WCB) insurance with trades to be hired.
11. Arrange builder's construction insurance for fire and liability protection.
12. Apply for warranty insurance (if required by the lender).
13. Plan start date and notify most trades of your start date.
14. Order items to be manufactured including windows, roof trusses and cabinets.
15. Discuss power supply needs with foundation contractor (cribbing concrete footings and walls) and set up temporary power (make appropriate arrangements with the electrician).
16. Call (utility companies) before you excavate to mark underground service locations.
17. Complete a site inspection (with land developer) of sidewalks, curbs and services prior to excavation equipment arriving on site to note any damages prior to construction. Report any damaged services to land developer prior to starting (you may have paid a damage deposit to the land developer and don't want to pay for damage caused by someone else).
18. Arrange temporary fencing to be installed around site (if required by regulatory authority)
19. Provide the surveyor with a copy of the house plans, site plan and grade slip.
20. Meet with the excavator to walk around the site to discuss access location, placement of fill and trenching (now or later).
21. Apply for all utilities (power, gas, water, internet, phone, cable) and apply early as sometimes the wait for new construction can be quite long.

Sequence of Construction List - Stage One, To First Floor (subfloor)

- Survey, plan for it one day prior to excavation (to ensure stakes were not removed)
- Excavation, determine trenching for services now or later
- Delivery of lumber and rebar for cribbing footings, top of walls and material for electrical meter
- Deliver basement windows, or window frames or include 2x8 lumber to build bucks on site according to actual window rough opening measurements
- Elevation check by surveyor to ensure correct excavation during footing forming (cribbing) and before pouring concrete
- Soil inspection ordered by builder, completed by soil engineer (if required or poor soil, sand, loam exists)
- Soil bearing certificate required? Compaction test required?
- Crib footings (cribber), discuss weeping tile requirements if any
- Water and sewer lines under footings now or later (depends on trenching and discussion with plumber)
- Water and sewer lines inspected (arranged by the plumber)
- Water and sewer trench backfilled after inspection
- Pour concrete footings
- Strip footing forms (2x6 lumber can be used elsewhere during construction)
- Confirm locations for electrical meter, windows, weeping tile, and items to be in the concrete walls
- Crib walls for concrete, pour concrete, strip and remove forms (usually the next day)
- Delivery of main subfloor building materials (beams, joists, floor trusses and plywood or OSB board
- Carpenters (Framing crew) begin to install subfloor
- Electrician installs outside service (to be placed on a 2x8 wood plank set into concrete or other method as determined) and orders the electrical meter from the utility company
- Builder marks grade line with spray paint for either tar or other waterproofing application required below grade
- Install rigid insulation for frost protection (if required) for walk-out basements or entry ways as per drawings
- Tar tab the snap tie holes and spray tar or apply an approved foundation wrap
- Weeping tile installed (if required)
- Clean gravel (1-inch washed rock) placed over weeping tile for drainage

- Electrical service inspected (inspection arranged by electrician)
- Foundation Inspection by city or other prior to backfill (arranged by builder)
- Post building permit on site and mark name on foundation
- Backfill and rough grade site (if wood basement, wait until after concrete floor is poured)
- Install security fencing if required by the city (determine if and when required)
- Contact surveyor for survey certificate
- Deliver survey certificate and proof of construction insurance to the lawyer
- Book appointment to sign mortgage documents at the lawyer's office
- Request the first financial inspection to obtain the first mortgage advance (arranged by builder)

Framing to Lock-Up - Stage Two

- Lumber package delivered (main floor and walls)
- Framing of walls and garage
- Tentative delivery date set for roof trusses and windows (ordered earlier)
- Delivery of second floor framing materials, floor trusses, sheathing, beams and other materials
- Delivery of roof trusses and roof framing materials
- Pre-manufactured stairs ordered and installed by carpenters (framing crew)
- Delivery and installation of large tub enclosure, shower enclosure (protect with insulation and cardboard)
- Meet carpenters on site to discuss items such as fireplace hearth, tub surround, framing stairs and other items in drawings
- Framing of second storey walls, trusses and roof
- Delivery and installation of gas fireplace, frame around face and hearth
- Delivery of windows and doors to be installed by carpenters (remove screens for future installation to protect against damage)
- Install temporary locks (supplied by finishing materials supplier), obtain 5 keys (for builder and main trades) including one hidden on site
- Measure, order and install metal fireplace top (preferably ordered by fireplace supplier and installed with fireplace)
- Carpenters place scrap in bin on site and stack longer pieces for later use on blocking and backing (back-framing after rough-in mechanical and framing inspection)

Lock-up to Drywall - Stage Three

- Plumbing rough-in (note some overlap, plumbing and heating starts before framers leave)
- Heating rough-in (furnace is hung from the ceiling), interior gas line installed
- Framers finish odds and ends, tub surround, fireplace hearth, blocking, decks, outside stairs, outside window trim, battens, stucco relief, garage door trim, and other items
- Drywall contractor visits home for a board count, checks backing and other framing for straightness and level
- Finisher visits home to check door sizes and confirm materials for finishing package
- Hardwood installer measures and orders hardwood flooring
- Delivery and installation of garage door (door opener is installed after the ceiling drywall has been completed)
- Electrician and builder/owner walk through home to mark exact locations of all lights, plugs and switches
- Kitchen measured for pre-manufactured cabinets
- Inspections for plumbing and interior gas line connections (arranged by the plumber)
- Vacuum system rough-in
- Notify trades for planning the concrete floor, drywall and interior finishing
- Electrical rough-in (plugs, switches, lights, furnace, fireplace, fans, etc.)
- Rough-in telephone, cable TV, internet, security, intercom, home theatre, home office
- Electrical inspection (arranged by the electrician)
- Framing inspection (arranged by builder), framer returns to fix up any deficiencies
- Financial inspection by bank representative or appraiser to receive second mortgage draw (arranged by the builder)
- Exterior soffits, fascia and eavestrough to be installed after exterior is finished
- Concrete front steps supplied and installed, formed for concrete or built by carpenters
- Stone, brick or other masonry work (interior and/or exterior)
- Clean interior to prepare for basement gravel and delivery of drywall for main floors
- Basement gravel, poly, preparation and installation of plumbing access pieces
- Pour and finish concrete floor (after insulation if heat required)
- Interior caulking, poly vapor barrier, insulation
- Exterior siding or stucco paper and wire or other exterior finish

- Outside gas line installed by gas company, heating contractor returns to ignite furnace
- Drywall board, tape, mud and sand walls and ceilings (if painted) with three coats of paint
- Preparation of garage slab, outside walkway and driveway
- Textured ceilings (or paint), choose style, consideration for interior design
- Ceiling attic insulation blown-in in areas not previously installed

Interior Finishing to Painting - Stage Four

- Primer coat of paint
- Delivery of hardwood flooring one to two weeks before installation and store in house to allow flooring to adjust to new environment (expand or contract)
- Install hardwood flooring
- Delivery of interior finishing materials
- Interior finishing; carpenters install underlay in kitchen and bathrooms for areas requiring tile, stone or vinyl
- Kitchen cabinets and bathroom and laundry room vanities delivered and installed
- Kitchen and bathroom countertops installed by granite supplier or other
- Railings and handrails installed by finishing carpenters or railing supplier
- Install interior doors, door and window casings, interior closet shelving and other shelving
- Baseboards installed later (or now if white lacquered finish is applied)
- Sink templates provided to counter top supplier for cut-outs or to cabinet installer for arborite counter tops
- Other interior finishing; fireplace facing, custom ceiling and any other interior finishing
- Bathroom ceramic tiles, foyer tiles, kitchen floor and backsplash tiles supplied and installed by tilesetter
- Clean up, drywall contractor returns to touch up any nicks in the walls prior to painting
- Stain, lacquer wood finishing or paint interior doors, casings, baseboards and shelving
- Outside finish coat of stucco and parging
- Concrete driveway and walks poured and finished (block off driveway for a minimum of 7 days to allow concrete to cure and harden and wait 28 days before driving on concrete)
- Eavestrough installed after all other exterior siding, brick and trim is in place
- Paint interior walls (two coats on top of primer coat)
- Arrange financial inspection for a mortgage draw

Painting to Move-In - Stage Five

- Install bathroom flooring prior to setting toilets
- Delivery of electrical light fixtures (by supplier or builder/owner)
- Delivery of dishwasher to be installed by plumber and connected by electrician
- Finish electrical; plugs, switches, lights, smoke alarms, electrical panel
- Finish plumbing; toilets, sinks, taps, hot water heater, garburator, etc. (supplied by plumber)
- Finish vacuum system installation, intercom, security, phone, cable TV, internet
- Arrange plumbing and electrical inspections
- Outside work; painting doors and trims
- Measure, supply and install mirrors, mirror doors, shower doors
- Finishing carpenter installs hardware, interior door handles, bathroom accessories, closet shelving and rods and new exterior door locks to replace the temporary construction locks
- Clean home thoroughly
- Finish applied to hardwood floor, if not pre-finished (to prevent dust, no other trades should be allowed in the home while finishing the floors)
- Outside; finish grading and loam
- Broadloom supplied by carpet supplier and installed by floor covering mechanic
- Finish heating; clean ducts and install heat registers and cold air returns
- Install baseboards, if not installed earlier
- Complete any necessary touch-ups and clean house
- Arrange a final inspection by city inspector
- Arrange a financial inspection for mortgage advance
- Install appliances
- Move-In
- Arrange a final mortgage advance after the lien holdback period (example 10% for 30 days)
- Other items; blinds, landscaping, sod, trees, fence, decorating

Well Begun is Half Done !

Sample List of Inspections

Type of Inspection	When	Why	Who Arranges/ Calls for it	Who does the inspection
Site inspection	Before excavation	Notify developer of any damages to services or sidewalks	Builder	Builder
Soil test and compaction test	After excavation (if required by land developer)	May be building on a site that was filled or softer ground Soil type may require additives in concrete	Builder (as advised by land developer)	Soil Engineer
Elevation check	After excavation and before pouring footings	To ensure correct elevation before starting construction	Builder	Surveyor
Plumbing, water and sewer system inspection	After installed and before trench is backfilled	Required by Plumbing Inspection Branch to ensure proper installation and codes are met	Plumber	Plumbing Inspector
Electrical underground service to foundation inspection	Before backfill of foundation and electrical trench	Required by Electrical Inspection Branch to ensure proper installation and electrical codes are met	Electrician	Electrical Inspector
Foundation Inspection	Before backfill Note: cannot backfill a PWF (wood basement) until after the basement concrete floor is in place	Check workmanship on weeping tile (if required), damproofing (tar or other) and gravel placement Check quality of concrete	Builder	City Inspector and possibly Engineer if ICF or PWF
Survey Certificate	After foundation is in, usually after backfilling	To receive a Survey Certificate certifying house is placed properly on the lot Required by Lawyer to advance funds from Mortgage Company	Builder	Surveyor
Framing Inspection	Before insulating	Check framing codes are correct to ensure structure is strong and safe Check framing is done as per plans submitted	Builder	City or Town Building Inspector
Financial Inspection #1	Usually after building is closed in Whenever you request funds be advanced	To receive draw on mortgage or interim financing advance	Builder	Appraiser or Mortgage Company representative
Plumbing rough-in	Before insulating	Check plumbing codes are met	Plumber	Plumbing Inspector
Gas Inspection	After gas line hookup & pressurized (30 lbs air)	Check for leaks in gas line and proper installation	Plumber or HVAC	Gas Inspector from city
Electrical rough-in	Before Insulating	Check electrical codes are met	Electrician	Electrical Inspector

Sample List of Inspections

Type of Inspection	When	Why	Who Arranges/ Calls for it	Who does the inspection
Fireplace Inspection	Before boarding or covering with drywall	Check for proper installation of firestop, clearance of framing from chimney, builder has followed manufacturers directions	Builder	City/Town Building Inspector/ Fire Inspector
Insulating, caulking and vapor barrier	Before boarding or covering up with drywall	Check for holes in vapor barrier	Builder	Builder, sometime the City Inspector
Financial Inspection #2	After cabinets are installed and house has first coat of interior paint	To receive additional funding	Builder	Appraiser or Mortgage Company representative
Final Electrical	After all electrical is complete	Check work is all done as per proper electrical codes and to close file	Electrician	Electrical Inspector
Final Occupancy	Before moving in	Check structure is complete, safe and codes are met	Builder	City or Town Inspector
Final Financial #3	When 95% complete	To receive remaining mortgage funds	Builder	Appraiser or Mortgage Company representative

Use this Sample List of Inspections to ensure all inspections are done. Edit as needed and fill in any extra inspections that you may specifically require in the blank spaces provided.

Safety Checklist

- Check to ensure that every trade has WCB coverage (Workers' Compensation Board)
- Homeowner has Builders Insurance for fire, theft and liability
- All trades should follow OH&S standards at minimum and Occupational Health and Safety (eye protection, hard hat, protective footwear)
- Trades should be using PPE (personal protective equipment)
- Follow safety procedures and wear proper protection when removing mold or asbestos or hire a certified person
- Wear proper mask protection when sawing materials like OSB board which has resins that are toxic
- Wear a respirator when spraying stain and lacquer or stay away while this work is being done
- Trades should have first aid training and first aid equipment on site. Make sure everyone knows where the first aid kit and eye wash station is located
- Fall protection mandatory for framers and roofers, supplied by trade contractor
- Monitor hazardous material disposal by trades to make sure they meet local and provincial laws
- Know where the underground lines are and call before you dig (check for a 1-800 number for this service)
- Backfill soon after inspections to level excavated area and close in open trenches
- Check if site should be fenced (may be a mandatory city requirement)
- Post a "no trespassing" sign on site
- Framers should construct temporary 2 x 4 railings where stairs exist and around any stair openings (or cover up the opening)
- Have stairs delivered on time
- Identify any danger area (like a covered hole) with spray paint
- Remove nails from wood or bend them over
- Maintain a clean site
- Bring to lock-up quickly and add job locks to secure property
- Review items on this list with your tradespeople

Action Exercises:

What goals can I set now to begin the pre-construction schedule?
    1.
    2.
    3.
    4.

List 4 items I will need to begin the process of job scheduling.
    1.
    2.
    3.
    4.

Chapter 19

Construction Tips and Checklists for Profit

"We all have dreams. But in order to make dreams come into reality, it takes an awful lot of determination, dedication, self-discipline, and effort."
Jesse Owens, Olympic Athlete

We have already covered dozens of construction tips and money saving ideas. This chapter will give you more of the skill-set to guide you as a builder or renovator by diving deeper into each trade speciality. Many of the check points listed will be performed by your tradesperson. They are mentioned here for discussion points for you to be more knowledgeable when you meet with tradespeople to discuss the contract and when you meet on site they guide you with tips and ideas for saving time, effort and money.

To build or renovate a home, a lot of shopping is required. In some cases you will spend hundreds of thousands of dollars. To turn all this spending into profit means you are applying some appraisal principles that were covered in previous chapters. As well, these construction checklists compliment the chapters "Contracting for Profit" and "Scheduling for Profit".

I've said this before, "I'm proud of the fact that I've never had a lien placed on a property". My plan was to develop good relationships with everyone I contracted with. The construction checklists are not intended for you to use for micro-management. However, it is important for you to be on the same page with all tradespeople regarding work expectations and have an increased awareness of what's going on because you are the manager, the person who is paying the bills. Reviewing contracts and the scope of work is something that should be done with each trade and you will see it mentioned several times as a reminder.

As you progress, highlight the relevant points in each section that pertain to your project to customize a list suitable for your needs. Do this when you deal with each specific trade, not all at once in advance, or you may never start. Using this increased knowledge and later adding the experience gained following each trade, your confidence and self-esteem will grow and you will evolve as a skilled project manager. Remember to always have respect for others and you will gain respect from others.

The remainder of this chapter covers checklists pertaining to the major construction trades. The points listed were originally created for the construction of new homes, however many points can be applied to an addition or a renovation. As you scroll through the list with your tradesperson, it's a good idea to have a highlighter to identify those points that apply to your project. These checklists include items to reference prior to starting work and are meant to be used as a guide for discussion and questions while the work is being performed. Good luck with your building/renovating and making a profit.

Excavation Backfill Grading Checklist

- Call before you dig to have all existing underground service locations marked (you do not want to accidentally dig up any service cables, especially high power cables and fiber optics cables)
- Check for savings offered by lumping the excavation, trenching, backfill, grading and the supply and spreading of loam all into one contract with one reputable company
- Check what type of machine is best for your job and discuss how the machine will enter onto the property without damaging services or sidewalks (in winter you may require a cat (heavier bulldozer) to dig through frost, it may also be possible to excavate and dig trenches all at the same time)
- Make certain excavation will not be too low or too high, check against survey markings and visual check cuts against existing homes (surveyor may be required to return to perform an elevation check, also timing of an elevation check is important and should be be done during the construction of the footings and prior to pouring concrete into the footing forms)
- Discuss with the excavator the location of fill and ensure it is not piled on an adjacent lot without permission
- Discuss excavation areas including jogs in walls, garage excavation, decks, trenching for services and any other areas affected by excavation, trenching and grading
- Check placement of fill to allow ease of backfill
- Discuss the finished grade for drainage (on lots where a 'Grade Slip" is issued, grades must be checked at locations on the grade slip, usually corners of the home and the lot)
- Discuss with excavator the location of access ramps, a place for lumber and materials to be dropped off for footings, walls and subfloor construction
- Discuss location of service trenches and fill before digging
- Perform a safety check for sufficient space between foundation and sides of excavation for cribbers to work in (if depth of cut is deep and soil unstable, excavation walls may need to be lowered)
- Check for hauling away fill or hauling in extra fill
- Check building requirements for a soil bearing test prior to placement of footings
- Before backfill, check to ensure electrical service is installed and inspected
- Check to see if you will require window wells
- Check grading after completion, should be smooth (the better the grading job, the better the loam coverage)
- In some areas the water table may dictate how deep you can dig for a basement (for those areas close to water or with high water tables, you must be very careful with drainage requirements)

Concrete Cribbing Checklist

Cribbing involves forming for the concrete footings and walls. It's a carpentry function and usually there are carpenters who specialize in doing cribbing and concrete forming. I would ask the cribbers to double check all measurements before the concrete is delivered. On one home I built, the entire basement was cribbed, formed and poured four feet too long because the tradesperson misread the measurements on the drawings. The saying "measure twice, cut once" applies to all carpentry work. Here's a few items for checking and discussing with your cribbers. It's a good plan to visit the work site before concrete is poured to discuss some of these items with your tradespeople.

- Cribber will need working drawings and materials delivered beforehand (work will begin following the excavation)
- Review the working drawings with the cribbing carpenter to determine what materials are supplied by the cribbing contractor and what needs to be purchased (prior to obtaining a quote from the lumber supplier)
- Show the contractor the lumber estimate on the basement package you received from the lumber supplier to ensure the right material and quantities are being supplied (check for sufficient footing material, sill plates, ladder material and rebar on the lumber list and following delivery, confirm supplies arrived as per estimate)
- Verify dimensions of footings with cribber (check details of fireplace, garage, telepost pads, bearing walls and protect from frost, if winter construction)
- Check with cribbers for power requirements (set up a temporary power supply if they do not have a generator)
- Cribber should loosen dirt or make preparations for locations where electrical, plumbing and weeping tile go through or under the footings
- Check with cribber that rebar was placed properly in footings (i.e. two rows six inches apart or as per drawing or building code requirements)
- Ensure compaction test was done (if required) and footing elevation was checked by surveyor prior to pouring concrete footings
- Discuss footing/wall design (a notch/shear keyway in the footing and/or rebar from footings protruding up into the wall or as per code or engineered designed drawings)
- Confirm proper placement of basement windows and doors prior to pouring basement concrete walls
- Cribber to check that forms are oiled and in good shape to prevent the loss of concrete
- Check for proper placement of rebar in walls, especially around corners and openings
- Check that all footing post pads are at correct locations
- Check to ensure all beams and joists are in the right place and level
- Advise cribber to clean away all waste material from within and around the basement
- Examine poured basement walls after the forms are removed and advise cribbers or concrete company to repair (patch) all voids and honeycomb areas
- Allow concrete seven days to cure before backfilling

Damproofing, Weeping Tile and Gravel Checklist

- Ensure snap tie holes are individually sealed before applying two coats of damproofing to entire foundation wall from footing up to finished grade level and mark wall with spray paint to show height of coating (an alternative method of water proofing is a foundation wrap)
- Check the footing wall junction is well sealed
- Check local weeping tile and sump requirements
- Weeping tile should be straight and start at a high point on the opposite side of the house from storm sewer connection sloping toward the connection or sump box
- Check coverage of gravel over weeping tile to ensure six inches of washed gravel
- Check alternative methods of placing gravel within basement (might be best to spread gravel after footings are in and before cribbing the basement walls as this could reduce shoveling by hand, however, gravel will be present during plumbing rough-in)
- Check for plumbing inspection on underground rough-in plumbing before pouring concrete floor
- Check level of the gravel bed according to height of the drain, height of the furnace and stairs (if installed after framing)
- Tamp with a plate vibrator to a hard smooth surface then re-check the level of the gravel to ensure you will get an even spread of concrete
- Install 6 mil poly between gravel and basement floor

Slab on Grade Checklist

- Check the soil conditions and take every precaution to ensure dryness
- Must have a well-drained site with the finished landscape grade sloping away from the house for adequate surface drainage
- Install a base of clean gravel or crushed rock (the gravel base will absorb water and keep the slab dry)
- Install a drainage system to carry away any excess water
- Install a six mil polyethylene vapor barrier just prior to pouring the slab to prevent moisture entering the slab from the soil below
- Ensure frost protection if in an area where you receive frost
- There are many methods of constructing a slab on grade foundation depending on soil conditions, requirements for frost coverage, requirements for drainage and the intended use of the building, i.e. summer camp or year round home (research technical data and consult your designer and engineer as they can provide useful data on soil compaction and soil types and make recommendations for better construction)

Note: It's always best to seek professional advice before spending a large amount of money and possibly making costly construction mistakes.

Cinder Block Foundation

- Depending on circumstances such as availability of concrete and distance for a concrete truck to travel, a block basement may be the right choice.
- Find an mason who is a certified bricklayer or otherwise proven to be qualified by experience and time in the trade (follow the contracting list in the Chapter 15 "Contracting for Profit")
- Consult with a structural engineer to ensure the proper size of footing, depth of foundation if frost exists and other construction details
- The footing must be level to ensure the top of the wall and subfloor is level
- Make sure you install a proper waterproofing system, no foundation wall will be any good if it isn't waterproofed
- Follow local codes for backfill material as large stones/rocks will move with frost and damage/compromise the weatherproofing
- Search the internet for "building a cinder block foundation" for information on estimating, safety and additional construction tips

Framing Checklist

- Meet with the framing carpenter to confirm start date, delivery date of material packages (subfloor, walls, trusses) and provide copies of plans for review, discussion of all areas including exterior walls, partitions, stairs, beams, trusses, sizes of interior doors, fireplace hearth, decks and windows and size of medicine cabinet rough opening (if required)
- Discuss contract and process to resolve inconsistencies, omissions and/or mistakes or changes to plans
- Discuss billing procedure and the payment schedule
- Advise if there is a large fiberglass tub or shower to be supplied before walls are built (ensure it is delivered early in the framing process)
- Give framer a copy of the rough opening window and door measurements provided by the window supplier (discuss arrival date on site, usually before last day of framing)
- Many of the items listed below will be checked by the framing inspector (if there is no framing inspection then you should perform this task with the lead carpenter or hire someone independent to check the framing)
- Check placement of sill gasket at top of foundation and behind end studs of interior partitions, against outside walls, and on top plates of inner partitions at roof, along stairs and outside walls
- Check for poly under subfloor on all heated cantilevers and overhangs (consider spray foam)
- Check backing for drywall, blocking for curtain rods, kitchen cabinets, range hood, flat screen TV mounts, medicine cabinets, bathroom accessories, attic hatch, thermostat, door chimes, fireplace fire-stop, handrail backing in the stairwell and soffits and fascia on the outside
- Ensure correct size of attic hatch and adequate headroom above
- Check for false ceiling in fireplace chase (if one exists) at ceiling height (follow fireplace manufacturer's installation guide)
- Check nailing of subfloor, remove nails that miss joists, check for spots requiring additional nailing and add screws in key traffic areas (if necessary)
- Check framing method of the eaves and ladders (is it strong enough to support the roof?)
- Check if gables are dropped 1.5 inches to allow for 2x4 lumber lookouts and ventilation
- Check for ridge blocks between trusses to support trusses and roof sheathing, blocking and/or sheathing support in valleys and blocking at hips
- Ensure roof trusses are secured to gable ends and toe nailed to inner partitions, exterior walls and braced according to manufacturer's design
- Check for installation of insulation stops
- For forced air heating check for cut-outs for heat registers and cold air returns (ensure no joists, beams or blocking were cut)
- Check walls for bends due to warped studs

- Check if door openings are correct sizes, plumb and square using a level
- Check for square of bathroom walls where mirrors will be installed and showers where tiles and shower doors will be installed
- Check for installation of metal joist hangers where floor joists are not supported (ensure all nails are correct size and all holes in the joist hangers are nailed)
- Check adequate nailing of sill plates, bottom plates to subfloor, around door openings, beams, and top plates, exterior wall corners, tall wall members and attachment details (if applicable)
- Check wall for main plumbing stack is 2 x 6 or larger to accommodate width and request studs line up with floor joists above and below plumbing wall for ease of mechanical installation
- Check that floor joists are laid out so that they are not under the waste outlet of your toilets or directly beneath tub and shower drains
- Check that there are no floor joists parallel and under the plumbing wall
- Review this list and construction scheduling list of items to ensure all work is complete before the framing carpenters leave to go to their next job
- Notify framers of any pot lights, ceiling lights, fans or other areas requiring wood members needed to support electrical fixtures
- Provide drywall access chute in second floor exterior wall for second floor drywall delivery to eliminate the need to go through (and possibly damage) a window
- Check that all point loads from the floor system and truss system have proper bearing to the foundation
- Ensure uniform placement and adequate number of roof vents have been cut into roof sheathing
- Check with mechanical and plumbing contractors to see if they need any openings cut in roof sheathing
- Ensure sill pans, and provisions for proper building paper lap is correct before window installation
- Ensure any build outs, eaves that run into walls, decorative roofs, and all components installed at the framing stage have building paper installed behind them

Roofing Checklist

- Discuss roofing contract including roofing materials, installation sequence, desired method of valley construction, i.e. open with metal flashing shown or closed, other flashing, method of eaves protection, building paper or installing a roof membrane, installing a drip edge flashing, payment terms, start and completion times (include the option to hire an outside inspector to approve the work before payment is processed)
- The contractor is responsible for clean up and removal of garbage (local laws may dictate that all construction refuse is to be taken to an approved site, not placed in with residential garbage)
- Discuss roof venting to ensure sufficient roof ventilation is put in place (the building code references provide what is required for all steps including a calculation on the number of vents which should be agreed on before work begins)
- Investigate various roofing materials, i.e. asphalt, rubber, tile, metal, slate and other roofing materials and if required, various flat roof applications and materials (compare cost differences referenced to the standard price of asphalt shingles)
- Select the appropriate roofing material and ensure it supports the weather conditions in the area and architectural controls if they exist as well as compliment the curb appeal
- Have the roof material and color approved by the developer (if required)
- Ensure the framing is capable of supporting the type of roofing material intended (a cedar shake roof requires ½ inch roof sheathing but a tile roof requires closer spacing of roof trusses to support the extra weight)
- For tile/slate roof systems you probably will be required to hire an engineer to rate and approve the application (include the price just in case it is necessary)
- If the roof is less than a 3/12 slope, a low-slope weatherproof membrane must be installed first (shingle systems are not meant to handle standing water and if not done properly, will result in premature failure within only a few years of installation resulting in major repairs to the under decking)
- Roofs with 3/12 slope or greater installed in regions having snow and ice must have an eaves and valley protection membrane, eve protection up 36 inches and valley protection for the full length of the valley (it's a good idea to install a roofing membrane under the shingles for the entire roof)
- Check for proper color co-ordination of roofing material before ordering
- When owner is supplying shingles, request they be delivered on a specified date and hoisted up onto the roof
- If wind uplift issues are magnified by location, upgrading to laminate shingles and a 6-nail pattern is more efficient to prevent blow-offs (consult manufacturer's literature)
- Co-ordinate plumbing and HVAC trades (it may be easier to install a plumbing stack after the shingles are installed, at least have the deck marked with a hole or otherwise noted on the deck or have the installers coordinate with the contractor about location)
- Ensure all flashings and collars for stacks and exhaust vents were installed and sealed
- Ensure all safety measures are being adhered to (check with the workplace health and safety authority on procedures relating to reporting safety violations and have it written in the contract so installers know that unsafe work will not be tolerated)
- Check if the manufacturer requires the installers to be certified by the manufacturer otherwise their warranty is void (roofers can also earn journeyperson trade certification)

Exterior Siding/Stucco Checklist

The building envelope must be properly installed prior to the exterior finish to prevent moisture from rotting away the wood structure.

- Discuss contract scope of work, materials, installation, payment terms, garbage removal
- Discuss installation of soffits, fascia and eaves, if in contract
- Ask siding contractor when to order materials, if supplied by builder
- Ensure your colors conform to the area and are approved by the architectural coordinator, if needed
- The following should be installed before siding and should have blocks behind each item with building paper behind them and/or provisions for proper flashing and siding trim
    - Hydro stack and meter box
    - Outside electrical outlets
    - Dryer vent, fresh air intake
    - Furnace and hot water tank venting and intakes
    - Outside water taps
- All windows and doors with brick moldings, window trim and other residential architectural cladding in place prior to siding being installed (ensure all sill pans and provisions for proper building paper lap is correct before window installation)
- Lot is backfilled before starting work (depending on grade levels)
- Mark location of brick or other type of siding on walls with spray paint
- Prior to installation of siding, check for proper installation (overlapping) of building paper or other wrap installed (ensure building paper is lapped over top of all flashing and is installed behind all trim and flashing and lapped correctly)
- Ensure any build outs, eaves that run into walls, decorative roofs, and all components installed at the framing stage have building paper installed behind them
- Ensure proper flashing above and below all horizontal changes in siding materials (stucco to siding, stucco to brick or stone, siding to horizontal trim)
- Check for all necessary pieces of trim on corners, around windows and doors
- Check all openings around trim work on doors and windows (ensure caulked and sealed on edges to prevent the passage of water)
- Important to caulk all cracks, joints, holes, around openings, pipes and vents, around fascia joints and roof corners
- Inform contractor to remove all garbage and debris at completion of work
- Add cultured (man made) stone using a polymer cement or a sand cement that is appropriate for sticking stone to a wall (bricklayer's refer to this as lick and stick and you don't require professional bricklaying trade skills to do this work, only basic knowledge to prepare the wall, apply the stone using the correct amount of concrete adhesive and ensure your work is level and square by stringing a line, level from side to side, across the front face)

Heating, Ventilation and Air Conditioning (HVAC) Checklist

- Plan the location of the utility room and allow enough space for all mechanical including the furnace, water heater, electrical panel, communication wiring and controls plus all other mechanical systems and controls
- Carefully investigate several heating systems and consult with more than one heating contractor to determine the best products to use
- A heat loss statement should be completed by a qualified heating expert to determine the proper size of the furnace
- The installation of a gas system will require a separate permit (check with you plumber or gas fitter)
- For your protection, the gas installation must be done by a certified installer/technician or gas fitter who can assume the responsibility for ensuring the gas fitting was completed in a safe manner in accordance with the applicable safety regulations and local codes
- All sheet metal work should be installed by a qualified (certified) sheet metal worker to ensure proper installation practices have been followed for safety reasons
- Consult your heating contractor regarding furnace capacity, codes, energy efficiency, furnace and water termination with Chlorinated PolyVinyl Chloride (CPVC) piping, location of furnace room, cold air returns, heat registers, dryer vent and other items including gas fireplaces, power humidifiers, air conditioners and Heat Recovery Ventilators (HRV)
- Mark location of gas meter on outside wall (check regulations regarding location)
- In winter, hang furnace from floor trusses (in summer, pour concrete floor prior to furnace install)
- After installation of furnace, inspect for damage, check for proper installation and duct sealant (a good trade practice is one screw minimum per joint of round pipe or fitting plus tape or sealant)
- After the heating rough-in work is complete, replace or add studs, floor joists or other wood members that were damaged or removed by the heating contractor
- For an air conditioner, consult with a reputable technician to get advice on the size of the unit required and where it should be installed
- Do whatever preparation work you are qualified to do to save time required by the crew and money
- Wait until fall when A/C units go on sale
- Consider alternative energy efficiency sources such as geothermal, solar, boiler/heat exchanger
- After home is complete, replace furnace filter and clean air ducts

Fireplace Checklist

The manufacturer of the fireplace will provide a "rough-in" framing drawing with the installation instructions. The drawing will indicate whether wood or steel framing is required and specifies all required clearances.

One creative installation I saw was a three-sided peninsula gas fireplace in a bungalow basement. The homeowner put some thought into saving on his heating costs. The peninsula that the fireplace was installed in was framed up and drywalled to a point approximately 3" below the floor joists in order to allow the warm air to escape between the floor joists. He installed a dropped ceiling using T-Bar ceiling tiles leaving 4" between the ceiling panels and the floor joists for heat to travel and warm the main floor. The fireplace has a thermostat set to come on similar to a furnace. The homeowner said, "it heats the entire house and the furnace hardly ever comes on". The bottom line is for you to put lots of thought when planning to install a fireplace. Here are some pointers to consider.

- It may be unlawful to install your own fireplace so consult with the supplier and check inspections and permits (fireplaces are usually inspected by a city/town inspector or fire inspectors before they are closed in)
- It is the responsibility of the licensed installer to check all clearances and obey fire codes
- The manufacturing company should specify whether to use cement board or drywall on the enclosure
- It pays to shop around (avoiding brand names could save you hundreds of dollars)
- Gas fireplaces and electric simulations installed on exterior walls are the most common types
- Fireplaces and wood burning stoves have different heating capacities (shop around for the fireplace that suits your heating needs and carefully choose the most appropriate fireplace for your property)
- Build the frame plumb and square, otherwise you may see flaws in the finished appearance
- It is important to consider the outside venting as well as the fresh air intake (in some cases the vent must be at least one meter above grade, a determined distance from windows and at least 12 inches away from any outside structures or plants as the vent can cause fire)
- For a masonry fireplace, hire a certified/qualified bricklayer with specialized knowledge and experience with masonry fireplace construction (some things to consider are foundation support, size of firebox, brick style, jointing/raking between bricks, fresh air intake, operation of the damper and damper seal, hearth size and design, pattern on front face i.e. basket weave, etc., corner miters, chase/chimney construction and design of the top of the fireplace chase i.e. concrete with rowlock around top edges)
- The interior face of a brick fireplace must be completed to perfection as this is regarded as an item of beauty, meant to be viewed and admired

Plumbing Checklist

Plumbing in many regions is a compulsory trade which means plumbers must be licensed or certified tradespersons or apprentices supervised by a certified journeyperson. The reason is public safety for proper venting of sewer gases. You have probably experienced plumbing issues such as venting sewer gases, noisy pipes, flushing problems and so on. A good designer will consider the location of bathrooms, vents and plumbing walls in the design. A good plumber will consider the location of shut off valves and perform their work without taking short cuts that can result in future plumbing issues.

- Review the plumbing layout with the plumber during the contracting stage (discuss where the plumber may or may not have to run piping that might need to be boxed in) Provide a list of fixtures, sinks, taps, tubs, etc. to be supplied by the plumber and advise of any items to supplied by the builder such as a large tub or pre-purchased items
- Discuss location of water and sewer connections on property and calculate the distance from inverts to house (completed by the plumbing estimator)
- Co-ordinate with the plumber the trenching and installation of services under the footings
- If building in winter and ground is frozen, dirt under footings where services will be installed should be loosened prior to pouring concrete (this will ease digging afterwards)
- Check for weeping tile requirements and whether or not your property has storm sewers
- Plan and co-ordinate with your plumber the exact location of basement rough-in plumbing, floor drain, washing machine drain, water heater, water softener, outside taps, garage water lines, wash basin, shut off valves and controls for other plumbing according to the plans
- During construction, check for clearances with framing members and reframe as necessary any studs or joists that need to be moved to accommodate the plumbing (all walls and floor trusses should be lined up properly for the plumbing to fit)
- Check fixture sizes for installation (any oversized bathtubs or one-piece showers are installed during the framing stage before walls are finished)
- During the rough-in, the plumber will mark or set the locations of toilets and other drains and check for proper location and clearances according to plans
- Check for required plumbing inspections prior to covering sewer lines in the basement and prior to backfilling the water and sewer trench
- Plumber or builder should mark the location of outside water services and gas meter on the outside of the house
- Check gas meter location meets requirements by the gas company
- Check with the municipality on well and septic system requirements and certificates (plans, permits and inspections are usually required)

Electrical Checklist

- Plan so that electricity works for you and not you working for it
- For an older home being renovated, discuss the changes needed to upgrade the service and the electrical panel to meet your new requirements and codes
- Your tender for electrical will be based on the layout and information provided in the drawings so it's a good idea to discuss some aspects of this layout with the draftsperson beforehand (a couple of items worth discussing is the location of the electrical panel, the plugs and lights in the kitchen area and any other specific electrical needs)
- Prior to starting construction you may want to check with the electrical inspection department for their rules and regulations on underground services, temporary power, inspections and any code requirements (the electrical code book is like a phone book so the code requirements would be only what applies to installing the service and your electrician must obey all electrical codes and will apply for the permit)
- Consult with the electrician regarding plan details, service location, inspections and temporary power and when you should call for rough-in wiring (which is best after other mechanical trades have completed their work first)
- Check with the electrician regarding what material and size should be available for the installation of the electrical panel including communication, internet, security and other components to be supplied and installed next to the electrical panel (mark location on plan)
- When the home is framed in, complete a comprehensive walk through with the electrician marking all locations for plugs, switches and lights (your objective with the walk-through is to make the necessary adjustments to height of switches, right handed or left handed, size and location of master bed, location of kitchen outlets, exact location of ceiling lights, outside plugs and extra items, etc.)
- Check the location of the thermostat (should be centrally located on an interior wall on the main floor and away from direct sunlight)
- Check to ensure sufficient number of circuits in the kitchen to accommodate major appliances and countertop appliances
- Check for ground fault breakers for bathroom plug and razor and arc fault breakers for bedrooms
- Include extra items during the rough-in stage (e.g. basement, ceiling fan, freezer outlet, water softener outlet, built-in vacuum outlet, home theatre outlets)
- Always set up temporary power first to ensure a continuous, reliable source for the trades
- Check for underground inspection prior to backfill of the electrical trench
- Following rough-in, check all outlets and switches are in accordance with the plan in the proper locations according to the walk through (e.g. location of outside plugs, washer and dryer, stove, ovens or other cooktop, microwave, range hood, garborator, dishwasher, fridge, smoke detector, door chimes, vacuum system plugs and plugs for entertainment systems)
- Contact other cable or utility providers for any prewire service that you may require

Caulking, Insulating and Poly Vapor Barrier Checklist

Closing off avenues of escape of warm air is a high priority in cutting heating costs. In the average home, nearly every hour, or more than 20 times a day, the entire volume of air inside the house is replaced by air from the outside. An airtight home requires an air exchanger to ensure a consistent supply of fresh air.

If you analyzed all the ways to make a home more energy efficient whether that be with a solar system, an ICF (insulated concrete form) building, a passive architecturally designed system, hot water heating or any system other than the standard forced air furnace, you would find the best bang for your buck is simply by doing a good job with the critical vapor barrier. The word "critical" applies because without this thin polyethylene barrier, air will find ways to blow right through those insulated walls. It's the vapor barrier and caulking of all the holes and cracks that adds value to your insulation. An energy efficient well insulated and sealed home will also be cheaper to cool in hot climates or in the summer time. Here's a checklist to ensure the home you build is constructed with energy efficiency in mind.

- Select triple glazed windows and consider other energy features to lower heating costs
- Walls should be built with 2x6 exterior wall studs with a minimum of R20 insulation
- Framers must install poly along end walls where they join the exterior walls and on all top plates
- Framers who install windows should have a caulking tube to run a bead around the window prior to installation
- There should be a 16-inch roll of poly and a bag of insulation on site during the framing stage (the insulation is used to fill gaps that cannot be insulated later)
- Attic hatch should be framed up with 18-inch plywood sides to ensure blown-in insulation is held in place
- Caulk all areas on exterior walls between double studs, top plates and bottom plates with proper acoustical sealant which does not harden
- Caulk all holes through floor and ceiling plates to seal and aide as a fire stop
- Select a high quality insulation with a higher "R" value
- Ceiling should be R35 to R40 insulation (blown-in insulation should have an even application with no voids)
- Use 6 mil poly, take care installing and inspect for holes prior to applying gypsum board
- Ensure no gaps or holes in insulation (if you can fit a pencil in a hole then it needs to be re-fitted)
- Ensure the gap between window frames and windows are foam insulated with window and door foam insulation and sealed to the vapor barrier with tuck tape to prevent drafts
- Ensure poly hats are used on outside walls around electrical plugs
- Use spray foam for the rim joist area because this area is difficult to insulate and is a common area for heat loss
- Insulate and poly basement walls

Drywall Checklist

- Review the drywall contract with your contractor and discuss how long the job will take and the payment terms (if a deposit is required to order material, you should pay the supplier directly)
  Note: Money paid should be for work completed or after materials are delivered on site
- Check contract for materials supplied (5/8 drywall on ceiling is better than ½ inch board for both strength and to prevent sagging)
- Your drywall contractor should visit the site beforehand to do an accurate board count and check straightness of walls using a laser pointer aimed perpendicular along walls
- Material should be delivered and in place, or work completed prior to making a payment or deposit on the contract
- Discuss the finish for ceilings as painted ceilings require a smooth finish
- Discuss precutting for electrical outlets on all exterior walls to ensure no damage is done to the critical vapor barrier
- Discuss heating requirements and co-ordinate temporary heat if necessary for mud to dry
- Check for completion of all framing including blocking, drywall backing, fireplace framing and sufficient framing to support all the kitchen cabinets
- Sweep the house clean before receiving drywall which should be placed in each room during delivery
- Take photos and measurements of walls in kitchen, bathrooms and television locations for future reference of locations of construction studs and backing
- Check with contractor requirements for heat (you may need to co-ordinate temporary heat with the taper a couple days before boarding to dry out the wall studs)
  Note: Avoid using propane if possible, it releases moisture
- Have board placed into the rooms (larger sheets in the larger rooms)
- Inform drywall contractor to take care not to puncture poly during installation and precut holes for all outside wall board
- Do not cut away poly from around window openings as it provides protection for windows while home is being painted
- Inform the contractor of ceilings not to be textured
- Check required corner beads on closet openings (some openings may not require corner bead, depending on the wood door frames and finishing)
- Check nailing and screwing of drywall boards (nailing is often done first around edges to install board followed by rows of drywall screws)
- Check walls and corners for smoothness
- Check sanding after completion
- Co-ordinate clean up and removal of garbage
- While work is being done, do whatever other jobs you can do on the exterior (e.g. installing front steps, decks, grading and landscaping work)

Painting Checklist

New Walls

- Always inspect walls before priming for dirt, dust, blemishes, holes and damage around electrical boxes (repair with a drywall patching compound)
- Dust walls with a rag on a pole sander or microfiber wand
- Sand and complete minor repairs a second time, wipe clean
- Use a quality primer that provides a good foundation for succeeding coats (cost is the best measure, the more expensive products have more pigments and resins and provide better coverage)
- If spray priming walls, have someone back roll the spray primer to even it out
- Check for drywall imperfections after priming
- Patch imperfections and then be sure to spot prime all patches to avoid uneven paint spots (flashing)
- Pole sand with 120 grit sandpaper
- Always better to cut-in the primer around trim, ceiling lines and corners
- Primer can be tinted if using a mid-tone to dark color paint

Repainting Existing Walls

- Inspect for mold, dirt, oil, grease, hair spray, holes and minor damages
- Wash oily contaminants with TSP or a degreaser and rinse well (kitchen, bathrooms, high traffic areas)
- When walls are in decent condition, spot prime wall patches
- Repaint with two coats of the product of choice
- For dark colors or badly damaged walls it's beneficial to use a quality primer before the top finish coat
- Life expectancy of one coat is 2 to 3 years (two coats is 5 to 7 years)
- Select a contractor grade paint or higher quality grade
- Recommend using brand new rollers to prime first coat (wash out roller to remove the lint and condition the roller for paint)
- Use a 2.5 inch angled sash brush for cutting in wall corners, ceilings and trim
- A quality angular sash brush with a polyester/nylon bristle works best with waterborne paints
- For oil-based paints, use a pure bristle brush (clean with paint thinner, hang brushes)
- For repainting walls using latex over oil paint, use an all-purpose primer first (these primers are designed to adhere to most surfaces including previous coats of alkyd paint)

Ceilings

- To handle stains, spray with a "flat" oil-based product designed for ceilings
- If needed, apply a top coat with a "flat" latex
- Paint ceilings before walls for ease of masking and prepping walls (work from top down)

Painting Checklist
Safety
- Work in a ventilated room, crack a window open (some air movement is good to allow paint to dry)
- Wear a dust mask (min N95) when sanding walls and a cartridge mask when spraying lacquers and oil-based stains
-

Finishing Checklist
- The finished look is very important for value (if you intend on doing some work yourself you should first consult with a professional to learn the techniques rather than learn by trial and error (if you have no experience you can easily ruin expensive material so do only the work you feel qualified to complete to get professional results)
- Allow sufficient time to complete all the finishing and to get the job done right (once you move in, the unfinished jobs never seem to get completed)
- There are several methods of installing and finishing the interior doors, windows, casings, closets and other millwork
- Review the contract and discuss the sequence and procedures with your finishing carpenters so you know who does what and when
- Review the materials list of items you will be supplying as well as any materials to be supplied by the finishing carpenters
- Discuss with finishing carpenters the millwork and installation of railings, stair finishing, fireplace finishing, built-in cabinets, closets, interior doors and casings, window casings, baseboards and any other millwork detailed in the contract
- Discuss level of finished product quality, paint or wood finish, size of gaps allowable for filling, and how you want it done (refer to pictures in design books/websites)
- Discuss clean-up, required daily following finishing work (furnace cleaning following completion)
- Check codes for proper height of handrails and maximum distance between spindles
- Contracting work separately to different crews who are expert in their field such as a stair and railing company, kitchen cabinet installers, closet experts and a glass company for mirrors and shower doors is usually necessary and can save time during the finishing stage
- Common procedure is to prime walls, install unstained/unpainted finishing material, fill holes, sand smooth and stain or paint as per selected finish prior to painting drywall
- On wood materials, holes are usually filled after stain and sealer coat (most painters want to fill holes themselves, discuss these procedures with your painter)
- Some finishing carpenters perform both the finish material installation and the wood staining/lacquering functions which can save you contracting time and money during construction

Flooring Checklist

There are many flooring products to choose from depending on your budget and interior design. My preference is hardwood and tile and also some styles of attractive engineered laminated hardwood. A good way to start the selection is to build a board with samples of all flooring products, samples of paint chips and a sample of the kitchen woodwork which is often supplied by the kitchen supplier.

- Compare products and prices from independent suppliers as well as the big box stores
- The more neutral the colors of carpet and other flooring products, the more acceptable for resale
- Colors of floor coverings should complement tile, paint, woodwork and furniture
- Laminate has some advantages like ease of installation, less waste, no finishing required plus an abundance of products to choose from (some quality wood laminates have a full 1/8-inch wood top and others only a paper thin finish)
  Note: Laminate is easy to install and generally only requires a chop saw, a few hand tools and maybe a table saw to cut the end pieces to fit in
- An experienced or journeyman tilesetter will know all the proper procedures and be able to establish the right pattern, cuts and levelness needed for a professional look (obtain samples of kitchen cabinet doors, paint chips, a piece of hardwood, carpeting, or any other flooring that will be adjacent to the tile to ensure all products complement each other)
- Sweep and vacuum before delivery of flooring products
- When installing hardwood, protect finished hardwood by laying out rolls of cardboard, mats or other flooring protection to protect from scratches while floor is being finished
- Check domestic vs imported hardwood, imported may have more shrinkage
- Hardwood flooring must sit in the home for a few weeks prior to installation otherwise it may shrink showing large cracks (hygroscopicity is the property of wood to attract moisture from surrounding atmosphere)
- Check subfloor nailing and smoothness and repair any squeaks prior to installation
- Check to ensure the floor covering contract includes all extras such as nailing strips, steps, stringers, stair nosing, under-pad, installation and a guarantee on the installation
- Be sure to have a guaranteed price on flooring contracts that include material and labor (exact measurements may differ slightly from blueprints so installer should pre-measure home before cutting carpets)
- Tile floors require a strong plywood underlay with no movement (oriented strand board (OSB), flakeboard, sterling board, aspenite, K3 board and other particle boards are not good products for tile adhesion due to the outer layer of resins and glues)
- Linoleum floors require a very smooth surface, usually K3 board stapled or screwed with holes and edges filled by the installer (vinyl composite flooring provides both attractive finishes/patterns and a durable surface)

- Remember when ordering tiles, hardwood, laminate and other flooring products, "it's better to be looking at it than looking for it" (order extra material because a percentage of product will become waste)

Action Exercises:
1. Review each list prior to signing a contract and while work is being performed.
2. Expand on the items listed whenever you have a new idea.
3. Review Chapter 12 "Renovating for Profit" for additional construction tips.

Chapter 20

Selling for Profit

*"DREAM BIG! There are no limitations to how good
you can become or how high you can rise
except the limits you put on yourself".*
Brain Tracy

This chapter will provide you with a list of ideas for selling your home. It's a fact of nature that we all get emotionally attached to our own home and view it with different eyes than a potential buyer. Your first task is to walk through your home as though you are the buyer, much like they do on the home buying television shows. Walk into each room, assess it and ask yourself how a potential buyer might feel. Consider any easy and inexpensive improvements that would make the room look more appealing. It's quite simple when you think about it.

It is not about being an interior designer. I have difficulty understanding what is contemporary and what is traditional. It's more about creating the right atmosphere for the buyer. One important concept for selling for profit is to achieve a balance. Too much dark paint or dark wood will make the room look dark and dreary. Too much clutter will make the room look disorganized, draw the wrong attention and create a negative perception. Visible water stains, visible damage to drywall or trim or other flaws will create a negative feeling of repairs that need to be done and more money that needs to be spent.

A professional real estate agent will do more than pull up a few comparable sales. He or she will compare properties conducting a similar evaluation to what a professional appraiser would do. They provide pluses and minuses to compare features of houses sold against your home they are listing. They should come prepared having done their homework prior to your first meeting. As they say in sales, you have one chance to make a good first impression. Expect those agents to come prepared and make their pitch to gain the listing. You should also expect to hear about their marketing plans, the home evaluation, comparable homes sold, fees and about the real estate broker or company they represent. The marketing plans will include photos, the website listing service, the signage, literature, advertising, showings, open house, other networking plans and consulting with the seller on options that could improve general appearance to help sell the home.

All the natural emotions of mood, stress, feelings of anxiety, doubt, passion and joy can come into play during the process of selling. The old saying "patience is a virtue" might have been invented by someone selling their home. It's not unreasonable to take several months to sell a property, one reason the bulk of agreements are a minimum of three months. We took eight months to sell one home due to economic and political conditions. The right buyer will eventually turn up if you have patience and keep your finger on the pulse of activities.

The first home we sold was one we built. It was in a small growing town of about 5,000 located 10 miles from the city. It backed onto a mushroom plant which had a field where the peat moss and cow manurer were mixed using heavy equipment. When the wind blew from that direction, you could say the odor was rich but truthfully it stunk really bad. We hired a top city real estate agent who we knew would drive clients out to do the showings. One day he called and asked, "Which way is the wind blowing?". I said it was good to come out. On the way he asked his client if he liked mushrooms. The client said "yes" and the real estate agent said "fresh mushrooms right here every day!". A good salesman will look for the positive things and have a positive attitude. In our case he turned a negative situation into a positive one.

We scrambled to tidy and clean the place for the showing and I mistakenly left a pair of underwear on the kitchen counter. Fortunately, the client bought the home, so the first house we built for $56,000 in 1980 sold for $92,000.00 a year later. A $36,000.00 tax free gain 38 years ago was a handsome profit for building one 1172 square foot bi-level home with no garage.

The key strategy was to hire the right real estate agent. One who likes to sell his own listings and also liked the area. As it turned out, our agent worked with another agent in his office who found the client for the property. The agents networking together proved all-important in getting the home sold.

I'm a fan of selling my home through a professional listing service. I wouldn't say selling yourself is a flat out bad idea as there may be certain situations when that works. It worked for me when we sold a home we renovated to one of the tradespeople after I discussed with him the idea of owning a rental property. I made a deal with the listing agent that if I found a buyer myself, he would cut the commission in half. He agreed and he assisted with supplying the selling contract and the signing by both parties. From then on I always made that a part of the listing. It makes sense that if you find the client through your own personal network that you get the "selling" commission knocked off the total. The agent assists in the negotiations and closing as he or she normally would anyway. This is a win/win deal and on more than one occasion it helped me to cut commissions by 50%.

You might be thinking "why did I list in the first place?". We could have started the process to sell it by owner first. It's a matter of choice. When we made the decision to sell we decided to pull out all the stops and get it done. I know that people who list their own home are often not seriously motivated because they are not reaching all the potential buyers unless they have it professionally listed. It's all part of the marketing effort which starts like a campaign. Part of my campaign was to network through my contacts to find a buyer before another selling agent came along with a buyer. The probability of you selling your home yourself is less than one of the thousands of agents who have access to sell your home but there is a small chance that a friend or neighbor will talk to you about it. That is why I like to have the option available. Your listing agent might roll his eyes a bit when you ask for this because they would like every chance to double end a commission without the potential for agent/client competition, due to a clause in the listing contract.

On another home, our Real Estate Agent asked me if I could replace the dusty rose broadloom which ran up the stairs and through the three bedrooms. He knew I had contacts in construction and he said, "How much would it cost to replace this carpeting?". I went to my flooring supplier and got a quote. For only a few thousand dollars we were able to change the carpet to a modern neutral color which greatly enhanced the visual appearance when you entered the home. The carpeting was the only negative thing and I had originally held back because I didn't want to spend the money. I learned from this experience that sometimes you need to spend a little if you want to impress buyers, sell quicker and get a better price. It also helped to have hired an experienced agent, who is not afraid to point out something he thinks should be done.

In some cases you should consider supporting your agent allowing both a real estate agent open house and public open houses. There are plusses and minuses to running open houses. Personally, and more so today, we do not like open houses where any Joe Blow from Kokomo can walk through. During an open house the agent often stays in one room while the visitors walk about. Every possession is on display and visitors can check out everything from personal photos to teenager wall posters. On one open house I had a hand held personal recorder taken. The Real estate firm replaced it but the point is you don't know who is coming through your home and definitely you will get many unqualified buyers and strangers walking through. Some agents recommend open houses while others say they don't offer much success finding buyers. It's one of those things that depends on a number of factors including your preferences as well as your agent's, how the home will show, the current market, your motivation to sell and the increased exposure with signs and advertising for the open house which can cost the listing agent some time and money.

A good agent will have the communication skills to ask their clients to clean out all the junk, remove personal photos, take the fridge magnets off, put away items of value and so on to prepare for an open house and showing. I have walked through dozens of open houses and I can easily say there are many sellers (and agents) who show little effort when hosting an open house that's not ready for showings. When we did agree with the agent to host open houses, visitors thought they were walking through a show home and some asked if there were people living in the home. This is what you should be shooting for if you are considering an open house.

An open house for real estate agents when they do their Tuesday morning tour is one I would not miss simply for the immediate exposure to many agents and the resulting networking that can come from this awareness. I'll ask our agent to plan an open house promoted just to real estate professionals within the first week of the listing. It's very important to get off to a strong start and this campaign has helped me in the past. Today, with wide angle photos and visual tours posted on the web, agents and the public can see everything right on their electronic devices. I'm still a fan of the personal invite and the benefit of the influence of all senses which is only achieved by getting people out to see in person what you have to sell. We can see the Grand Canyon on our computers but there's nothing close to seeing it in person where all your senses are activated. You get a feel and an appreciation for a home when you walk through the front door. There's a presence of sense when you're in a home, a certain vibe you can feel which you can't get on a website.

I have often wished I had kept every property I owned. This is certainly true for the four half duplexes that were generating a positive cash flow and would be clear title today. It's also true for one we sold at the wrong time. Values were appreciating and it seemed like a good time to sell. That decision to sell would cost $150,000.00 in lost appreciation over the next year. It was not the right time. You will benefit financially knowing and using the concepts from Chapter 3, identifying the principles of appraisal and Chapter 4, identifying the many factors that influence values by understanding what is happening right now in the marketplace. Keep these two chapters in mind when you are considering selling for profit.

Some real estate experts will say that the only time you will lose money is when you sell. There is truth to that and most real estate agents would agree. However, there are times when selling is necessary and your objective is to sell quickly for as much profit as possible. One example is when you are dealing with an estate sale. My sister, her husband and myself had to get the home ready to sell. We rented a twenty foot moving van to make two trips to the dump plus one to Value Village (used clothing store) and there were still many items left for charity. Here is a full list of what was done to prepare for the listing. Every home will be different and you should start by making a list. This list can provide you with some ideas to begin the process.

Example of Activities Completed Prior to Listing with a Real Estate Agent

- Emptied the home of everything except for a few of the nicer furniture items and a couple of paintings (some items remained in the garage in boxes)
- Cleaned everywhere! (the kitchen taps, sinks, and bathroom fixtures required some special cleaning to remove old dirt, rust and hard water deposits)
- Replaced 35-year old carpeting with new pre-finished engineered hardwood
- Replaced one set of taps
- Replaced old wrought iron railings inside with new wood railings
- Removed the old curtains
- Cleaned and painted the basement floor
- Drywall repairs to one wall in the basement, primed with a sealer and painted to cover up murals painted on walls
- Filled small holes in walls and painted rooms which had poor color choices
- Checked electrical outlets and completed some minor electrical work to avoid home inspection deficiencies
- Replaced the furnace filter, cleaned the top of the water heater and emptied the vacuum system
- Cut lawn and fixed loose railings on the deck
- Cleaned out the garage, cleaned the concrete floor and removed the old workbench and tools
- Interviewed three real estate associates for opinions on value and selected one for listing the home

We could have replaced the entire kitchen adding new appliances and a dishwasher. The cost/benefit or contribution to profit was not enough to warrant this work. It would have been too time consuming plus we did not live in the city and had no contacts for trades and suppliers. We needed to stage the home quickly using our own labor for most of the work. Get it done, listed and leave.

I like to use Brian Tracy's "GOSPA" acronym which once again stands for goals, objectives, strategies, priorities and activities. Here's an example.

Goals	To sell my home within 90 days
	To establish a listing price and a reasonable pre-anticipated selling price
Objectives	Prepare home
	Interview three real estate agents and hire one
Strategies	Get the property listed under a multiple listing service by a reputable real estate team
Priorities	Prepare home before hiring an agent by cleaning, removing junk and any other necessary pre-listing activities
Activities	Declutter the home
	Go to the dump
	Drop off household items at the goodwill or other charitable store
	Have a garage sale
	Paint
	Fix taps, clean inside, cut lawns
	Interview three real estate agents, list home with chosen agent
	Choose a lawyer, choose moving firm, fill in change of address forms
	Prepare for a real estate agent open house

Refer to the following detailed checklist of pre-listing activities for things to check and do before inviting real estate agents or appraisers into your home. These preparations can take some time but for certain, if you do them, they will help you obtain a quicker sale and more money.

A good agent will employ a professional photographer who uses a wide angle lens to capture the best pictures for the listing. If you have ever sold anything on E-Bay, Kijiji, Auto Trader or other sites you know the importance of having good photos posted on the web. This is something you should discuss with your listing agent.

When we sold our homes, buyers thought they were show homes. That was our competition in the area. New homes are fresh, staged with show home furniture and move-in ready. They sell well because there is no clutter, no toys everywhere, it's clean, attractive, not dated with old tile and carpet and no negative thoughts of it being work, work, work! If this is your competition, get ready to compete. Follow this checklist as a guide to creating you own to-do list so you can sell your home quicker and for more money.

Preparing To Sell Checklist

If you stop and think about it, it's just a matter of applying a lot of common sense. Interior design takes into consideration style, lighting, colors, furniture and scale. It's to your benefit to make a few easy improvements to prepare for selling by creating a positive mood, atmosphere and design that feels comforting.

Valid Survey Certificate

- Obtain a valid Survey Certificate or Real Property Report before you list for sale as proof that it's compliant with the city bi-laws and has a compliance stamp on it (if any changes were made, it could take a week or more to arrange a survey and obtain a compliance stamp)

Color (paint) Helps Set the Mood for the Room

- Choose fresh, neutral, modern, earth tone and up-to-date colors (lighter colors tend to make rooms appear larger and neutral colors prevent some buyers from being turned off right away
- Paint areas in need of paint and change colors if necessary (touch up front door trims, first impressions are important)

Declutter Before Listing for Sale

- Declutter by removing and storing any unnecessary items, selling items, taking stuff to the dump, dropping off items to a thrift store, Good Will, Value Village, Salvation Army or other charity
- Take away garbage and recycle items, boxes, garage junk
- Put away personal family photos, calendars and art that could be considered inappropriate and remove anything that could create a negative vibe (photos of children or pets are nice to look at but can also give the impression to a buyer of wear and tear on a home)
- Put away laundry
- Remove items from bathroom counter tops including shampoo bottles and personal care items (store out of site or purge unwanted items)
- Minimize items on kitchen counter tops including bread, sugar, coffee, tea, vitamins, etc.
- Remove old or unwanted items from cupboards then clean and organize
- Clear off table tops by removing papers, magazines, ash trays, etc.

Clean Prior to Listing

- Clean it up as much as you can! (also see tenant clean-up list in Chapter 10)
- Clean all floors and stairs (flooring is very important, it's the first thing buyers see and it covers a large area) or resurface/replace with new flooring
- Clean toilets, sinks and taps (use chrome cleaner on taps, remove water stains and rust in sinks and tubs, clean fridge, oven, microwave, clean windows inside and out)
- Clean dust from lights, ceiling fan and other fixtures and dust furniture

Prepare for the Home Inspection

- Prepare by eliminating items that can hinder your sale or cause a reduction in price
- Have the furnace professionally serviced and cleaned (a new dated sticker will be applied to the furnace)
- Clean and remove any calcium or rust from the top of the water heater
- Empty the built-in vacuum system and clean the lint from the dryer vent
- Ensure taps are working properly with no leaks
- Ensure there are no missing shingles
- Fix any loose electrical wiring, repair drywall damage (holes in walls, noticeable cracks or screws popping)
- Tighten any loose handles and toilet seats
- Clean up outer buildings, repair broken boards on decks or other areas and add a coat of paint or stain if needed
- Repair any damaged areas and paint using "Kiltz" spray primer or other sealer and ceiling paint (stain marks on ceilings are a sign of water damage)
- Touch up nicks on white door frames and trim using white out or white paint and a small brush
- Ensure basement water stains are not visible (a sign of previous water problems)
- Mold needs to be remediated by a professional who can certify it's been removed
- Best flooring items are hardwood, engineered flooring, laminate, tile, travertine, slate, quality neutral carpet

Easy Do-It-Yourself Staging

- The yard should look like it's well taken care of (lawns cut and driveway/walks shoveled)
- Leave a nice soap dispenser by sink, clean set of towels hanging, toilet paper on the roll
- Add a fresh bouquet of flowers which look and smell nice, potpourri in a nice dish or bowl of fresh fruit (eliminate odors in the home from cooking or pets)
- Organize the garage area and kids play areas (put toys away for a cleaner look)
- Can add an attractive front entrance area rug to offset an older floor
- Place a small sign which says please remove footwear
- More of an updated look is better, heavy old drapes and big bold patterns on bedspreads or furniture coverings are a turn off (cover them up or get rid of them)
- Stage interior like a show home, make beds and arrange things neatly (other people need to visualize living there)
- Everything should be to scale for the room (typically the larger the piece of furniture, the larger the room should be)

- Have all lights on, drapes open and blinds open, unless it's a bad view (the more light you have the bigger, brighter, cheerier it looks)
- Look for ways to add more lighting, check all light bulbs are working and consider adding floor or table lamps in an area needing light
- During showings turn lights on
- Determine what is the best time of day for showing as the home could be dark in the morning or afternoon
- People who are interested in buying your home may take a drive by at night (good lighting will make the home look more appealing and may increase value)
- If located by a daycare, showings should not be at drop off or pick up times
- Discuss with the listing agent the desired process for showings, hosting any open house events and appointments

---

Action Exercises:

1. Write out on paper a "To Do List" of items prior to listing a home for sale.
2. Make a plan to stage the home or, if empty, consider hiring a firm which does staging.
3. Research local real estate agents and select three who will provide an opinion of value and show comparisons of homes listed as well as homes recently sold.
4. Make a list of all the home improvements that have been made which show that you have kept the home in good condition and review this list when you tour the home with your listing agent.
5. Choose the best agent to represent your sale. Discuss list price, commissions, showings, booking appointments and other items of importance before signing a contract.
6. Discuss the selling strategy with your agent. Are you listing a bit high now and prepared to reduce the price later? Are you listing at a determined sale price leaving some room for negotiations? Are you listing at (or below) the appraised market value to be the most competitive now?
7. Discuss what advertising and marketing plans your real estate agent has in mind and whether or not they will be hosting an open house for real estate agents or the public.
8. Review applicable contents in Chapter 11 "Flipping for Profit".

Chapter 21

Becoming a Contractor for Profit

*"The more you know about your customers,
the more you can provide them information
that is increasingly useful, relevant and persuasive."*
Jay Baer

My dear friend, you've come a long way to get to this chapter. You now have many tools to help you buy, renovate, build or sell your own home for profit. This last chapter is for those who are taking everything they have learned to start their own contracting business for profit. I'm sure you'll agree that starting a business is a big step requiring a lot of trade knowledge, business sense and entrepreneurial desire. Here's a short summary of what's in this chapter that can propel you to a quick start.

- Starting a Contracting Business
- Values
- Nothing Happens Until You Start Selling
- Contractor Checklist
- Questions for Your Client to Ask
- Gaining Acceptance, Hot Button, Follow UP
- Steps to Construction (to advise clients)
- Owning Versus Renting (a business shop location)
- Government Programs and Grants
- Procurement
- A Fair and Complete Building/Renovating Contract
- Project Terms and Conditions and Change Orders
- Statutory Declaration
- Letter to Neighbors
- Site Notices

Every successful contracting business I know, and I do know hundreds, has one thing in common. Their business gets a reputation from their excellent work which leads to good references and repeat business. These contracting businesses seldom need to advertise because of repeat business gained from constant word of mouth by satisfied clients. Performing excellent work and dealing with everyone in a polite and courteous manner is the only way to achieving success. The flip side of this is far too costly with no referrals and no repeat business. Plan to be the best in your field. Make sure everyone who works with you or for you feels the need to tell others about their incredible experience.

Starting a Contracting Business

Owning your own business has many advantages. You are the boss, you make all the decisions and you reap the profits. Sounds good doesn't it. Now whats the cost? Consider the price you must be prepared to pay, including hard work and long hours. One look at this list and it's easy to see why ten out of eleven businesses that start fail within the first couple of years. You need big shoulders and you must be prepared to be proactive in many of these areas.

Business Activities List

- Sales and marketing, includes knowing your customers
- Procurement, estimating, negotiating
- Trade work, contracting or subcontracting
- Human resources, hiring, firing
- Scheduling
- Project management activities
- Co-ordinating permits, insurance, legal matters, etc.
- Safety
- Customer service
- Purchasing
- Business administration handling payables, invoicing, collections, business taxes
- Book keeping, accounting, payroll taxes and source deductions, banking

When I met with tradespeople in their own business I would often joke with them by saying "I guess being in your own business you get to work half days". After receiving the dirty look I would follow by saying "that's 12 hours, right?". Then they would understand what I meant by working half days. Be prepared to work many evenings and weekends until you are in a position financially to delegate some of the tasks listed above.

Starting a business, becoming an entrepreneur and working long hours is much easier when you have a passion for what you are doing. Without passion it will be very difficult to put in the full effort needed for success. Bringing passion into your business promotes excellence in the work you do which in turn cycles back to you as clients show appreciation and respect for your work and services. This gives you the self motivation and energy to do more, sell more and build or renovate more. The best way to perform well is with passion.

Practically it would apply to every entrepreneur, when you start a new business it's you that has to perform nearly all of the job functions until you reach a point where you can hire others. A partnership has advantages if one partner has strengths to carry some of the load. Partners bring a different set of skills and a different perspective to solving problems but partnerships have disadvantages also. The work load may not be even and you might not agree on things which could lead to disagreements. Consider a buy or sell clause in the partnership agreement where one partner can offer a price to buy out the other partner. The one who receives the offer has the option to purchase at that price or sell to the other partner at a negotiated and agreed upon price.

It's likely you will start off as a sole proprietor with a registered trade name and later when income and taxes reach a certain level incorporate to form a limited company. One big advantage of a limited company is that you are limited to your liability. When you are in a construction contracting business a limited company will give you some smart protection, to protect what assets you currently own in the event of a lawsuit and reduce your liability. Some builders will open up a new company for every large project then close the company when done to limit liability.

If you are just starting out, select a trade name for your company that you can register. Take the certificate of trade name to your bank and establish a business bank account. Next you can apply for contractor's cards and discounts at various suppliers. These are both wholesale suppliers of building products as well as those big retail outlets. Set up a file and accounting system so you are organized and have a place for various documents, forms, estimates and invoices. You will need contractor estimating or procurement forms and agreements. It's best to reduce paper whenever possible so think paperless when you can but agreements in my opinion are still best in writing and on paper.

Values

What do you value and what's important for the successful operation of your business? Values govern how you want your business to run and how you interact with others. These values are the internal characteristics that govern you and your employees during all day to day activities. Determine four values for your company. Some good examples are honesty, integrity, respect, responsibility and accountability. Some bad examples are; act dumb, look surprised, show concern and deny everything. All joking aside, decide from the start to never be a bad contractor because, like karma, what goes around comes around. You will never get the priceless reputation of being a good builder, contractor or renovator if you have the wrong attitude and values.

Nothing Happens Until You Start Selling

Many years ago I met a lady working in sales for a cabinet manufacturer. She told me she was making over 100 thousand per year. I was a bit stunned by this because it was back sometime around the early 1980's. I asked her that one word "How?". She explained that not all her clients were buying but her boss was very positive and told her just to bid, bid, bid, bid on every kitchen with every client that walks in the door. She was very busy designing and estimating kitchens and had little time to follow up with closing sales. The odds worked in her favor as many clients returned and placed orders for cabinets. The lesson here is you have to get into the game and start bidding on work. Remember the Tony Robbins question he asked an audience, "How do you get everything you want out of life?". After everyone pulled out their writing pads and got ready to write down the big answer to that question, he said one little word "Ask!". Never feel uncomfortable or invasive asking questions about the contractor or renovator. This is true for both parties, clients as well as contractors. The following checklists give examples of questions you can ask contractors and questions clients can ask their builder. As a builder you should know the answers to all of these questions. This is important to gain the confidence of the client and to close the sale.

Contractor Checklist

- Have they done this type of work before?
- Can they provide some references?
- Are they listed with the Better Business Bureau (BBB)?
- Do they have a recent project you can look at?
- How long have they been in business? What's their story?
- Are they current with Worker's Compensation Board and/or Worker's Safety Board?
- Do they have up-to-date liability insurance?
- Do they have a city or township business license?
- Are they bonded?
- Are they doing the work themselves or subcontracting out all work?
- Are they certified for compulsory certification work?
- Who are their professional trade partners?
- Do they have any lawsuits current or pending? If so, why?
- Do they have a clearly written contract with details of the scope of work and specifications?
- Are they requiring a deposit prior to starting work and supplying materials?
- How do they handle change orders?
- How do they handle permits and inspections?

Worksite Safety Awareness Checklist

- Is the area safe to work in?
- Will the activities of other crews interfere with safe operations?
- Do workers understand their work assignments?
- Is a pre-job hazard assessment needed to get the job done safely? Is the assessment needed for the work being done?
- Have the proper tools and equipment been provided?
- Has the proper personal protective equipment (PPE) been provided?
- Is the crew knowledgeable on how to properly use all personal protective equipment?
- Can the crew communicate effectively with each other or are there restrictions due to high noise, restricted vision or language barriers?
- If chemical products or compounds are being used, is the crew aware of hazards and safety controls required to safely complete work assignments?
- Have workers been encouraged to make suggestions to assist in completing job assignments safely?
- Has the crew been advised to report any unsafe acts or unsafe conditions to their supervisor or project manager?

Questions for Clients to Ask

- Can we live in the home during the renovation?
- Should we have a contingency amount for changes and upgrades?
- Do you offer a fixed price, a price based on cost plus or a blended option?
- How much is too much for a renovation?
- Should I renovate, buy new or build?
- What is the residential market doing right now?
- What are the steps or processes we need to take (see flowchart)?
- What inspections are required and who is responsible for them? (see Chapter 18 "Scheduling for Profit" for a sample list of inspections)

Gaining Acceptance

Having dealt with thousands of small businesses as a government consultant, I can recall many instances where individuals gained success in their trade and/or business. The ability to gain acceptance, develop rapport and build trust was common with many of these success stories.

One technique a hairstylist used to rapidly build a repeat clientele was to "FORM" her clients. This word is an acronym for Family, Occupation, Recreation and Message. All she did was engage in conversations using "FORM" as a reminder of the key conversation subjects then following the service wrote down information about the client on a 3x5 card for future reference. The Message could be something like "let's look at adding a color during your next visit". When the client returned for service six weeks later, she used the "FORM" information as a reminder of the previous conversation. After checking her 3x5 client card, she was able to reference the things said during the previous visit demonstrating she listened and showed interest in them. Clients were overwhelmed that she remembered so much personal information from a conversation that happened many weeks earlier. They were so impressed by her displaying interest in them that many become repeat clients who would provide referrals.

When the client left her salon she would give them three business cards with the client's name hand written on the back. She would ask them to please pass them along to a friend or relative because she was just starting out and was building her client base. Then she said, "tell them to show the card when they come in and I'll know you sent them. I'll keep a record of any referrals and offer you a special discount for helping me expand my client base." By using this sales approach her business multiplied very quickly and she soon became fully booked and able to make a good living.

The point here is that repeat business and positive word of mouth will have a profound effect on your business success and survival. You will save marketing and advertising dollars as well as build a valuable client base giving you repeat business and referrals. Successful contractors who perform excellent work are often hard to find because they seldom need to advertise. They are always booked with work from referrals passed along from satisfied customers.

Hot Button

Listen very carefully to clients to determine their needs and to take note of any items they would consider to be the most important. On one occasion, when I was a builder, a client wanted 4-inch oak baseboards. I ignored this as trivial and almost lost the deal to build a large new custom home. What's important to you may not seem important to the client. It's always a good idea as well as a professional selling skill to match the clients needs with your products explaining the features and benefits you can offer to meet the client's needs.

Follow Up

I developed and ran workshops for individuals unemployed looking to find work in the trades. The workshop taught people the sales process and how to sell themselves. Having knowledge of the steps involved has helped many speed up the process of finding a job in far less time than it would without knowing the steps. The cover letter, resume, building a large prospect list from all resources, contacting employers, how to make calls, what to say, how to gain an appointment and following up are all part of getting a job. It's also a sales process that can take up to six attempts. The process eventually become quicker once you know and practice the steps.

When you start out as a builder, contractor or renovator you are also a salesperson. As a sales person you need to understand the sales process. The process can take up to six times before closing and sometimes more. Six times means six events, presentations and follow-up meetings to answer questions, clarify items, negotiate items, resolve unknowns, develop confidence, gain acceptance, determine the final price and eventually sign a contract. Knowing this upfront will keep you from getting prematurely discouraged and walking away from a potentially profitable opportunity. Brian Tracy teaches this using a bell curve to illustrate that some clients will buy early, illustrated by the small area under the front part of the bell curve. More clients will buy after two or three meetings which is the middle (average) or fatter part on the bell curve and some will take five or six meetings represented by the tail on the right side of the curve. People will react differently according to their personality types. The key to success in selling is to recognize this and use it to your advantage. Guide your clients through the sales process knowing it could take six or more meetings before you finally agree on everything and close the sale. Then afterwards make sure you follow up with them as this leads to future business. You can share these seven steps with your clients to inform them of the process. If you need to see visual examples and further explanations on bell curves, the internet has plenty.

Steps to Construction

1. Dreaming stage
2. First meeting, consultation and ballpark estimate
3. Architectural design drawings
4. Preliminary budget, permits required
5. Working drawings
6. Contractor final estimate and agreement
7. Begin construction

Owning Versus Renting a Shop

Chances are you may not need a shop but when you reach a certain size there will become a need to have a location for storage, millwork, painting and other construction work. Think this over carefully. I know of several businesses where the owners went from renting to owning. Their net worth from owning will eventually allow them to retire. The hair college, the hair salon, the auto repair shop, the bricklayer who built his own building and the cleaning company owner who owns the building are just a few examples of business owners who made the decision not to rent. That decision in some cases is the difference between building equity and having a retirement plan or not. I asked one heavy equipment shop owner, who was paying large rents every month, how he was ever going to retire and he said he couldn't. Think long term and what your progression or exit plan will look like.

Government Support Programs

We covered the long list of topics you need to know to run a business. One more thing, you may want to research government support programs pertaining to household improvements or your relatable scope of contracting. For every new venture ask the question, "Is there a government incentive for this project or client?". Some areas where incentives have been targeted in the past include home improvements related to energy (solar, wind) or water efficiency, low income housing, seniors housing, job creation, apprenticeship training and other areas where government financial incentives are offered to attract investment.

Procurement

Refer to Chapter 14 "Estimating for Profit" for the Building and Renovating for Profit checklists to complete your job procurement. You may require a more detailed breakdown, depending on the size and complexity of the contract, to complete calculations of man hours being supplied by yourself and other employees. A procurement spreadsheet might have titles including trade function, hourly rate, quantity, units or number of hours, description of work and cost. You can source these forms or create your own custom procurement sheets.

Fair and Complete Contract

Having a fair and complete contract for work is extremely important for you as a contractor. You should design a contract to suit your work. The following template can provide you with the titles to help you get this started. Since this is only a sample, you should have your contract reviewed with your lawyer beforehand to ensure it is drafted with all proper articles, terms and conditions. In the example provided, the terms of payment can be based on either a fixed cost or a cost plus basis. The payment option chosen is often determined by the type of project and the contractors ability to provide an accurate price. Renovations that have many unknown factors are often on a cost plus basis. A ballpark estimate requires knowledge and experience behind it. A fixed project (i.e. a new home) on the other hand, may be best using a fixed price. Using this agreement as an example would mean you would cross out the terms of payment option that is not applicable and both parties initial beside the change.

BUILDING / RENOVATION CONTRACT

THIS AGREEMENT made in duplicate this ____day of _____, 20____

BETWEEN

_____
Name of Contractor (hereinafter called "The Builder")

of the first part

- and -

_____
Names of Purchasers (hereinafter called "The Client")

WHEREAS The Clients are registered owners of the following described lands:

_____
Building Address

In the City/Township of _____, in the State, Province, of (hereinafter called "the said lands"); and

WHEREAS "The Builder" has agreed with "The Client" to renovate/construct a dwelling on the said lands in accordance with the terms and conditions hereinafter set forth:

NOW, THEREFORE, THIS AGREEMENT WITNESSED as follows;

ARTICLE 1.   PLANS AND SPECIFICATIONS

- The Builder agrees to build/renovate a dwelling house on the said lands in accordance with the detailed plans and specifications. Each of the parties hereto acknowledge as having received the said plans and specifications signed by the other party. Specifications are attached hereto and marked as **Schedule"A"**.
- Designs and blueprints remain the property of "The Client" unless produced by "The Builder", in which case they remain the property of The Builder.
- Designs provided will reflect the layout of walls, rooflines and finish details as required to assist in defining the scope of work.

ARTICLE 2.   TERMS OF PAYMENT - Cost Plus or Fixed Amount

Cost Plus
The full cost of the renovation will be based on the cost of construction plus____%.
Schedule "C" attached hereto outlines the project estimate.

In the absence of agreed upon unit prices and in accordance with the contract between The Client and The Builder, the subcontractor's allowed markup for changes is 10% (overhead & profit) OH&P and the contractor's markup is 5% OH&P.

or

Fixed Amount
The price to be paid to "The Builder" hereunder shall be the sum of _____

Written amount in dollars

Payment to be made in the manner prescribed in **Schedule "B"** attached hereto.

ARTICLE 3.   COMMENCEMENT

This agreement is open for acceptance for 30 days from the date of presentation.
Commencement date on or before: _____
Estimated completion date on or before: _____
Attached and included as part of this agreement is:

Schedule A	The Specifications and Plans
Schedule B	The Payment Schedule and Terms
Schedule C	The Project Estimate
Schedule D	List of Allowances

© David Pocock All rights reserved. The contents or parts thereof, may not be reproduced, for any reason, without permission from the author.

ARTICLE 4. BUILDER WARRANTY

- The Builder provides a one year warranty on all materials and/or workmanship provided in the listed scope of work from date of substantial completion. The Client agrees to give written notice of such defects within a reasonable time.
- This warranty does not cover:
    - Equipment that includes a manufacturer's warranty or supplies that come with a separate supplier's warranty.
    - Changes, alterations or additions to the scope of work made by other parties other than The Builder.
    - Loss or damage that The Client has not taken timely action to minimize.
    - The quality, performance or condition of client supplied products or fixtures.
    - Further, the warranty on The Builder supplied materials and products will be invalid if the failure is directly attributable to the failure of the client supplied project components.
    - Any defect in the work or existing structure caused by or resulting from any pre-existing defects on the site.
    - Normal wear and tear or aging of any of the work.
    - Existing items on the site not identified in this agreement.
    - Warranties applicable to supplied materials or services are honored according to those provided by the manufacturer or supplier, not The Builder.

ARTICLE 5. PERMITS / INSPECTIONS / ENGINEER'S REPORT

- Building permit is included as required.
- A development permit, if required, is included.
- Structural engineer's report and stamp will be obtained as required.
- Necessary mechanical, electrical, framing, gas permits and inspections if required will be obtained at appropriate stages of the project.

Exclusions
Items not included in the scope of work to be performed by The Builder, unless specified in the estimate.
- Sales Tax
- Window coverings
- Landscape Remediation
- Appliances
- Mold and asbestos remediation
- Heavy Furniture moving (e.g. piano)
- Electrical and gas meter relocations
- Utility line relocations and connections

- Repairs to hidden water lines
- Hidden electrical violations that require repairs
- Repairs to cast iron drain lines
- Wallpaper removal
- Security systems

Other specific details may be noted in the attached project estimate.

ARTICLE 6. GENERAL SCOPE OF WORK

Project Preparation
- To include tarps, masking, duct and electrical tape, dust barrier, fire extinguisher, first aid kit, ear and eye protection, dust masks and other useful miscellaneous items placed on site.
- Any preliminary work will be completed and a garbage bin will be present on the job site at all times. A second tote may be made available for small items that need to be removed and saved.
- Project preparation is to include a walk-through, at which time you will become acquainted with the site foreman and he will become acquainted with the job and yourselves.
- See the attached Schedule "A" for further information related to project preparation.

Demolition
- Garbage bin(s) will be placed on site. Clean up will be on an on-going basis and if more bins are needed they will be dumped periodically.
- Specific details may be noted in the attached project estimate.

Excavation and Cribbing the Foundation
- Excavation is conducted with a minimum of 5 foot depth to a maximum of 7 feet where specified and/or required.
- Excavation must and will be to a level of stable or undisturbed ground. Excavation beyond 7 feet requires a notification of change in costs.
- Specific details may be noted in the attached project estimate.

Framing and Roofing
- Framing to be standard construction materials and constructed to meet all building codes and design requirements.
- Exterior wall studs 2x6 kiln dried spruce @ 16 inches on center (O.C.)
- Interior wall studs 2x4 kiln dried spruce @ 16 inches O.C.
- Exterior wall sheathing - 3/8 OSB or 3/8 spruce plywood

- Roof sheathing 3/8 OSB or 3/8 Spruce plywood with H clips.
- Roof trusses, engineered roof trusses @ 24 inch O.C. or as per supplier layout.
- Specific details may be noted in the attached project estimate.

Exterior Doors and Windows
- Window and door types as per specifications provided by the supplier and agreed upon by The Client. Specific details may be noted in the attached project estimate.
- Garage doors, if applicable, details as noted in the project estimate provided by the supplier and agreed upon by The Client.

Heating
- Where applicable, heating changes to include relocation of new heat vents and registers in renovated areas as noted in the attached project estimate.

Plumbing
- Plumbing to include rough-in, supply and installation as specified. Shutoffs will be provided at all new locations of supply lines to fixtures. Specific details may be noted in the attached project schedule.
- Exterior irrigation is not included and if needed should be provided by others.

Electrical
- To include rough-in, supply and installation of plugs, switches and wiring as per drawing.
- Electrician or a data communication firm will be responsible for wiring all telephone and cable connections for the renovation project. The electrician is not responsible for the activation of these services.
- Wiring will meet or exceed current electrical code requirements.
- Scope of work will be listed on the attached project estimate.

Insulation
- Where applicable, insulation is to be batts of at least R-20 in exterior 2x6 walls and R12 in any remaining 2x4 walls.
- Ceilings R-40 loose fill where required and if applicable.
- Where applicable, insulation on exterior walls and ceiling will be covered by 6-mil polyethylene vapor barrier and sealed with acoustical caulking.

Drywall
- Where applicable, 1/2 inch drywall is to be added to walls and drywall to ceilings in areas affected by renovation. All joints taped and sealed. Drywall is to be primed, ready for painting.
- Repairs, where required due to removal of cabinetry, will be performed. Concrete board, taped and waterproofed, will be used in shower areas.

Interior Finish and Details

Flooring
- Preparation of subfloor for tile installation is with 3/8 plywood glued and stapled. Areas with linoleum or vinyl are prepared with 3/8 K3 board glued and stapled. Areas with hardwood will receive new 3/4 inch plywood if required and screwed and glued to floor joists. For areas with carpet, the new or existing subfloor will be screwed in areas to remove any existing squeaks. All other flooring areas as noted above are screwed down to prevent squeaks prior to installation of 3/8 inch sub flooring.
- **Tile** in areas specified as noted in the attached project estimate.
- **Carpeting** specified as noted in the attached project estimate.
- **Hardwood flooring** specified as noted on line items of the attached project estimate.

Interior Doors
- Where applicable new doors to match existing or specified. Standard is hollow core slab door with laminate and three hinges per door.
- Where applicable, closet doors to match existing as specified.
- Specific details may be noted in the attached project estimate.

Painting/Staining and Ceiling Finish
- Painting is typically considered for new construction areas only. Walls and ceilings will receive primer and walls will then receive two coats of paint. Primer is sometimes tinted to improve the finish and coverage of the final color.
- New ceiling finished with a knock down (flattened) stipple finish unless specified to be painted or other finish.
- Specific details may be noted in the attached project estimate.

Millwork
- New built-in cabinets, closet shelving, custom mantels, to be supplied or constructed as specified on the attached project estimate.

Trim
- Baseboards and trim to match existing in areas indicated on plans as best as possible or as noted in the attached project estimate.

Cabinets and Countertops
- Detailed specifications of cabinets and countertops are according to plans and noted in the attached project estimate.

<u>Exterior Finish and Details</u> (cont'd)

- All exterior finish materials, masonry, stucco, battens, parging, siding, soffit, fascia and eaves to be supplied and installed according to plans and specifications in the attached project estimate.
- Decks, if applicable, designed and construction according to plans and specifications in the attached project estimate.
- Site will be cleaned and landscaping to a rough grade only. Additional landscaping to be charged as extra unless otherwise specified in the project estimate.

ARTICLE 7. FINAL PHASE
- A final walk through of the project will occur when the project is deemed to be substantially complete. At this time, The Client and The Renovator will view and inspect the quality of work and make note of any deficiencies.
- The final interior cleaning will be performed by professional cleaners and the cost to be invoiced separately.
- Furnace and heating ducts will be cleaned.
- Following the substantial completion invoice, a final invoice will be created once the remaining project work is complete and the expenses can be accounted for.
- Refer to the project estimate payment schedule for clarification.

ARTICLE 8. CONSTRUCTION NOTES
- The site is to be kept in a tidy and organized fashion.
- Gates, doors and windows are secured at the end of each day.
- Work will be performed in a fashion to minimize upset to neighbors.
- Unknown conditions such as dry rot, mould, ants, mice, termites, hidden plumbing deficiencies, non-code electrical wiring and out of level (plumb) structural components (beams) discovered during demolition can materially alter the time, work and cost of conducting the renovation beyond the originally intended scope of work. The client will be advised to the extent of the additional work and any applicable additional costs will be charged as an extra to the contract.

ARTICLE 9. CHANGE ORDERS
- A change order is required to make changes or have additional work done following the execution of this agreement. We will provide information outlining the change and the associated costs for your review and approval. A change must be agreed to in writing and a form for accepting the change will be provided to the client prior to proceeding with the changes.
- Change orders will in some cases impact the schedule of work currently underway, thus extending the duration of construction time.

- If and when a major change occurs, the change will be presented to all parties with the intentions of keeping all informed and appraised of the casual effects these changes have to expedite the decision process. Many of the items in a renovation are ordered well in advance of their installation. Request for changes can carry extra costs for re-stocking, and re-work. Often they cannot be accepted beyond critical stages. If you are requesting a change, please discuss it with us as soon as possible so that we can assist you in making a final decision as quickly as possible.

ARTICLE 10. PROTECTION OF PRIVACY

- We respect your right regarding the protection of your personal information. We collect, use and may disclose personal information for the purpose of providing you with our products and services but only after you have requested and ordered products and services from us. We are in the business of renovations and new home construction and selling. During the course of providing our products and services to you we may disclose some of your personal contact information to reliable third parties including agents, supplier and trade contractors. These third parties are responsible to us for ensuring the privacy of your personal information.

ARTICLE 11. TERMS

Getting Started and Meeting Deadlines

- The start date, as outlined above, is subject to being able to obtain all the required materials, services, and permit approvals. The client acknowledges that it is their responsibility to arrange and meet with all The Builder suppliers and to finalize all details necessary so the start of construction is not delayed.

Plans and Specifications

- In the event of a conflict between the blueprints and these specifications, these specifications shall govern. The project is to be built according to these specifications unless otherwise designated by way of amendment to the agreement or by a change order signed by The Client and accepted and approved by The Builder.

Construction

- All construction shall meet or exceed the local building codes. Due to onsite conditions and procedures, specification and dimensions can vary within reasonable limits. The locations of mechanical equipment may vary from the locations specified on the blueprints. Exterior finish items such as final grading, driveways and exterior painting cannot always be completed due to weather. The Builder will complete such seasonal items as weather permits.

Substitutions
- The Builder reserves the right to substitute equivalent or better materials or products where a manufacturer's name brand or product becomes unavailable or discontinued for any reason.

Entire Agreement
- This agreement and specification shall constitute the entire proposal made between The Builder and The Client and no representations, warranties, or statements made by any employee or agent of the Renovator unless otherwise specified in writing shall be binding as to vary the terms hereof.

No Assignment
- Neither party to this Agreement shall assign the same without consent of the other, provided however, that nothing herein contained shall be construed so as to restrict the right of The Builder to employ sub-contractors in the construction of the said dwelling house.

Non-Competition
- The Client agrees not to contract any work directly related to this agreement with The Builder's sub-contractors, suppliers or sub-trades. All business related to this agreement will be conducted through The Builder.

Builders Lien Act Requirement
- Pursuant to the appropriate legislation, a lien holdback payment amount will be required as outlined in the payments in Schedule B.

Completion Date
- The Builder is committed to completing your renovation as quickly as possible. However, due to weather, material or labor shortages and our commitment to the quality of your renovation, delays to the specified completion date may become necessary. The Builder will not compromise the quality of the renovation by working towards an unreasonable or rushed deadline. We trust that you agree with this philosophy.
- Substantial completion occurs when the work described herein is at least 97% completed and that the area of the work is either ready for use or is already being used for the intended purpose. The Substantial Completion date determines the payment date of the lien holdback as outlined in schedule B.
- Where the further work that is required to fulfill the contract due to seasonal specific items exceeds 3% of the contract, a mutually agreed holdback will be negotiated.

ARTICLE 12. FINANCING AND MORTGAGE PROCEEDS

- The Client covenant forthwith upon receipt thereof to assign to the Builder proceeds of the said mortgage or other financing to which The Builder is entitled pursuant to the terms of this agreement and further to covenant to assign the proceeds payable under such fire insurance policies respecting the said dwelling as may be required to rebuild the said house.

ARTICLE 13. CANCELLATION

- You may cancel this contract by providing a written notice of cancellation by registered mail or personal delivery. In such event, work will cease and an accounting shall be undertaken between The Client and The Builder in which the costs incurred by The Builder shall be offset against payment amounts received. Any difference in costs shall be paid by either The Client or The Builder.

ARTICLE 14. NOTICE

- Any notice required to be pursuant to the terms hereof shall be given by either party hereto in writing and mailed by registered mail or delivered to the other at the following addresses:

    Builder's Address: _____
                            _____

    Purchaser's Address   _____
                            _____

    Any notice so delivered by mail shall be deemed to have been received by the other party forty-eight (48) hours after the same has been posted for delivery.

ARTICLE 15. BINDING EFFECT

- This agreement shall extend to, be binding upon and ensure to the benefit of the heirs, executors, administrators and assigns of the parties hereto.

ARTICLE 16. TIME ESSENCE

- It is agreed that time is to be considered of the essence of this agreement.

In Witness Whereof the parties hereto have hereunto executed this agreement on the day and year first above written.

    The Builder: _____
                         (The Builder, Contractor/Renovator)

                 PER: _____
                            Authorized Representative

Signed, Sealed and Delivered
in the presence of :

_____	_____
Witness	The Client (Purchaser)
_____	_____
Witness	The Client (Purchaser)

Project Terms and Conditions

- No Smoking on the job site. Keep cigarettes in your vehicle. Failure to comply is grounds for loss of contract or dismissal.
- We hire professional sub-trades. The prime contractor and our clients expect top quality professional work.
- Wear personal protection equipment (PPE) and always practice safety first for yourself and others.
- We expect workers on site when scheduled.
- Respect the site supervisor. They are there to assist you to complete your work.
- Present the upmost courtesy to our clients and their property.
- Conduct yourself in a professional manner (language, music, etc.)
- Take extra care and attention to client's appliances, washroom fixtures (bathtub and shower bases), electrical fixtures, countertops, etc. Counter tops are never to be used as work surfaces. Do not stand on counter tops.
- Any damage to a clients property will be photographed and back charges will be applied for repair or replacement.
- Any and all damages must be reported ASAP to the Site Supervisor.
- No heavy vehicles or equipment on clients driveway or sidewalks. Back charges for repairs will apply.
- No parking on clients driveway. Only loading and unloading permitted. Oil stains on driveway will be cleaned and back charges will apply.
- A general cleanup of your work area is expected as a common courtesy for the next trade and the client.
- Please dispose all garbage in the provided garbage can/bin on site. If you create a large amount of garbage, please make arrangements to remove it.
- Do not place extra signage on the property. Vehicle signage is acceptable.
- Inform all your employees, sub-trades and delivery persons who will visit the job site of these terms and conditions.

We thank you for your cooperation.

Change Order

Contractor name _____   Date _____
Address _____
Phone _____

Site Location _____

Item #	Description	Cost
	Shipping	$
	Tax	$
	Total Estimated Cost of Change Order	$
	Updated Project Estimate	$

Approved by:

Client Signature _____   Site Manager _____

Client Signature _____   Initial

STATUTORY DECLARATION

Company name _____ IN THE MATTER OF:
Address _____
                                         (Project Address)

I, _____ of the City/Town of _____, in the State/Province of
    (name of company representative)
of _____ do solemnly and sincerely declare that:
    (State/Province)

1.   I have completed the renovation contract undertaken between

         (client name)   and   *(contractor name)*

2.   I have satisfied and paid all subcontractors and suppliers who have submitted invoices to the date of this Statutory Declaration and I undertake to pay all future subcontractor's invoices as they relate to this contract.

AND, I make this solemn Declaration conscientiously believing it to be true and knowing that it is of the same force and effect as if made under oath and by virtue of the appropriate Act and Legislation.

Declared before me at _____)
)
_____,_____,)
)
this ____ day of _____, 20___.)   _____
)   Name of Contractor
_____)
A Commissioner of Oaths in and   )
)
For the _____ of _____)
        (City/Town)   (State/Province)

Notices

Think safety all the time. Avoid conflict by taking measures to prevent a conflict and show everyone what the rules are. Posting a few notices can help inform those who need to know; employees, sub-trades, suppliers, clients and neighbors. Post any notice that is necessary especially if there is any danger like an open pit or stairwell. These notices can make the project safer and easier for everyone.

Dear neighbors

XYZ Construction and Renovations has been contracted to provide home renovations to a home at _____. We are writing you to assure you that we shall do our best during the performance of our contract to not disrupt the enjoyment of your neighborhood.

We have instructed our sub-trades to time their delivery and completion of their work during reasonable hours and to exercise caution and respect while at the place of work. We will work hard to complete the project as soon as possible.

If at any time you have reason to be concerned about any disruption, please do not hesitate to contact the office at _____ and we will address the problem immediately.

If you would like to discuss a renovation which you have been considering, we would be pleased to meet with you to hear your ideas and to help you develop them into reality. We love talking renovations.

Sincerely,

_____
(Contractor Name)

_____
(General Manager)

_____
(Phone Number)

Site Notices

ATTENTION
SUBCONTRACTORS / TRADES / SUPPLIERS
FOR SITE ACCESS
PLEASE CALL
JOHN CONTRACTOR ___ ___ ____
OR
CALL THE XYZ CONTRACTING OFFICE AT ___ ___ ____

No Smoking on the Job Site
Smoke and Leave Your Cigarette Butts In Your Vehicle
Not on the Property, Sidewalk or Road
Strictly Enforced

ATTENTION

TRADES PEOPLE / SUBCONTRACTORS

LAST PERSON OUT -

PLEASE ENSURE ALL LIGHTS ARE
OFF, WINDOWS ARE CLOSED AND
DOORS ARE LOCKED WITH THE KEY
BACK IN THE LOCK BOX

For a final comment, the startling statistic is that over 85% of new and small businesses fail due to lack of proper business administration. So be diligent and make sure that you set up a proper business administration system to deal with human resources, accounting, payables, receivables, taxes, estimating and other items.

Action Exercises:

1. Choose four values for your company.
2. Using the example, create your own construction contract.
3. Choose a company trade name and set up a business account with a bank.
4. Obtain letterhead and create forms you will need using the examples in this book as a reference.
5. Create a client information page with all contact information, e-mail, phone numbers and room for notes during presentations and meetings. Enter information on paper during the meeting with clients. (Turn phone off and give your clients your full attention)
6. Create a client introduction/thank you letter and short survey to obtain feedback to continually improve performance.
7. Protect yourself against possible losses due to unforeseen events. As the "prime contractor" responsible for safety of workers, contractor liability insurance is necessary as well as ensuring all workers are covered with workers compensation and liability insurance.
8. Sell your service, perform excellent work, take immediate action towards achieving your goals and profit in a positive way by helping others!
9. Refer to Brian Tracy at www.briantracy.com to further enhance your personal, sales and business knowledge.

Here's a final quote by Douglas Adams that applies to everyone who wants to be successful in their own business.

"To give real service, you must add something which
cannot be bought or measured with money,
and that is sincerity and integrity."

To your success!

Dave Pocock

www.ingramcontent.com/pod-product-compliance
Lightning Source LLC
Chambersburg PA
CBHW081407080526
44589CB00016B/2489